THE
UNITED NATIONS
AS A POLITICAL
INSTITUTION

THE
UNITED NATIONS
AS A POLITICAL
INSTITUTION

―――

H. G. NICHOLAS

―――

FIFTH EDITION

OXFORD UNIVERSITY PRESS
London   Oxford   New York
1975

Oxford University Press

LONDON   OXFORD   NEW YORK
GLASGOW   TORONTO   MELBOURNE   WELLINGTON
CAPE TOWN   IBADAN   NAIROBI   DAR ES SALAAM   LUSAKA   ADDIS ABABA
DELHI   BOMBAY   CALCUTTA   MADRAS   KARACHI   LAHORE   DACCA
KUALA LUMPUR   SINGAPORE   HONG KONG   TOKYO

© Oxford University Press 1959, 1962, 1967, 1971, 1975
First published by Oxford University Press, London, 1959
Second edition 1962
Third edition published as an Oxford University Press
paperback 1967; reprinted with corrections 1968
Fourth edition 1971
Fifth edition 1975
Printed in the United States of America
This reprint, 1976

CONTENTS

IN MEMORIAM
W. D. N.

FOREWORD

WHEN an institution embracing almost all the states of the world is well launched into the second decade of its existence there is little point any longer in asking about it, 'Is it a good thing?' In these pages I am not concerned to be 'for' or 'against' the United Nations; the questions I want to answer are 'What is it like?' and 'How does it work?' I shall try to look at the Organization as I should look at Parliament or Congress, that is to say as an established political institution which has a right to be examined in terms of its processes as well as its products and which must be understood through its politics as well as its constitution. Though some incidental expressions of praise or blame may be found in these pages, my primary purpose is not to endorse or condemn, but to describe.

Accordingly, what follows, though making no pretence to originality, is at least based as much as possible on first-hand observation at the United Nations Headquarters itself. It goes without saying that such observation depended in great part upon the co-operation of a host of persons, members of the Organization and others, in New York and elsewhere, who placed their experience and their knowledge of the United Nations at my disposal. It is impossible to thank them individually, but any merits the book may have are attributable to their patience and generosity.

February 1959   H. G. N.

NOTE TO SECOND EDITION

YOU never step twice into the same U.N.; the Organization about which I wrote in 1959 had already undergone some change by the time my book appeared. The present edition cannot hope to escape the same fate, but at least it has given me the opportunity to record the major developments of the past two years as well as to benefit by the advice given me by many kindly readers of the earlier version.

November 1961   H. G. N.

NOTE TO THIRD EDITION

IN a restlessly fluid world international institutions refuse to stay still while authors write about them. I have taken advantage of this third edition to try to catch up with an institution more restless than most, but if the reader finds that some details are already outdated I hope he will be indulgent to the vicissitudes of authorship and publishing.

December 1966   H. G. N.

NOTE TO FOURTH EDITION

THE twenty-fifth anniversary of the U.N. is a good moment to take fresh stock of the Organization's development and functioning. This I have tried to do, revising and updating the record in a mood of what I would venture to call congratulatory realism.

June 1970   H. G. N.

NOTE TO FIFTH EDITION

SINCE 1970 a good deal has happened to the U.N. The membership has expanded, notably by the admission of Communist China and the two Germanies. Its politics have been affected by the new American relationship with Russia, China, and Indo-China. Its economics have been complicated by the new pattern of trade in basic world commodities. Its organization has been modified, particularly in the Security Council, and in its economic, social, and environmental activities. Finally its involvement in the conflicts of the powers has continued, conspicuously in the Middle East and Asia. I have taken the opportunity of a fifth edition to up-date my account in relation to all these developments.

October 1974   H. G. N.

1 · ORIGINS

IN a real sense the origins of the U.N. lie far back in history, in every attempt from the Achaean League to the League of Nations to construct an organization which would harmonize and control the discrepant operations of states and nations. The immediate stimulus, however, for its establishment is to be found in the events of World War II. Paradoxically, as with the League before it, war provided the impulse for creating a new organization for peace. Not that the cynics' relish of this paradox need delay us long; there is nothing discreditable about attempting to give concrete expression to the sentiment 'Never again!', and since, for all its inadequacies, the nation state has sheltered so much that civilized man rightly prizes, it is not surprising that it takes a world cataclysm to break the mould in which it holds him. Indeed, inasmuch as the war which created the United Nations was fought against the deification of the nation state, it is not unnatural that the organization should have had its inception in the coalition of victors. It was in the London Declaration of 12 June 1941 that all the nations then fighting against Hitler announced their intention of working together, with other free peoples, to establish 'a world in which, relieved of the menace of aggression, all may enjoy economic and social security'. On 1 January 1942 at Washington the anti-Axis coalition, then numbering twenty-six states, expanded this affirmation into the United Nations Declaration. This embodied an endorsement of the Atlantic Charter of 14 August 1941, which, in somewhat vague terms, had spoken of the establishment of 'a peace which will afford to all nations the means of dwelling in safety within their own boundaries', of 'freedom from fear and want', of the disarmament of the aggressors and subsequently the creation 'of a wider and permanent system of general security'. The main business of the Washington Declaration, however, was with war, not peace; it was to emphasize co-operation in an all-out struggle and to give mutual undertakings not to make a separate peace. The phrase 'United Nations' was a coinage of President Roosevelt's and its initial emphasis was on unity against a common foe. As a title for a permanent organization it is no doubt open to the logician's objection that it assumes as an historic fact a unity which the organization has been created to promote; there is either a tautology or a contradiction about the preamble to the Charter of the U.N., with its phrase, 'We, the peoples of the United Nations, determined . . . to unite our strength'. If so, it merely enshrines a paradox common to many forms of human endeavour, that some concept of the end must inhere in the beginning—alternatively that even a beginning cannot be made until there has been some progress towards the end.

By 1942, of course, considerable progress had already been made towards uniting for peace and security. There was the war-time coalition and there was also the still formally existent League of Nations. Why did the leaders of the coalition not build upon the Geneva structure? Mr. Cordell Hull curtly announces in his memoirs, 'As to whether to revive the League of Nations or set up a new international organization, we decided in favour of the latter.' Mr. Churchill is hardly more explanatory, but he is known to have preferred an organization more regional in character than the League had been. The truth was, of course, that by 1942, fairly or unfairly, the League reeked with the odour of failure; Russian pride had been mortally offended by the League's condemnation and subsequent expulsion of her at the time of the Russo-Finnish war; and in the United States it was generally thought that it would be much better to try to enlist public support for a new organization than to risk reviving the stale and bitter controversy over American entry into the League.

Accordingly, agreement was general that there should be a new organization and that it should be built upon the structure of the United Nations coalition. The next collective stage in foundation-laying was on 30 October 1943, when in the Moscow Declaration of the Four Nations on General Security, Britain, China, the U.S.A., and the U.S.S.R. announced 'that they recognize the necessity of establishing at the earliest practicable date a general international organization, based on the principle of the sovereign equality of all peace-loving states, and open to membership by all such states, large or small, for the maintenance of international peace and security'. This was soon followed by the more loosely and rhetorically worded Teheran Declaration of 1 December 1943, which referred to seeking 'the co-operation and active participation of all nations, large and small, whose peoples in heart and mind are dedicated, as are our own peoples, to the elimination of tyranny and slavery, oppression and intolerance. We 'will welcome them, as they may choose to come, into a world family of Democratic Nations.'

Meanwhile, plans for the world organization were being elaborated in Washington and London (and, presumably, in Moscow). The evolution of British official thinking, only recently exposed to view with the opening up of the wartime records, was dominated by one consideration above all others, the imperative necessity of securing American membership. All American designs for the new world organization were similarly dominated by the imperative necessity of securing congressional co-operation and, at the very least, the benevolent neutrality of the Republican Party. This involved continuous liaison between State Department and Congress as well as conversations between the administration and Mr. John Foster Dulles, as the foreign policy spokesman for Governor Dewey, the Republican presidential candidate. By February 1944 the American domestic consensus had developed to a point where the State Department felt it safe to suggest to the British and Soviet governments that they should exchange their ideas and drafts. Accordingly arrangements went forward for an informal Great Power conference at Washington which would hammer out agreement on fundamental points. On 21 August the conference met at Dumbarton Oaks, where the semi-tropical climate of a Washington summer is moderated by the spaciousness and greenery of what might almost be an English country house. The conversations were organized in two parts, the first from 21 August to 28 September, between Britain, the

U.S.A., and the U.S.S.R., the second from 29 September to 7 October, with China taking the place of the Soviets. This arrangement, formally necessitated by the U.S.S.R.'s neutrality in the Far Eastern war, also reflected the ambiguous position of China, half in, half out of the Great Power Club. Britain was represented by Sir Alexander Cadogan, the U.S.A. by Mr. Stettinius, the U.S.S.R. by their Washington ambassador, Mr. Gromyko, and China by Dr. Wellington Koo. The talks were private.

The general atmosphere of the meetings was cordial and co-operative and there was almost immediate agreement on the main structure of the new organization—an Assembly in which all members should be represented and a Council with a Great Power nucleus which would carry the main responsibility for peace and security. Beyond this each power had certain preferences and prejudices which it argued and bargained for, but the communiqué of 9 October 1944 which published the 'Proposals for the Establishment of a General International Organization' recorded a far-reaching agreement not only on main principles but also on a good deal of detail. The U.N. as we know it now, in all its main features, was outlined to public view; the main gap was on the trusteeship and colonial territories side, where British sensitiveness as the major colonial power and America's prospective interest as a legatee of Japanese colonialism equally dictated avoidance of this topic at this stage. There were, however, certain silences which reflected serious disagreements at the conversations, notably on the voting arrangements in the Security Council, where the Soviets wanted a comprehensive Great Power veto, and on the membership of the organization, where the agreed formula 'open to all peace-loving States' left open the question whether the sixteen constituent republics of the U.S.S.R. were, as the Russians claimed, each of them, a State, and whether 'peace-loving' meant 'signatories of the U.N. Declaration' only. With another meeting of the Big Three impending it was agreed to leave these delicate issues over for decision at the highest level.

Thus room had to be found at Yalta, on the agenda of that

over-crowded and unhappy conference, for filling these gaps in the Dumbarton Oaks Proposals. Like so much that was decided then, the agreements on U.N. issues bore the marks of haste and wishful thinking; they papered over the deep differences between the national interests and policies of the Big Three with formulas which would not stand the strain of the world's inspection and the wear and tear of the organization's own functioning. For the voting arrangements in the Security Council it was proposed by the U.S.A. and Britain and agreed by the U.S.S.R. that the Great Power veto would not apply to 'decisions on procedural matters', that a party to a dispute would not vote where peaceful adjustment of disputes was involved, but that in all decisions involving enforcement measures Great Power unanimity should be required, even if one of the Great Powers was itself a party to a dispute. As to U.N. membership, it was agreed that all governments which had declared war on the Axis by 1 March 1945 should be eligible to join and Stalin scaled down his demand for the admission of all sixteen Soviet republics and contented himself with asking separate recognition only for the Ukraine and Byelorussia. Churchill, anxious for the separate admission of India in advance of her full Commonwealth independence, supported Stalin's demand. Roosevelt, however, insisted that the decision be left to the founding conference of the U.N., though he pledged the U.S.A. to vote then for the Russian proposal. The full drafting conference itself was fixed for San Francisco on 25 April 1945, and it was agreed that China and France should be invited, along with the Big Three, to act as sponsoring governments.

While the main structure of the U.N. was still being built, smaller and more specialized international agencies were also taking shape. They developed in part as responses to specific needs, as for example UNRRA (The United Nations Relief and Rehabilitation Administration), established in 1943 to cope with the pressing problems that sprouted in the rear of the retreating Axis armies everywhere. However, the impulse for their creation also owed a good deal to the efforts of those, in both Britain and the U.S.A., who advocated what was known as 'the functional

approach' to the problems of world organization. These advocates pointed to the ILO, an organization which still survived,
respected and active, amongst the ruins of the League world.
They claimed that there, in a body which shunned the mine-
strewn high road of international politics and concentrated on the
safer levels of the universal needs and problems of economic and
social man, you had the model of what international co-operation
should be. A network of such organizations, they argued, could
be created which would absorb, one by one, successive fields of
international activity and might even end, like the Lilliputians, in
tying down the Gulliver of politics while he slept, so that the
world would find itself governed and controlled without ever
having consciously yielded up those abstract rights of sovereignty which arouse such fierce political passions and prejudices.
Few political leaders were prepared to accept the functionalist
creed in its most optimistic flowering, but many were convinced
by functionalist advocacy of specific proposals. The first fruits of
this were seen in the United Nations conference at Hot Springs,
Virginia, in May and June 1943, which resulted in the establishment of the Food and Agriculture Organization. This was followed in July 1944 by the United Nations Monetary and Financial
Conference at Bretton Woods in New Hampshire, out of which
eventually emerged (in December 1945) the two international
lending agencies—the International Bank for Reconstruction and
Development and the International Monetary Fund. Similarly,
in Chicago in November 1944 an international conference on
civil aviation set up an International Civil Aviation Organization,
though its full establishment was delayed until 1947. Each of
these bodies operated under its own constitution and was responsible only to those states which had chosen to become members;
membership was by no means identical. In a sense their objectives, though more specialized, were in harmony with those of
the U.N.; in a sense also they had interests, aspirations, and
sovereignties of their own.

Addressing the United States Congress on his return from
Yalta President Roosevelt declared, 'This time we shall not make
the mistake of waiting until the end of the war to set up the

machinery of peace. This time, as we fight together to get the war over quickly, we work together to keep it from happening again.' It was in accordance with this philosophy that arrangements were hustled on for the final charter-drafting conference at San Francisco, arrangements which not even the sudden death of the President was allowed to disrupt. Mr. Truman, with characteristic decisiveness, announced within an hour of his succession to the Presidency that the conference would proceed as planned and on 25 April 1945 the U.N. Conference on International Organization was opened in the Opera House in San Francisco, with Mr. Stettinius, as the U.S. Secretary of State, in the chair.

We still lack an adequate account of the proceedings at San Francisco. No participant has written anything which approaches the brilliant and vivid impressions of Versailles recorded by Keynes and Harold Nicolson. Still less do we have an equivalent to the matter-of-fact revelations of David Hunter Miller's *Diary at the Conference at Paris*. There are good reasons for this. In the first place the agreement of the Big Three to separate the peacemaking from the charter-drafting meant that much of the drama of Versailles was, as it were, banned in advance from San Francisco. And when one reflects on the course that the Peace Conference of World War II did take when it met in Paris in 1946, one can be truly grateful for the decision. Secondly, much of the groundwork for the U.N. had already been laid at Dumbarton Oaks, while almost the entire League structure had to be hammered out at Paris. These considerations, together with the fact that the war in Europe (until 8 May) and in Asia was still in progress, robbed the Conference of that galaxy of great leaders which provided Versailles with the glittering clash of personalities that history, no less than journalism, loves to feed on. San Francisco was graced by the near great, the foreign ministers, but the ultimate custodians of power stayed in their capitals thousands of miles away, the telephone and the radio enabling them, when occasion required, to apply an abrasive or obstructive touch to operations that for the most part they were happy to entrust to their subordinates on the spot. Finally, perhaps there hung about San Francisco a certain air of the derivative, the second-hand. The world had been through all this before, and though there was a pervasive hope that the U.N. would succeed where the League had failed, the peculiar thrill and promise that comes of doing something for the first time was inevitably absent. At San Francisco history was not so much being made as re-made. The world was having a second try.

Honouring Wilson's precept more than his practice, San Francisco also differed from Versailles in its genuine respect for the doctrine of 'Open covenants, openly arrived at'. From first to last the conference took place in a blaze of publicity. The Californian climate (physical and social), the pressures of the American journalistic tradition, the national rivalries for a place in the world's headlines, and, above all, the need to capture the interest and support of the American public and, through them, the U.S. Senate, all combined to make San Francisco the best reported international conference of the century. 2,636 correspondents reported daily on the conference's doings and all national delegations maintained a full flow of guidance and information to the press of their own and other countries. Of course, occasional meetings, especially of the Big Five or the Big Three, took place in private (though even here the privacy was more nominal than real) but otherwise the press, even when it was not actually present, was kept fully informed of what went on. In another important respect peace-building at San Francisco differed from the previous practice of Versailles. Decisions were taken by vote, a two-thirds majority being required, and the Charter and the proposed amendments were voted on clause by clause. Such a procedure would have been utterly impracticable had the conference not already had before it as an agenda the substantial and agreed basis of the Dumbarton Oaks 'proposals'. The procedure also depended on there being, in effect, as Sir Charles Webster says, 'a Great Power Conference inside the larger Conference', and on delegates showing a realistic respect for this inner circle's recommendations. As it was, the voting arrangements worked surprisingly well and introduced into the conference proceedings an element of the democratic process which was of real value.

The conference opened on the day the Russians announced that they had surrounded Berlin, and although it was nine weeks before it disbanded there hung over its sessions an almost constant awareness of the pressure of history in the making outside. Mr. Stettinius, in his opening speech, spoke for everyone when he emphasized that 'We have no time to lose'. The imminence of peace, or at least of armistice, was only too obviously loosening the bonds of the wartime coalition and endangering that unity of the Big Three which everyone agreed to be indispensable for the establishment of world order. Two days before victory in Europe was announced, the arrest in Moscow of the emissaries from the London Polish government dramatically demonstrated the contrast between the notions of international propriety entertained in Moscow and those obtaining in the West. Indeed, throughout the entire conference the absence of any spokesman for Poland constituted a silent reminder of the consequences of Great Power disagreement. For this reason—and also because leaders from every country had pressing domestic problems clamouring for their attention—the proceedings were always hard-driven and sometimes hurried. This left its marks on the Charter at many points in loose and wordy or untidy drafting. But it does not follow that a more leisurely tempo would have produced better results; had the pressure been relaxed the filibusterers and the utopians would have had a field day and agreement would have been sacrificed on the altar of perfection.

The conference opened with Mr. Molotov objecting to any permanent presidency for Mr. Stettinius, although he represented the conference's host country. Instead, Mr. Molotov insisted on a presidency rotating among the sponsoring powers. Again the U.S.S.R. objected to the admission of Argentina, whom the Latin-American countries wished to have as a participant. In the voting on this issue San Francisco showed forth the solidarity of two blocs which were to become familiar in the functioning of the U.N. itself, the Soviet and the Latin-American, with Yugoslavia, Czechoslovakia, and Greece siding with the U.S.S.R. (the Ukraine and Byelorussia were not yet admitted), and the rest of the world either abstaining or supporting the

Latin-Americans. Of the substantive disagreements in the Charter-drafting the first serious one concerned the relationship between regional organizations and the U.N.'s Security Council. Superficially this too was a Pan-American problem, created by the separate and prior action of the Inter-American Conference at Mexico City in staking out a claim to have inter-American disputes handled by themselves. Underlying this, however, was of course the universal desire to have some insurance, in the form of possible regional or other alliances, against the risk that the U.N. security system would not function as planned. If fully indulged, this desire would obviously have ended by siphoning off all authority from the Security Council and leaving it a mere bystander, yet the anxiety was a real one and, since it was widely shared, argument on the issue, though protracted, was not really bitter and agreement was finally reached on the formula which now appears as Article 51 of the Charter.

Dumbarton Oaks, as we have seen, was silent on the question of trusteeships and colonial territories, and this was a gap which it was San Francisco's recognized role to fill. At Yalta little more had been done than to agree that trusteeship should apply to existing League mandates, ex-World War II colonies, and any other territory that might voluntarily be placed under trustee-ship. The Big Five were to consult on the question before San Francisco. In fact, however, no such consultation took place and agreement had to be hammered out in the conference itself. Disagreements were prolonged and at times sharp, with the main line of fissure corresponding, as might be imagined, to the distinction between colonial and ex-colonial or anti-colonial powers, the U.S.S.R. mainly voting as one of the latter. The discussions lasted for most of the conference and the eventual agreements were embodied in Chapters XI, XII, and XIII of the Charter.

The crucial controversy, however, was over the veto. Ostensibly this had been settled at Yalta, but when the Formula came under fire from the smaller powers led by Australia and New Zealand, who objected to the veto applying to procedures for pacific settlement, it soon became apparent that the Great Powers themselves had divergent conceptions of what the Yalta Formula meant. On 22 May the delegates of the smaller powers presented a list of twenty-three questions to the sponsoring powers designed to clarify the Formula; when they came to concert their replies, Russia emerged alone as a fairly constant exponent of a 100 per cent. veto power, wishing to apply the veto even to the decision of whether a question was 'procedural' or not, and, even more disconcertingly, to the question of whether to put an item on the agenda or not. The acute crisis created by this seemed to endanger the whole conference, and for a week proceedings virtually stalled, while the Great Powers transferred their altercations from San Francisco to their respective capitals, and in particular to Moscow. There Harry Hopkins, present on a mission of reconciliation and fresh from negotiating what looked like an agreement on the Polish question, was instructed by Truman to take the matter up directly with Stalin. He persuaded the dictator in a matter of hours to modify the Russian stand and on 7 June the conference learnt with relief that Great Power unanimity had been restored. Not a word was altered in the Yalta Formula, which now appears in the Charter as Article 27; nor were explicit answers returned to the twenty-three questions. Instead the sponsoring powers issued a statement giving their interpretations of what the Formula meant. The key clauses in the statement were those which affirmed,

No individual member of the Council can alone prevent consideration and discussion by the Council of a dispute or situation brought to its attention. . . . Nor can parties to such dispute be prevented by these means from being heard by the Council. . . .

Beyond this point, decisions and actions by the Security Council may well have major political consequences and may even initiate a chain of events which might, in the end, require the Council under its responsibilities to invoke measures of enforcement. . . . This chain of events begins when the Council decides to make an investigation, or determines that the time has come to call upon states to settle their differences, or make recommendations to the parties. It is to such decisions and actions that unanimity of the permanent members applies, with the important proviso, referred to above, for abstention from voting by parties to a dispute.

Unpalatable as this response was to many delegates, and particularly to Australia's Evatt, criticism eventually gave way before the recognition of the need for Great Power unity. Finally, as a slight concession to the disgruntled who felt that even in this form the veto would give trouble, a loophole for subsequent revision was introduced. It was provided that if after ten years the Charter had not been amended by the ordinary machinery, the Assembly by a majority vote, plus the Security Council by a vote to which the veto would *not* apply, could together summon a Charter review conference.

With the clearance of this hurdle the major worries of the conference were over. The U.S.S.R. caused a last-minute flurry by seeking to reverse the decision by which the powers of the General Assembly had been liberalized and to go back to the tight limitation imposed in the Dumbarton Oaks draft. However, a compromise (embodied in Articles 10, 11, and 13 of the Charter) was hammered out which preserved for the smaller powers most of the concessions they had won.

Indeed at many other points the revised Charter showed the influence of the critics of Dumbarton Oaks. The 'middle powers', particularly Canada, had much to show for their labours—e.g. Article 44 which provides that if a country not on the Security Council is called on to provide troops to enforce peace it shall be entitled to join in the Security Council's discussions, and vote on the use of its forces. The smaller powers, in addition to their role in everything that touched on 'colonialism', also exercised effective pressure to have the economic and social functions of the organization expanded—e.g. the upgrading of the Trusteeship and Economic and Social Councils to the level of 'principal organs', and the expansion of those clauses which prescribe U.N. obligations and codes of conduct in these fields.

Finally, the Charter was ready for signature—no mean formality, since, with five documents to be signed, and over two hundred delegates from fifty nations to affix their names, the proceedings took all of eight hours to complete. On 26 June President Truman bade the delegates farewell in a speech whose qualified or, one might say, conditional optimism reflected the mood of most of them. Six days later he presented the Charter to the U.S. Senate; when on 28 July that body approved it by 89 votes to 2 the world could feel that something at least had been learnt from the blunders of a previous generation. Truman's America would not, like Wilson's, abandon its own brain-child. It would accept obligations proportionate to its power and place in the world. Other states quickly followed suit. Under Article 110 it needed ratification by all the Big Five, together with a majority of the other signatory states, to bring the Charter into effect. By 24 October this had been attained, and thus twenty-six years after the inception of the League the world embarked on its second experiment in organizing itself for peace.

2 · COVENANT AND CHARTER

In all the excitement that attended the accouchement of the new order, little attention had been paid to the obsequies of the old. In line with the American tactic of emphasizing the novelty of the U.N., the League had been virtually ignored at San Francisco. Its representation there was 'unofficial' and had been restricted to 'two or three persons': the Acting Secretary-General, Mr. Sean Lester, the Treasurer, Mr. Jacklin, and the senior Director, Mr. Loveday. Mr. Stettinius's speech of welcome to the delegates had pointedly omitted any reference to the League—as if even a word of allusion might set the ghost of Woodrow Wilson's failure walking the stage of the San Francisco Opera House. In the Charter, even where convenience would have dictated identity of nomenclature, pains seemed to have been taken to avoid it— e.g. in the substitution of 'Trusteeship' for 'Mandate', or 'The International Court of Justice' for 'The Permanent Court of Justice'.

In fact, however, at San Francisco as at Dumbarton Oaks, the delegates paid the League a much more profound tribute than any formal eulogy could have expressed: they copied it. Attention then and since naturally concentrated on the points of difference between the Covenant and the Charter, but the most obvious fact, so obvious as to be taken for granted, is the basic identity of objectives and methods, of plan and structure. 'Peace and security' are the main goals, however important and desirable the social and economic aims may be. Voluntary association in accordance with certain agreed codes of behaviour remains the accepted method of procedure. The sovereign state is still the unit of membership. In each body four main organs of basically the same character discharge roughly the same functions—an assembly, to which all members belong; a council, built around a nucleus of great powers; a secretariat, permanent and international, under an elected secretary-general; and a court, as it were adjacent to rather than incorporated in the main structure.

The General Assembly, in composition, is the League Assembly over again, the forum in which all member states are represented with equal rights of speech and vote. After San Francisco it was at first widely thought that the U.N. had drawn a clearer line than the League between the functions of its Assembly and its Council, giving the latter a more nearly exclusive responsibility in face of threats to peace and security. Whereas the Covenant had rather sweepingly permitted the League Assembly, like the Council, to 'deal . . . with any matter within the sphere of action of the League or affecting the peace of the world' (Article III, paragraph 3), the Charter, while leaving the General Assembly equally wide powers of discussion, sharply restricts it in the making of recommendations. Where matters of peace and security are concerned the Security Council has priority, and the General Assembly may make recommendations only when the Security Council is not dealing with a question or when, for any reason, the Security Council asks the General Assembly to recommend. In fact, as we shall see, this distinction has become, to say the least of it, considerably blurred in practice.

In one direction the Charter enlarged the Assembly's powers. Where economic, social, and mandate questions were concerned the League had entrusted principal responsibility to its Council, charging it with the direction of the League's technical bodies and the supervision of the Mandates Commission. The Charter, virtually restricting the Security Council to 'peace and security', gives to the General Assembly an exclusive ultimate authority in the other fields. This, however, must be read against the background of two facts, the first that the Charter also established two specialized Councils, the Economic and Social Council (ECOSOC) and the Trusteeship Council, with proximate authority in their own spheres, and the second that much of the enormous expansion of international activity in the social and economic fields has in fact escaped the U.N.'s parental control, the separate specialized agencies having sprouted up alongside with a strong independent life of their own.

In procedure the U.N. introduced one important novelty. It abandoned the League's principle of unanimity. In both the Assembly and the Council of the League one hostile vote could prevent a decision (although, as we shall see, the League had its own devices for escaping from this strait-jacket). The U.N. Assembly was empowered, by contrast, to make decisions by majority vote—in the case of 'important decisions', by a two-thirds majority. Similarly, the Security Council, as we have seen, reserves its veto for its permanent members; if they concur, an affirmative vote of nine out of its fifteen members carries the day.

In structure the Security Council closely parallels its League predecessor, with its core of permanent Great Power members and its elected non-permanent members. The League Council, however, was more fluid, permitting changes in the composition of the Great Power core and the numbers of the elected members, and even the emergence of a category of 'semi-permanents'. Such fluidity was possible because the League Assembly was given authority to control the Council's composition. The Security Council structure is rooted in the Charter itself, and its form of composition can only be changed by Charter amendment. Thus the enlargement of its membership, from eleven to fifteen, was made possible in 1965 only by the amendment of Articles 23 and 27.

More specialized in its function, the Security Council was also designed to be more potent in its operation. It was empowered to decide on behalf of the whole U.N. whether peace is threatened and whether sanctions should be applied, and such decisions, when taken, were to be binding on all members. For this purpose the Security Council was to be equipped with a special organ, a Military Staff Committee composed of the Chiefs of Staff of all the permanent members. This body would make advance plans for the organization and deployment of military forces which member states would place at the disposal of the organization and, when the Council acted, the Committee would serve as its strategic adviser.

The Charter says a good deal more about economic and social objectives than the Covenant did. Nevertheless, by 1939 the

League's work in this sphere had so greatly expanded as to lead to a proposal that a new League organization, the Central Committee for Economic and Social Questions, should be created to supervise what the League was doing in this field. This proposal was the seed which in the Charter flowered as ECOSOC, a separate organ of the U.N., 'under the authority of the General Assembly', to which it must report. ECOSOC was made responsible for the work of the U.N. in these fields. It was also charged with the task of co-ordinating the work of the specialized agencies, though it was given no coercive powers for this purpose. Its membership was originally restricted to eighteen, with, in theory, no reserved seats for Great Powers or anyone else. In 1965, however, by a Charter amendment passed at the same time as that affecting the Security Council, its membership was raised to twenty-seven.

To look after its mandates and its mandatories the League had established a Commission on which sat nine (subsequently ten) independent experts, in no way official spokesmen of their governments, four of whom were always from mandatory countries. The Permanent Mandates Commission was advisory to the League Council, in which ultimate responsibility was lodged, though in fact the League Assembly also made its voice heard frequently on mandates questions. The U.N. confined ultimate authority to the General Assembly, but, in effect, raised the Mandates Commission to the level of a separate organ under the title of the Trusteeship Council. As under the League, oversight can only be exercised by agreement with the controlling trusteeship power and moral pressure is the Council's only weapon. The Council was, however, given one power the Commission never enjoyed; it can visit trust territories for itself. Moreover, Chapter XI of the Charter, the Declaration Regarding Non-Self-Governing Territories, though only an unenforceable statement of professions, does impose on all member states who have colonies an administrative code which is morally binding on them. The Trusteeship Council consists not of experts but of representatives of member states—all the administering powers, together with all non-administering members of the Big Five, plus members elected by the General Assembly. The General Assembly elects as many members as are needed to make the numbers of trusteeship and non-trusteeship states equal.

The Charter provided for a Secretariat to serve all these bodies and its provisions in this regard adhered closely to League practice. There was, however, one significant exception: the Secretary-General, under Article 99, was given an explicit political role, by being empowered, of his own initiative, to bring to the attention of the Security Council any matter which might endanger peace and security.

The League system included a Permanent Court of International Justice, set up in 1921. It functioned at the Hague and while not actually a League body (its membership was not identical with that of the League) its fifteen judges were elected by the Council and the Assembly and the League paid its bills. It turned out to be 'Permanent', however, only in name, the San Francisco Conference preferring to establish a new U.N. organ in its place. The Conference did, however, admit its inability substantially to improve on the original model by formally recording that the new court's statute was based on its predecessor's. In fact the only significant difference is that the new International Court of Justice is an integral part of the Organization. All U.N. members are automatically members of it, though provision is also made for non-members to join.

Just as the structure of the U.N. rested upon a League basis, so its philosophical foundations went down into a Geneva subsoil and indeed beyond. In *The League of Nations and the Rule of Law* the late Sir Alfred Zimmern disentangled the ideas which underlay the League Covenant and traced them back to their origins in the earlier history of international organization. It is instructive to examine the Charter in the same way and see what diverse, and at points, discrepant, concepts were combined in it and also how far it re-embodied the ideas of the Covenant and of the working League.

Zimmern found the first influence upon the Covenant in the concept of the Concert of the Great Powers with its roots going back at least as far as the 'Congress System' of Castlereagh. The essence of this system was to be found in the regular conferences of the powers whose strength both permitted and obliged them to accept special responsibility for the organization of international order. The League Council was essentially the embodiment of this concept, with the privileged position of its permanent members and its regular meetings.

From the start the thinking of the architects of the U.N. revolved around this concept. The events of 1940-5, which provided the context for the work of Charter-making, were dominated by 'the Grand Alliance', as Churchill called it. The successful prosecution of the war, the indispensable precondition of any successful organization for peace, had depended on a continuous harmonization of Great Power policies through the mechanism of meetings of heads of state, foreign ministers, or military chiefs. The harmonization had often been imperfect, but recognition was general, apparently even in Russia, that without it victory would probably not have been achieved. It seemed only logical therefore to build any permanent organization for peace and security upon the same corner-stone.

Consequently the idea of the Concert is to be found at the heart of the Charter. The Security Council gives it structural embodiment, as in the League, with the Great Powers given permanent seats, the five of them being actually named in the constitutional document (Article 23). The veto is the symbol of their privileged position and the constitutional weapon by which they defend it. The other members explicitly recognize their role; they 'confer on the Security Council primary responsibility for the maintenance of peace and security, and agree that in carrying out its duties under this responsibility the Security Council acts on their behalf' (Article 24). Moreover, (Article 25) 'the Members of the U.N. agree to accept and carry out decisions of the Security Council in accordance with the Charter', even when these decisions involve (Chapter VII) calling upon the members to apply sanctions, up to and including armed force. This indeed was going beyond the Castlereagh concept of the Concert, just as it was going beyond the League Council's potency. It was practically a return, in institutional form, to the Quadruple Alliance system, with the Great Powers acting jointly to keep the peace amongst the rest. To this end the Security Council was to be equipped with its Military Staff Committee; it was to be a permanent policeman of the world.

The Assembly of the League had originally been conceived as a sort of outer circle of conferring powers, without exceptional privileges or responsibilities, meeting less often—perhaps even (so the Foreign Office had originally contemplated) at four-yearly intervals. In fact, as the Covenant took shape, and still more obviously as the League began to function, the Assembly became something very much more than this. Exactly what it was—an annual conference of the whole League world, a 'parliament' to the Council's 'cabinet', a universal forum for debate and complaint—no one quite liked to say. It was more than some of these labels implied, less than others claimed. It was, indeed, *sui generis*; whether intentionally or not it was the League's nearest approach to a political invention.

The framers of the Charter seem to have approached this section of their work with no clearer concept to guide them than the Wilsonians had had. There was never any shadow of doubt amongst them (not even, apparently, amongst the Russians) that there must be an Assembly; that—provided certain qualifications were met—the U.N. must include, at this level, all the powers, however impotent, and that the obvious model was the Assembly of the League. The exact powers and functions of the General Assembly appear to have been determined, however, not in accordance with any particular theory but as the result of a tug-of-war between (broadly speaking) the Great Powers and the rest. The Great Powers, provided they got their Security Council, were prepared to make concessions to the Assembly elsewhere—e.g. in the social, economic, and trusteeship fields; the other powers aspired to share in as much of the Concert as they could and pressed for as extensive a participation of the General Assembly in all fields as they could obtain. Such black and white terms, of course, do violence to the many shades of opinion that were represented at San Francisco, but it is broadly true to say that the Charter's allocation of power between Council and Assembly reflects some such division of views.

Zimmern and many other writers have traced the development of international organization on its non-political side, in respect of the provision of what he called 'World Services', back to the establishment of the Universal Postal Union in 1874. The Covenant, as is well known, incorporated a good deal of 'international functionalism', in the role it envisaged for the League in social and economic matters, in its provision of a permanent Secretariat which would collect and provide information, and in the way it enthroned the League (under Article XXIV) as a kind of super-directorate for all existing international bureaux. Functionalism, as we have seen, was a strong influence playing upon the thinking of the Charter-framers, both at Dumbarton Oaks and at San Francisco, and the impact of this 'World Services' concept is even more marked in the Charter than it was in the Covenant. Structurally it manifests itself in the Economic and Social Council, and administratively in the co-ordinating role accorded to it in relation to other international organizations (Articles 63 and 64). In fact, however, the concept has been so expanded as almost to be transformed. Just as the nation-state has carried its provision of domestic services far beyond such bare essentials as roads and post offices and now provides for health, employment, and higher productivity to such an extent that we speak of 'the welfare state', so at the international level by 1945 expectations of what world organization could and should do had passed far beyond the limited, though solid, achievements of the 'World Services' side of the League. There was a demand for a sort of 'Welfare Internationalism' which would do far more than regulate; it would promote and share; promote health, education, productivity, and full employment, share raw materials, technical skills, and perhaps even capital. 'Welfare Internationalism' very seldom took the form of a clearly argued and thought-out theory of international action or organization; it was rather the reflection of a diffused set of dissatisfactions and aspirations— unevenly felt, but where felt, as in the so-called 'under-developed areas', capable of generating a head of steam which the otherwise indifferent powers could not ignore. The result of this, as far as the Charter was concerned, was what might be expected. Far more than the Covenant, the Charter was lavish with pledges and good intentions. There is not a word in the Covenant to say that people should not starve, but the Preamble to the Charter talks about a determination 'to promote social progress and better standards of life' and 'the economic and social advancement of all peoples'; the Purposes of the U.N., as defined in Article 1, include 'co-operation in solving international problems of an economic, social, cultural, or humanitarian character', etc.; the obligations of the organization, as set out in Article 55, include the promotion of 'higher standards of living, full employment, and conditions of economic and social progress and development'. The catalogue of such phrases is not exhaustive. But compared with the precision of the Charter's provisions in the political field what strikes one about the 'Welfare Internationalism' of the Charter is its vagueness, both structurally (as we shall see when we examine the Economic and Social Council) and procedurally, in the lack of clear indications as to the processes by which the organization is to realize its pledges in these fields. Some of this vagueness, of course, is due to the success of the most practical 'functionalists' in setting up their own independent agencies outside the U.N. proper, but most of it is due to the comparative novelty of the whole concept and the disposition, in what most of the Charter-framers felt to be a secondary matter, to let verbal inflation be a substitute for hard thinking.

The Concert and World Services concepts between them would have accounted, even by themselves, for most of the U.N. structure as the Charter adumbrates it. But the mode of functioning of the U.N., like that of the League before it, was an expression of other ideas as well, especially where the primary purpose of the two organizations, the maintenance of peace and security, was involved. Zimmern isolated one of these ideas as a distinctively Wilsonian one and gave to it the not altogether happy label of the 'Monroe Doctrine System', a name which more accurately describes its ancestry than its functioning. In the Covenant it finds its most explicit expression in Article X, the Article of Mutual Guarantee, by which members 'undertake to respect and preserve as against external aggression the territorial integrity and existing political independence' of each other's countries. The Covenant, viewed in this aspect, becomes an extension, to the point of becoming a universalization, of the old-fashioned bilateral treaty of guarantee, by which A undertakes to protect B or (if the two parties are of more equal strength) A and B undertake to protect each other. This is the concept of 'one for all and all for one' which later earns the name of Collective Security.

In the Charter, Article 2, § 4 affirms: 'All Members shall refrain in their international relations from the threat or use of force against the territorial integrity or political independence of any state', a pledge which clearly reproduces half of the undertaking that League members assumed in Article X. What is notably absent is the obligation to *preserve* as well as *respect*—in other words the positive as opposed to the merely negative aspect of the Mutual Guarantee. Why is this? In the British Government's official commentary on the Dumbarton Oaks proposals (Cmd. 6571) this failure to reproduce *in toto* the guarantee of Article X is explained on the ground that, literally interpreted, such a guarantee would freeze the territorial *status quo* 'for all time', that the recognition given elsewhere (Article 2, § 1) to the general principle of 'sovereign equality' protects states against arbitrary molestation, and above all that the Charter contains elsewhere an 'absolute' undertaking to prevent war together with much more definite obligations on states to secure that end. The reference is to the authority given to the Security Council by Articles 39, 41, and 42 to act to the full in face of a breach of the peace, threatened or actual, and the powers given to it to call on other members for support. In other words the Guarantee loses something of its complete Mutuality, becoming instead more of a Guarantee by the Strong of the Weak. Such was certainly the main thinking of those who drew up the Charter, particularly the Great Powers. In fact, as events were to show, the failure of the permanent members of the Security Council to agree led to the atrophying of this concept to a point where it virtually reverted, in so far as it retained vitality at all, to something like the Mutual Guarantee concept of the League.

Closely allied to the Mutual Guarantee concept in the framing of the League Covenant was what in 1918 the British Judge, Lord Parker, called the principle of the 'Hue and Cry' and which found contemporaneous expression in a memorandum of Mr. Elihu Root. This was, in essence, the idea that war, as such, was a matter of universal concern, no matter where it occurred, and also a crime against the world community. The world organization should therefore organize a joint and mutual guarantee of all its members, not primarily in defence of their territory and their independence, but against any act of war however arising. This found partial expression in the Covenant's Article XI with its assertion that 'Any war or threat of war, whether immediately affecting any of the Members of the League or not, is hereby declared a matter of concern to the whole League'. The force of the principle was, however, sensibly abated by the lack of any clear and automatic machinery to give effect to it. Individual states were left free to decide whether or not they would join in the 'Hue and Cry' and, by Article XII, resort to war was still permitted under certain limited circumstances.

In 1928 the Pact of Paris, or the Kellogg–Briand Pact, sought to carry the idea of 'the outlawry of war' a step further. By this the sixty-five states which ultimately adhered to the Pact declared 'that they condemn recourse to war . . . and renounce it as an instrument of national policy' and accepted an obligation to settle all disputes or conflicts 'by pacific means'. As a profession of good intentions the Pact was unexceptionable, but the claim that it 'outlawed war' was excessive. War was only 'condemned' and 'renounced' and no enforcement machinery of any kind was provided. Above all, signatory states made it clear that they did not interpret the Pact as in any way limiting the right of 'self-defence', with all the possibilities of broad interpretation therein implied.

It was contended in respect of the 'Hue and Cry' concept that it assumed the existence of the rudiments of a world community, and some critics of the League, after its failures over Manchuria and Ethiopia, argued that its experiences then proved that no such rudiments existed. When the U.N. was being framed a slightly different assumption prevailed—that whether or not a world community existed there was a Five Power community with world-wide strength. The logical deduction from this assumption was that the primary responsibility for organizing the Hue and Cry should rest on the Big Five—in other words on that expanded and strengthened manifestation of the Concert which is the Security Council, functioning continuously and equipped with force. Thus in one sense the universal concern over any outbreak of war is narrowed; in the first instance, as in Article 39, it is the Security Council's business to 'determine the existence of any threat to the peace', etc., and to 'decide what measures shall be taken'. On the other hand, once the Security Council has made a decision it may call upon all the members, under Article 41, to apply it—and such a call is mandatory; the members are pledged by Articles 25 and 49 to respond. Thus, although the Charter contains no phrase explicitly paralleling Article XI's sweeping assertion that 'any war' is 'a matter of concern to the whole' membership, the U.N. system is, in effect, organized on that assumption. Furthermore, its founders would have claimed, it goes far beyond the League or the Pact of Paris in the provisions contained in the Charter for giving effect to this belief. As the British official commentary on the Dumbarton Oaks proposals put it: 'While the Covenant in certain cases allowed war to be made legally . . . the new organization would not only try to abolish the use of all violence between States but could intervene even when violence is merely threatened.'

Wider than the Concert, weaker than the Hue and Cry, there was a third instrument of the pre-1918 world that had provided the League founders with a set of habits and techniques which they sought to incorporate in the Covenant. This was the Hague Conference system. The essence of the system lay in the procedures it developed for the peaceful settlement of disputes by the processes of mediation, conciliation and inquiry, laying down a workable body of rules, and making available a permanent secretariat and a body of arbitrators. The system of itself cannot stop aggression; its function is to facilitate a settlement where the disputants want one and to mobilize public opinion in favour of a peaceful solution even where they do not.

This system was taken over virtually in its entirety by the League and may be found embodied in the Covenant in all those Articles from XII to XV inclusive which set out the agreed processes for settling disputes, either by arbitration, or by judicial settlement through the Permanent Court, or by submission to the Council and ultimately to the Assembly. The Covenant, however, put a novel coping-stone on this structure by Article XVI, providing that any power which flouted this machinery and resorted to war should have invoked against it automatic financial and economic sanctions and conditional military sanctions. (There was a loophole in this procedure, as in the Hue and Cry system; it consisted in the exemption from these procedures of any dispute arising out of a matter solely within the domestic jurisdiction of a member.)

The U.N. took over practically the whole of what the League had incorporated of the Hague Conference system. In Article 1, § 1, the Charter announces its purpose 'to bring about by peaceful means, and in conformity with the principles of justice and international law, adjustment or settlement of international disputes or situations which might lead to a breach of the peace'. The whole of Chapter VI of the Charter, 'Pacific Settlement of Disputes', is devoted to an elaboration of the processes which give effect to this purpose, while Chapter XIV outlines the functioning of the International Court in this connexion. The processes set out in Chapter VI run the gamut from direct negotiation between the affected parties, inquiry, mediation, conciliation, arbitration, judicial settlement, and recommendation by the Security Council. The following Chapter VII sets out the ensuing sequence of more militant U.N. action if the dispute, still unsettled after the exhaustion of these processes, becomes a threat to the peace. Although Article 35 permits disputes to be brought before the General Assembly as well, the emphasis in the wording throughout is on *Security Council* action, and clearly the framers expected that in this sphere, as in the sphere of enforcement, the Council would be the prime mover. The Charter does not, of course, any more than the Covenant, give to the world organization any power to impose a settlement of its members' disputes. It provides an elaborate adaptable machinery for settlement which it expects them to use, but no organ of the U.N., not even the Security Council, is empowered to impose a decision. In the event of the dispute developing into a threat to peace and security the Council can certainly act, but again not to impose a decision, but only to preserve the peace. The U.N. is not a world government.

These are the main strands of thought which were woven into the Charter. Subsidiary to them, but still important, are a number of other concepts which found their way, at one level or another, into the Charter, just as in many instances they had found their way into the Covenant. One of these was disarmament. The thinking of the first Hague Conference on this subject became the thinking of Geneva—that armaments were not only an instrument of war but also a cause of war; consequently disarmament was a proper concern of a world organization. In the Covenant this had found expression in Article VIII, by which members, recognizing 'that the maintenance of peace requires the reduction of national armaments to the lowest point consistent with national safety and the enforcement by common action of international obligations', gave to the League Council power to produce a disarmament plan which, once accepted by governments, would set upper limits to their forces. The experience of the inter-war years had weakened enthusiasm for disarmament *per se*; the events of the thirties seemed to suggest that it was not armaments as such, but armaments in the wrong hands which endangered peace, that indeed the 'peace-loving' nations ought to remain armed if aggression was to be prevented or repulsed. This line of thinking is reflected in the Charter in a much reduced emphasis on disarmament for its own sake. There are two references to the idea:

in Article 11 the General Assembly is empowered to consider and make recommendations about the 'principles governing disarmament and the regulation of armaments', and in Article 26, in order to establish peace and security 'with the least diversion for armaments of the world's human and economic resources', the Security Council is made responsible, with the aid of the Military Staff Committee, for formulating plans 'for the establishment of a system for the regulation of armaments'. There is here no recognition that peace requires 'the reduction of armaments'; the emphasis is more on regulation and much less on disarmament; and nothing is said anywhere about that 'interchange of full and frank information' about national armaments which members of the League had sworn to provide (though they notably failed to live up to their promises). Indeed the whole concept of a policing Security Council with a Military Staff Committee implies that adequate force must always be available to the organization. This reflects, of course, the pervasive Churchill-Roosevelt conviction that World War II had been due as much to the weakness of the democracies as to the aggressiveness of the Axis and that the greatest mistake of the victors after World War I had been the precipitate dismantling of their military structure. It is quite possible, too, that the thinking of the Charter on this subject might have been different if the San Francisco Conference had been held after Hiroshima, instead of ending a month before.

We have seen how, so far as structure is concerned, the League's Mandates Commission had been made over, expanded and strengthened, as the U.N.'s Trusteeship Council. The theory of international action in this field had similarly developed in the years between Versailles and San Francisco. Broadly speaking, three sets of ideas can be traced in the Covenant's provisions for a Mandates system: first, the concept of *condominium*, joint supervision of certain disputed areas (such as had been practised in the Congo); second, the concept of trusteeship exercised by an imperial power on behalf of its dependent peoples (as by Britain in India or France in Africa); and third, the concept of the Great Powers as a Concert exercising a collective responsibility to co-ordinate and promote their interests in areas, like the Ottoman Empire or the Congo, which were 'unsettled' or 'backward'. The League system, with its recognition of the power and privilege of the mandatory and its safeguards, sometimes more nominal than real, for the 'mandated', represented an imperfect blend of these three concepts. The inter-war years had been marked by a growing demand all over the world for the application of the principle of 'self-determination' to dependent peoples. Most of the colonial powers in varying degrees accepted self-government as the goal of their administration, as for example the British in India and the Americans in the Philippines. Little remained after the Versailles Treaty of any outright imperialist theory that colonies existed merely for the interest of the imperial powers. Argument was confined to the question in what forms and with what sincerity colonial powers were discharging their responsibilities in their territories. Furthermore the war had simultaneously weakened the prestige of the imperial powers—particularly in the Far East—and accelerated the drive for self-determination among hitherto dependent peoples. Finally two of the Great Powers at San Francisco were in a crusading anti-imperialist mood (with, of course, appropriate private reservations)—the U.S.A. under the influence of the Legend of 1776 and the promptings of Franklin Roosevelt, and the U.S.S.R. in accordance with the principles of Marxism-Leninism as interpreted by Stalin.

The impact of these forces on the Charter is observable not only in the status of the Trusteeship Council—a separate and 'principal' organ—but still more in the extension of the U.N.'s interest to cover not just mandated territories but others as well. Article XXIIIb of the League Covenant had pledged League members to secure 'just treatment of the native inhabitants of territories under their control', but this unenforceable expression of good intent was the only mention in the Covenant of colonial peoples, except for those who having lost their wartime masters were put under the mandates system. The Charter, by contrast, contains a lengthy 'Declaration concerning Non-Self-Governing

Territories' (Chapter XI). This, admittedly, is no more enforceable than the Covenant's article but its range and precision create a stronger moral pressure on members and demonstrate how far the concept of an international responsibility for dependent peoples had developed since Geneva. In place of the indefinable 'just treatment' of the Covenant we have a recognition that the interests of the natives are to be paramount, that their *political*, as well as economic, social, and educational advancement is to be ensured, that 'self-government' is to be developed, that 'constructive measures of development' are to be promoted and 'research' encouraged; above all, that imperial powers are 'to transmit regularly to the Secretary-General for information purposes, subject to such limitation as security and constitutional considerations may require, statistical and other information of a technical nature relating to economic, social, and educational conditions'. The careful wording of these clauses reveals immediately that the imperial powers did not accept at San Francisco any administrative role for the U.N. in their colonial territories, any more than they admitted the U.N. into the domestic business of their homelands. For all that, these clauses undoubtedly represent the admission of a new concept—the claim of an international organization in principle to interest itself in the affairs of dependent peoples, even those who do not come under the umbrella of its mandates.

The same disposition to expand the concept of what is legitimately of international concern is to be seen in the language of the Charter about 'human rights'. The League Covenant had admitted, in Article XXIII, to a marginal interest in these fields, but only where labour conditions were concerned (the ILO, of course, was a fuller exemplification of this) and where the traffic in women and children was involved. The Charter, by contrast, not only sounds off in wide terms in its Preamble—'determined . . . to reaffirm faith in fundamental human rights, in the dignity and worth of the human person, in the equal rights of men and women and of nations large and small'—and in its Purposes Article (1, § 3)—'to achieve international co-operation . . . in promoting and encouraging respect for human rights and for fundamental freedoms for all without distinction as to race, sex, language, or religion'—but also, in Article 55c, commits the U.N. to promoting 'universal respect for, and observance of, human rights and fundamental freedoms', etc. Article 62 directs the Economic and Social Council to make recommendations in pursuance of this, and finally, Article 68 bids it set up a separate commission 'for the promotion of human rights'.

Behind this plenitude of language there stood no very clearly defined philosophy of international action such as would explain how an international agency whose members were sovereign states was going to be able to protect the rights of individuals dwelling within the boundaries of those same sovereign states. Still less did the Charter explain how this could be done without infringing Article 2, §7, which expressly forbids intervention 'in matters which are essentially within the domestic jurisdiction' of states. Historically, however, the appearance of this concept in the Charter is explicable enough. By 1945 the world had become fully and sickeningly aware of the outrages perpetrated against humanity by the Nazi and Japanese régimes (though much less aware of what went on in the U.S.S.R.). The Nuremberg prosecutions were an indication of the widespread demand for an authority which could go behind national sovereignty and 'reasons of state' and bring the perpetrators of such outrages to book. The human rights clauses of the Charter, like so many other clauses, looked backward in a 'never again' spirit and drew their inspiration more from a revulsion at the past than from any very clear programme for the future. They also received a powerful impetus at San Francisco from the American sentiment that saw their place in the Charter as analogous to the position occupied in the American Constitution by the 'Bill of Rights'. It may even be significant that it was Senator Vandenberg and Mr. John Foster Dulles who particularly pressed for them, leading spokesmen of that Republican Party which had been instrumental, after the American Civil War, in extending the long arm of federal authority so as to protect civil rights even in those fields which the Constitution in 1789 had specifically recognized as under the sovereignty of the several States. However this may be, the idea, for all its vagueness—largely because of its vagueness—was popular at San Francisco, not least amongst those countries whose domestic record in the field of civil liberties left most to be desired. Meanwhile, those countries which were sceptical contented themselves with the reflection that these humanitarian clauses were merely recommendatory and did not endow the organization with any powers of enforcement.

The time had been, in the heyday of Cobdenism, when free trade appeared to be, of itself, an adequate solvent of war, as well as an essential ingredient of peace. There remained in 1919 enough vitality in this Victorian concept to secure it some recognition in the League Covenant. The third of Woodrow Wilson's Fourteen Points had called for the 'removal, as far as possible, of all economic barriers and the establishment of an equality of trade conditions among all the nations consenting to the peace'. This had appeared, considerably modified, as Article XXIIIe of the Covenant: 'The Members of the League will make provision to secure and maintain . . . equitable treatment for the commerce of all Members of the League.'

After World War II the principal apostle of the Cobdenite faith was Mr. Cordell Hull. That an American Secretary of State, representing a traditionally protectionist power, should preach the gospel of free trade is explicable largely by the fact that Mr. Hull, like Wilson before him, was both a Democrat and a Southerner, and in each capacity had been engaged in trying to convert his fellow countrymen, as well as the rest of the world, to a belief in the virtues of non-discrimination. Under such impetus the U.S.A. during the war had used its Lend-Lease programme as a powerful lever to exact compliance from its allies in its liberal objectives; each Lend-Lease Agreement contained a clause by which the recipient agreed to the 'expansion . . . of production, employment, and the exchange and consumption of goods . . . the elimination of all forms of discriminatory treatment in international commerce . . . [and] the reduction of tariffs and other trade barriers'. However, when it came to Charter-drafting, it appeared that even the U.S.A. was not as wholeheartedly committed to these objectives as its language towards its allies made it appear. Strong conservative and protectionist elements made their influence felt in Washington and subsequently at San Francisco, while Britain, the homeland of Cobdenism, had now become more concerned to preserve the Commonwealth preferences than to gamble on her chances in a free-trade world. In any case the almost universal decline in *laissez faire* economics, domestic as well as foreign, meant that the emphasis even amongst the internationalists was now much less on the mere removal of trade barriers and much more on positive action to promote productivity and high levels of employment. The result is to be seen in the absence from the Charter of any reference at all to the desirability of freer trading, as such. In all the plenitude of language in the Preamble, Purposes, and Economic and Social Chapters there is nothing that goes as far even as the Covenant's Article XXIII. Instead, besides the 'International Welfare' references to 'higher living standards, full employment,' etc., already mentioned, there are references to 'international co-operation in solving international problems of an economic . . . character' (Article 1), or to 'promoting international co-operation in the economic . . . fields' (Article 13), or to 'conditions of economic . . . progress and development' (Article 55a). These are broad terms and it is open to members to read into them, if they wish, endorsement for liberal trade policies (as indeed was subsequently done by the promoters of the International Trade Organization and the General Agreement on Tariffs and Trade), but taken all together they constitute only the most shadowy relic of the Cobdenite faith in a world made safe from war by the unhindered enterprise of its producers and traders.

The League, though envisaged as a universal organization, with what might be described as a European-Atlantic core, had admitted into the Covenant a recognition of regionalism, inspired originally by the American sensitivity over the Monroe Doctrine, but persisting in its final form as a legalization of other regional arrangements as well. This was Article XXI: 'Nothing in this Covenant shall be deemed to affect the validity of international

engagements, such as treaties of arbitration or regional under-
standings like the Monroe Doctrine, for securing the maintenance
of peace.' This Article made possible the legalization of such
regional alliances as the Little Entente and the Balkan Entente
and such arrangements as Locarno. It also opened the door, in
some critics' opinion, to a revival of the pre-war alliance system
which, in the eyes of leaders such as Wilson, the League had been
created to supersede. What is certain is that it represented the
persistence into the League period of a reliance on security
arrangements originally belonging to a pre-League world.

The League's failure as a universal organization for the preservation of peace and security seemed to one veteran of the
inter-war years to point the need for constructing its successor
round a frankly regional core. We have seen how at one stage in
the evolution of the U.N. Mr. Churchill had advocated an
organization built out of a group of regional security systems.
At the time and in its original form this idea had been rejected
not only by the other Great Power architects of the U.N. but also,
it seems, by Mr. Churchill's Cabinet colleagues at home.
Instead, the verdict had been cast in favour of a universal
organization of security with a hard core of power and responsibility at the centre. Nothing, however, could obscure the plain
fact that over many areas of the world regional arrangements
were either in effect or in contemplation, such as gave their
members a closer community of interest and feeling and a
stronger guarantee of protection than a fledgling universal agency
could provide. Recognition of this was initially made at Dumbarton Oaks, where approval was accorded to such bodies, provided their powers of enforcement were to be employed only with
'the authorization of the Security Council'. At San Francisco the
pressures in favour of recognizing regional arrangements were
greater even than at Dumbarton Oaks. Not only were there Great
Power interests; there were also the pressures coming from
smaller states which were members, in fact or in contemplation,
of the Inter-American system, the British Commonwealth, or
the Arab League. They professed concern lest a Security Council
with a Great Power veto might prevent swift action by a regional

organization; accordingly the Dumbarton Oaks proviso was itself equipped with a loophole—it would not apply where action was being taken against a state which had been an 'enemy' in World War II (Article 53). More sweeping, however, was the licence accorded to regional alliances by the addition of an entirely novel Article, No. 51, which does not indeed in so many words contain any reference to regionalism or alliances. What it does, however, is to give explicit authorization to 'the inherent right of . . . self-defence', and by recognizing that 'self-defence' may be either 'individual or collective' goes far to give *carte blanche* to the establishment and free operation of almost any regional arrangement. Whether such a concept is incompatible with the essential purpose of the U.N., however, depends less on the conformity or inconsistency of the two ideas in the abstract than on the applications accorded to them in practice.

The same may be said of another concept which found lodgement in both Covenant and Charter, in the first implicitly and in the second explicitly. In Article 2, § 1, the Charter announces: 'The Organization is based on the principle of the sovereign equality of all its Members.' In the pre-1914 European state system this was the most central and fundamental principle from which all else flowed. To find it enshrined in the constitution of the second organization designed to supersede that system gives one at first a shock. Has the jungle strayed into the paddock? Has anarchy been reinstated as the corner-stone of world order? Friends and foes of the U.N. have in different ways pressed this question, but all too often have not stayed for an answer. Hasty and ill-conceived presumptions as to what the answer is, or ought to be, have probably been the single most fertile cause of misconceptions about the nature and purpose both of the League and of the U.N.

The Covenant's silence is perhaps the most eloquent testimony one could find as to its draftsmen's acceptance of 'sovereign and equal' as a basic assumption of the League system. It is an association that is being formed, more solemn perhaps, more inclusive certainly than any previous alliance, but still an association, which states freely join and can freely leave and which they do not recognize as having any power to act save with the voluntary compliance of its members. A phrase in the Preamble is loaded with this implication: 'The High Contracting Parties . . . agree to this Covenant.' This, as Zimmern in his *League of Nations and the Rule of Law* (p. 270) puts it, 'indicates that the League is composed of sovereign states who of their own free will sign what is before all things a moral—one might almost say a religious— engagement. By so doing they do not form a new state, a new sovereign body. They merely dedicate themselves in their individual activities to a new political way of life.' Again (p. 283) the League 'is a standing agency facilitating common action by states animated by the co-operative spirit'. And, of course, it is a corollary of this that the member states co-operate as equals, cf. the unanimity rule in the Council and in the Assembly, carrying over into the Geneva world the principle of the old conference system that conferring states could not be overborne or outvoted.

In fact, however, member states by undertaking to live their lives in accordance with the Covenant thereby accepted a limitation on their freedom to act as they chose. The undertaking was a voluntary act; none the less, for all its voluntariness, it was still a limitation. Similarly the concept of equality was *ab initio* bent and breached to enable the new organization to function in a world in which, whatever the jurists might say, states were not equal, in power, population, or responsibility. The establishment of the Council, with its Great Power core, was a recognition of this within the heart of the Covenant itself, while the Assembly in its very first session established the convention that, provided it called a resolution a wish, a *vœu*, it could adopt it by a majority vote, thus making possible a whole range of decisions which only a majority favoured but which a minority accepted.

At first sight the U.N. seems to go far beyond this. The veto in the Security Council still protects the Great Powers but at the expense of heightening the disparity between them and the other members, not only of the General Assembly but of the Security Council itself. If the Great Powers agree the Security Council can act by a majority of a mere 9 out of 15 (originally 7 out of 11).

In the Assembly unanimity has been cast to the winds. 'Important questions' need only a two-thirds majority for their decision; others only an ordinary majority of those present and voting. Far more significant, as an encroachment upon earlier concepts of sovereignty, the Security Council was, as we have seen, given the right and responsibility of taking decisions on behalf of other members of the U.N. and, by the provisions of Chapter VII of the Charter, of making these decisions binding upon other members. All this undoubtedly reflects an awareness from a world still rocking with the war struggles of the Titans that sovereignty, in any Austinian sense, has become for most states largely a fiction, and reflects also an admission that if all states are equal some states are certainly more equal than others.

So much is true, yet the assertion in Article 2, § 1, of the Charter remains: 'The Organization is based on the principle of the sovereign equality of all its Members.' More than this, there is the restrictive paragraph 7 of the same Article, debarring the U.N. from intervening in 'matters which are essentially within the domestic jurisdiction of any state'. The interpretation of such clauses provides considerable scope for the ingenuity and fertility of the international lawyers (as for instance when they argue that the acceptance of international obligations implies an exercise of sovereignty and not a restriction of it). The political observer cannot, however, fail to see in such clauses the expression of a distrust of too swift a growth of power in the international organization, of a determination to keep for member states the maximum freedom of action externally and the maximum control internally consistent with the existence of a U.N. at all. These clauses and the type of thinking they embody are the brakes on the organization—to be relaxed when members feel happy about the organization's speed and direction, to be applied whenever they are uneasy. They serve notice that while the wide range of purposes described above are all, in varying degrees, intended for the organization, one thing is not intended: it is not to be a government.

What is it then? Most of what it is will by now be apparent

from what has been said earlier in this chapter. It will also be
apparent that this entity, some way between a club and a government, defies any too simple and categorical a label. One term,
however, strikingly recurrent in the Charter, provides a further
clue as to its character. This is the term 'Organization'. The
Preamble to the Charter concludes '. . . do hereby establish an
international organization to be known as the United Nations'
and in the text of the Charter proper the term recurs on another
twenty-four occasions. The Preamble to the Covenant, by contrast, had concluded '. . . agree to this Covenant of the League of
Nations' and on the rare occasions when the Covenant referred
to the new creation in its corporate capacity the term 'the League'
was employed—e.g. Article VII, 'The Seat of the League is
established at Geneva'; the refrain, moreover, that runs through
the Covenant is 'The *Members* of the League'. The emphasis, in
other words, falls on the components, not on the construct. The
stress of the Charter falls differently. In Article 2 it is 'the Organization and its Members' who are to 'act in accordance with
the following principles' and 'the Organization' which 'shall
ensure' that non-member states act in accordance with them as
well. In Article 4 (Conditions of Membership) 'the judgment of
the Organization' is involved. In Article 56 members pledge
themselves to co-operate with 'the Organization' to achieve the
social and economic purposes of the Charter, while in Articles 58
and 59 'the Organization' is to 'make recommendations' for co-
ordinating the specialized agencies and 'initiate negotiations' for
establishing new ones. The Secretary-General, under Article 98,
is to make an annual report 'on the work of the Organization', and
he and his staff, by Article 100, are to be 'responsible only to the
Organization'. Finally, one may note that under Article 105 it is
'the Organization' which 'shall enjoy . . . such privileges and immunities as are necessary for the fulfilment of its purposes' (under
the Covenant it was only 'officials of the League' and 'the buildings and other property occupied by the League or its officials'
which were so safeguarded).

Too much must not be made of language, especially the language of a document not conspicuous for careful drafting. Nor

indeed is it likely that the draftsmen of the Charter had a calculated
intent to stress 'the Organization' to the degree that these cumu-
lative examples suggest. The term 'Organization' came in originally as an almost necessary pendant, once the phrase 'United
Nations' had been accepted as the main label of the new enterprise.
But it is also true that, unlike the draftsmen of the Covenant, the
men of Dumbarton Oaks and San Francisco had, whether always
consciously or not, grown up in a world where international
organization was a fact of life. The League, for all its failure to
save peace and security, had established its right to exist, nay, its
indispensability, as an international organization. For all the
silences and undertones of the Covenant, an organization had
grown up at Geneva which was, with all its inadequacies, something more than the sum of its members. Most conspicuously,
though by no means exclusively, this was manifested in the League
Secretariat, that remarkable growth which went so far beyond the
thinking of all but a very few of the draftsmen at Versailles. That
this was recognized by the framers of the U.N. can be seen from
Chapter XV of the Charter, where the powers and duties of the
Secretariat are laid down. Not only is the League advance maintained; at one important point, as we have seen, it is even carried
further, as in Article 99 which endows the Secretary-General
with a politico-diplomatic responsibility and initiative, that of
bringing 'to the attention of the Security Council any matter
which in his opinion may threaten' peace and security. We must
be careful not to over-inflate the concept, but here we certainly
find personified the idea of an Organization which is more than
its constituent members, which has not merely, like some inert
idol, its servants and ministers, but also has—or can have—a
voice, a mind, and even a conscience of its own.

'A constitution', said Napoleon, 'should be short and ambiguous.' The document which embodies the ideas we have been
elucidating satisfies one of these criteria much more nearly than
the other. Ambiguity, indeed, as must now be obvious, is imposed
upon it by the variety and contrariety of the interests, fears, and
aspirations to which it gives expression. The Charter is, after all,

the charter of a *world* organization; the diversity as well as the unity of mankind has gone into its making. The Covenant, for all its world-wide applicability, was basically a European creation—especially if the U.S.A be regarded in its moral and political manifestations as that extension, indeed quintessence, of Europe which it is. But in the making of the Charter most of the world had a say, and of those nations which were excluded it was the Europeans who were most conspicuously absent—only ten were represented at San Francisco out of a possible twenty-four and as compared with the twenty European powers which had been original members of the League. In such circumstances, to have expected brevity in the legal instruments which charted their areas of agreement would be optimistic indeed. There was too much to be said. The lawyers wanted space to define and refine. The diplomats and politicians wanted space to regain through one clause what they might be thought to have too rashly conceded at another. The prophetic and the blandiloquent wanted space to open windows on to the future and to lose themselves and others in an O Altitudo. And since these diverse personalities were not infrequently to be found cohabiting within the breast of one and the same delegate it was difficult, if not impossible, to resist their demands. The Charter embodies, after all, more even than the diversity of mankind; it embodies the contradictions that inhere in each of us as members of the human race. The result is a document of nineteen Chapters, 111 Articles, and over 8,000 words. Lord Bryce, contemplating the American Constitution, found it possible to read it through aloud in twenty-three minutes. The Covenant of the League, at the same tempo, would take just about as long. But the Charter, by the same standards, provides work for an hour. Nor does the tripling of length produce an improvement of quality; rather it gives more scope for stylistic inelegancies, ambiguities and repetitions. The Charter is in fact an imperfect blueprint for an imperfect structure. As such, it invites, and deserves, criticism. But first of all it has a right to be understood.

3 · EVOLUTION

WITH ratification of the Charter the skeleton of the U.N. was now complete; it remained to put on flesh and blood. This task San Francisco entrusted to a team of deputy Pygmalions, the Preparatory Commission, who met in London later in 1945. They met in fact in two stages. Between August and November an executive committee, drawn from the fourteen states who had constituted the executive committee at San Francisco, drew up a set of recommendations. These it presented to the full Commission (consisting of all member states) when it assembled at Church House, Westminster, on 26 November. The Executive Secretary throughout was Mr. Gladwyn Jebb; conspicuous amongst the other national delegations was the American deputy delegate, a young Chicago lawyer and temporary civil servant, Mr. Adlai Stevenson. The British delegation was headed by Mr. Philip Noel-Baker and the Soviet by Mr. Gromyko.

The Preparatory Commission was seized with the urgent need to summon the General Assembly as soon as possible and it gave the highest priority in its operations to the framing of a full set of draft rules of procedure, which were accepted virtually without change by the General Assembly at its second session. The Commission similarly equipped the Security Council, which also (though with slightly greater modifications) adopted them for its own. It also proposed that the Council should normally meet in public and envisaged three types of meetings—'regular' to be held at whatever intervals the Council might decide, 'periodic' to be held every quarter (the League Council met four times a year), and 'extraordinary' to be called by the President whenever necessary. These distinctions were blurred from the first and have not been maintained subsequently in the Council's operations. Much attention was given to equipping the Economic and Social Council and it was recommended that at its first session it should establish a Commission on Human Rights, an Economic and Employment Commission, a Temporary Social Commission, a Statistical Commission, and a Commission on Narcotic Drugs— all of which, and more, the Council did indeed create. For the first meetings of all these bodies provisional agendas were provided so that they could start their existence with a minimum of delay.

Thus far the Commission's work was generally uncontentious. It was not so when it came to organize the Trusteeship Council. Here there was a lawyer's problem arising from the fact that its nucleus was to consist of members who administered trust territories. But since there were not and could not be any such territories until they were created by agreements made between administering powers and the U.N., it followed that there could not be any 'trusteeship powers' and so no Council. This largely formalistic tangle provided a net in which were caught all the pro —and anti—colonial groupings that San Francisco had first exhibited, and although eventual agreement was reached on the main issues—e.g. that League mandatories should submit trusteeship agreements as soon as possible—it was agreement, in most cases, over the heads of dissenting minorities.

The Commission devoted a great deal of attention to amplifying the five brief articles of the Charter which deal with the U.N. Secretariat. It found that in doing so it was having to make some far-reaching decisions. It debated whether there should be an integrated Secretariat that would serve all the organs of the U.N. or (as the U.S.S.R. wanted) separate secretariats for each. Its decision in favour of integration undoubtedly rescued the U.N. from an 'infrastructure' of great divisive potentiality. A Yugoslav proposal that governments should enjoy a right of veto on the appointment of their nationals was rejected—fortunately for the international character of the Secretariat. The Secretary-General, the Commission advised, should initially be appointed for five years and the Commission also thought it desirable for the Security Council to 'proffer only one candidate for the consideration of the General Assembly, for debate on the nomination . . . to be avoided', and for the vote to be taken by secret ballot. All these recommendations were accepted.

Important though all these operations of the Preparatory Commission were, none of them excited half the public interest aroused by the last item on its agenda, 'Preparation of recommendations concerning the location of the permanent Headquarters of the Organization'. The announcement early in October that a majority of the Executive Committee favoured a site in the United States proved to be only the beginning of a long wrangle in which the rivalries of historic civilizations became jumbled up with the ambitions of municipal Chambers of Commerce. The majority recommendation of the Executive Committee was resisted in the full Commission by those states, mainly European, who wanted to continue the League tradition and have the U.N. housed if not in Geneva at any rate in Europe. In this Britain and France, who were the principal spokesmen for Europe, were opposed by China and, more significantly, by the U.S.S.R., on the grounds that to house the U.N. in Europe would be to diminish its global character and turn it into a merely regional organization. The U.S. government, as such, refrained from advocacy and merely announced that if the U.N. came to its shores it would be welcome, but Congress went a step further and passed a formal resolution inviting it to come. Meanwhile, beginning with Mayor Kelly of Chicago, there flew into London delegations from every American city that envisaged itself as the prospective capital of the world—San Francisco, of course, but Philadelphia, Boston, St. Louis, Denver, and Miami as well; not to mention Navy Island, Niagara, or Hyde Park and Gentryville, the homes respectively of Franklin Roosevelt and Abraham Lincoln. Perhaps most bizarre of all, there was the joint delegation from the States of Wyoming, Nebraska, and South Dakota, which offered a spacious site in the heart of the Black Hills, the Ararat where their three boundaries met. From the nearer side of the Atlantic the claims of various European cities, The Hague, Vienna, Prague (and even extra-European ones such as Tangier and Jerusalem) were urged in turn, but none was supported by any comparable demonstrations of civic enthusiasm. In the main debate of Europe versus America, two arguments were dominant. For Europe it was argued that this was the trouble zone where two world wars had started and where the U.N. must be located, since it was here that it would have most of its work to do. For America it was contended that an American headquarters was necessary to retain American interest and avoid a return to isolationism. But of course behind both arguments there was a contest of power and pride; Europeans wished to retain the supreme symbol of a Europe-centred world; Americans hailed the prospect of a new age dawning under American skies.

Not until 15 December did the relevant committee of the Preparatory Commission finally endorse an American site by a vote of 30-14-6. (U.N. voting is always given in this form, the order representing 'Ayes', 'Noes', and 'Abstentions'.) It then went on to approve a site in the eastern United States and by 28 December this had been narrowed down to a choice of sites around Boston and New York. An inspection group of seven members was dispatched to explore these areas early in 1946. With the arrival in New York of these seven emissaries in search of a site began a comedy worthy of Pirandello. The territory they had been instructed to explore contained some of the choicest hinterland of the richest cities in America, that 'exurbia' whose residents were as conspicuous for their wealth as their conservatism. When, after a month's inspection, the committee selected a forty-two-mile stretch which included some of the *crème de la crème* of this countryside, the embattled gentleman farmers of the townships involved gave voice in a storm of protests. The General Assembly bowed to this to the extent of instructing its committee (now nine-man strong) to produce alternative recommendations for sites ranging from forty square miles to as little as two, but it still clung to the central concept of an international semi-rural enclave.

Meanwhile, it was agreed, the temporary home of the Organization should be in New York City. But where, in a city racing back to 'normalcy' and crowded with ex-servicemen? The only immediate accommodation that could be found was in a building at Hunter College, a women's college in the Bronx. But by August the infant U.N. had to be on the move again. This time it was to Long Island. The General Assembly was housed in a converted skating rink at Flushing, which had once formed part of the buildings of the World's Fair. The Secretariat had to move to the suburban village of Lake Success, where a wartime Sperry Gyroscope factory had become vacant. Here for four years the U.N. made its headquarters, with delegates journeying to it often several times a day from down-town Manhattan, a minimum of forty-five minutes away.

During this time the pressure of local opposition to the chosen permanent site in no way diminished. For all its frequent absurdity (e.g. the complaint that the U.N. would affect the purity of the local water supplies), this made an impact on delegates and others. In August the sub-committee dropped from its recommendation the township of Greenwich, where hostility had been most vocal. However, when it announced its preference for Westchester County, this evoked a comparable furore there. All this encouraged the City of New York to press the claims of Flushing Meadow as a permanent home and the City of San Francisco to renew its earlier invitation in flattering terms. The natural consequence, of course, was to weaken the Assembly's faith in its earlier decision, and when on 5 November the American delegation broke a long silence of neutrality by advising consideration of sites in the area of New York *and* San Francisco the lines broke in all directions. The Soviets even for a moment advocated a return to Europe, until the Republican victory in the American midterm elections revived their fears of a New World isolationism if the U.N. were removed. The Assembly voted to send another touring mission to Philadelphia, San Francisco, Boston, and New York to see again what each had to offer. But when the mission reported lyrically in favour of San Francisco, the U.S.S.R. exploded with a threat to boycott any conferences held in so remote a spot. The British came out for Philadelphia, while the U.S.A., to general surprise, withdrew any support for San Francisco in favour of 'an East coast site'.

It was at this stage, with no consensus in sight and all tempers frayed with a year's accumulated frustrations, that New York

City played its trump card. In a manner characteristically American, private philanthropy succeeded where official action had failed. On 11 December Senator Warren Austin electrified an exhausted headquarters committee by reading them a letter from Mr. John D. Rockefeller, Jr., offering the U.N. a gift of $8½ million with which to purchase six blocks in midtown Manhattan, between 42nd and 48th Streets, where slums and slaughterhouses could be demolished to provide seventeen acres of building space along the shores of the East River at a spot known as Turtle Bay. It was the opposite of everything that the U.N. had always said that it wanted; it was intensely urban instead of semi-rural, it was cramped instead of spacious, it could hardly at any point be insulated from its American environment, much less made into an international island. But it was a home, and a home too in a city where, almost without knowing it, the U.N. had become acclimatized. After a most cursory survey of the site the Assembly on 14 December voted acceptance of the gift by a majority of 46 to 7.

Mr. Wallace Harrison, the architect of Rockefeller Center, was appointed Director of Planning. With him worked in unexpected harmony an international team of architects. By mid-May 1947 a final plan was agreed upon at an estimated cost of $65 million (subsequently raised to $68 million) which the U.S.A. agreed to lend interest-free, though it was not until August 1948 that Congress approved the loan. Work on the site began in September 1948 and by October 1952 the last structure, the Assembly Building, was completed. (There has since been added a library block, named after Mr. Hammarskjöld and given by the Ford Foundation.)

Opinions have differed about the merits of the U.N.'s 'permanent' home. There is a romantic *élan* about the buildings which to a considerable extent compensates for their functional inadequacy. Despite the lack of coherence between the two-dimensional skyscraper which houses the Secretariat and the low-domed Conference Building, a certain monumental symbolism, important for the Organization, has been achieved—more certainly than at the Palais des Nations at Geneva. But the Secretariat in particular suffers from having to operate in a vertical structure, with all that that implies of impaired circulation and rigid stratification. The lift is a poor substitute for the corridor. Finally, of course, as the activities of the U.N. expand, the inadequacies of the site itself, small and not easily extensible, become more apparent.

It is no part of the purpose of this book to give a history of the operations of the U.N. However, to understand the nature of the Organization and its present functioning it is essential to take some account of the changes wrought in the original conception as a result of the experiences that the U.N. and its member states have had since 1945. In its pure form the dream of San Francisco was quick to fade. When the first General Assembly opened at Central Hall, Westminster, on 10 January 1946, there was already hanging over it the blight cast by the failure of the Foreign Ministers' Conference. Though the infant U.N. undoubtedly escaped the full contagion of this by the wise decision of its parents to exclude the Organization from the processes of peace-making, it could not escape the moral infection of Great Power disagreement. This revealed itself immediately in the initial organizing operations, when East and West clashed over the Presidency of the Assembly, Mr. Gromyko offering the surprise nomination of Mr. Trygve Lie, Foreign Minister of Norway, in place of M. Spaak, the Foreign Minister of Belgium, who (it had been supposed) was the universally acceptable candidate. M. Spaak was elected, but by a deeply divided vote of 28 to 23, and Mr. Lie was thus left available for the greater office of Secretary-General. For this, though not the favourite candidate of the West, in whose eyes M. van Kleffens of the Netherlands or Mr. Lester Pearson of Canada would have been preferable, Mr. Lie had the supreme advantage of being unopposed by any major power. The Russians had put forward the name of M. Simič, Marshal Tito's Foreign Minister, but it was not a serious proposal and they were ready to compromise on Mr. Lie, who was elected by 46 votes to 3. Mr. Lie's election established the effective precedent that the Secretary-General-ship should not be held by the national of a Great Power.

By way of compensation the permanent members of the Security Council shared out amongst themselves five of the eight Assistant Secretary-Generalships (later Under-Secretaryships).

It might have been argued that these rivalries and disagreements were over mere matters of organization, the inescapable birth-pangs of the new creation. Unhappily it was at once revealed that East–West cleavages were substantive as well. On 19 January 1946 the Security Council received its first complaint; it came from Iran, and most unfortunately it was directed against the U.S.S.R., alleging Soviet refusal to withdraw her troops from Persian soil and interference in Persian internal affairs. Two days later the U.S.S.R., in clear retaliation as it seemed, complained of interference by British troops in the internal affairs of Greece. At once it was apparent that Great Power rivalry had penetrated the very citadel of the Organization and that the supposition of unity amongst the permanent members of the Security Council, on which the Charter had been based, was unlikely to be realized. A few days later the implications of this for the functioning of the Organization were painfully clarified when a dispute over the withdrawal of French forces from Syria and the Lebanon provoked the first use of the veto—by the U.S.S.R., and in a context in which Soviet national interests were not directly threatened *at all*.

All these disputes were in fact eventually resolved, though the Iranian issue paradoxically remained on the Security Council's agenda because too much loss of face would have attended any proposal to take it off. Fortunately these dissensions did not infect the work of the General Assembly, which, after organizing itself along the lines recommended by the Preparatory Commission, elected the six non-permanent members of the Security Council, the eighteen members of the Economic and Social Council, and the fifteen judges of the International Court, and finally went on to establish an Atomic Energy Commission. Adjourning on 15 February, the first Assembly met again in its temporary home in Flushing Meadow outside New York on 23 October. There it established the Trusteeship Council, the last of the 'principal organs' envisaged by the Charter, and admitted four new members. But despite the very reasonable measure of harmony in its own deliberations, the Assembly revealed its deeper anxiety for the general health of the Organization by the passage of a resolution requesting the permanent members of the Security Council to moderate the use of the veto in the interest of the Council's own efficiency. The children, in effect, were asking the parents, in the interests of the family, to patch up the marriage. The question this prompted, of course, was whether the moral authority of parenthood could be thus restored from below.

In the following year the question received a disquieting answer, when the persistent use of Soviet vetoes in the Security Council over the dispute between Greece and her Communist neighbours led the Western powers to resort to a tactic which, though within the terms of the Charter, was hardly in accordance with its original and central conception. Arguing that the Soviet vetoes had prevented the Council from living up to its intended role, Mr. Marshall, the American Secretary of State, proposed that the Assembly should be adapted to fill the gap in the functioning of the Organization. As finally adopted by the Assembly in November 1947, the American resolution provided for the establishment of an Interim Committee (or 'Little Assembly', as it was dubbed) which, like the Security Council, would be available for immediate summoning at any time when its parent body was not in session. This body was to handle any matter referred to it by the General Assembly and specifically 'any dispute or situation proposed for inclusion on the Assembly's agenda', though of course it had none of the enforcement powers of the Security Council.

As it turned out, the Interim Committee was more significant as a symbol of frustration than as an escape from an impasse. It never functioned as intended. It made a few recommendations, but mainly of a procedural and long-range kind. It never functioned as a real interim Assembly and, though renewed at intervals, it was given less and less to do and since 1955 has been adjourned *sine die*.

The same year, 1947, witnessed on another front, however, an enhancement of the General Assembly's prestige as a result of the action of the United Kingdom in calling it into special session in April to determine the future of the Palestine mandate. This use of the Assembly rather than the Security Council to handle a major political problem may have been a questionable success but it set an important precedent for the Assembly operating in fields that the framers of the Charter had intended to reserve for the Council.

In fact, of course, the Security Council was a victim of the growing estrangement of Russia and the West. March 1948 saw the signature of the Brussels Treaty, establishing the Brussels Treaty Organization. This came close on the heels of the Communist *coup d'état* in Czechoslovakia and was followed, in June, by the Berlin Blockade. On 26 July the U.N.'s Disarmament Commission reported that it had reached deadlock, and no one was surprised when on 10 August the Military Staff Committee announced a virtual cessation of activity—it had already reported to the Security Council in April 1947 its inability to agree on the armed contributions that permanent members should make. Its failure meant that the Security Council, whatever it might do, could not now discharge the policing role that the Charter had originally designed for it. The world could not repose in peace under the united strength of the permanent members of the Council. Though the parents had not actually applied for a divorce, the marriage was now an open failure. The children consequently sided, some with one party to the dispute, some with the other—and some with neither. Yet, though weakened and for certain purposes inoperative, the family, significantly enough, did not break up. For all their quarrelling, the parents, as so often in real life, went on living together; the children, though each going their separate ways, stopped short of abjuring their parents or of disowning their family connexion.

This was the situation when in 1950 the Organization was faced with a test more severe than any in its short history and every bit as severe as those, like Manchuria and Abyssinia, which had proved so ruinous to the League. The year began with a Soviet proposal to remove the representative of Nationalist China from his seat on the Security Council on the grounds that the Communist and not the Nationalist government really represented the people of China. The defeat of the proposal led to a Soviet boycott of the Security Council and all other U.N. organs. This was the position when, on 25 June, the U.N. Commission on Korea cabled from Seoul that South Korea had been invaded by North Korea. The Security Council, meeting immediately, accepted an American resolution declaring the invasion to be a breach of the peace, calling for an immediate cessation of fighting and withdrawal of the invading troops, and asking all members of the U.N. to help in the execution of this resolution. Two days later, on reports of continuing aggression and rapid progress of North Korean forces, the Security Council met to be informed that President Truman had ordered United States forces to assist the South Koreans, in response to the U.N. resolution of the 25th. The Council then adopted a second American resolution recommending (since Article 43, envisaging armed contingents at the disposal of the Security Council, had never been implemented, *recommending* was as much as the Council could do) members to furnish such assistance as was necessary to repel the attack and restore peace in the area. Britain, Australia, New Zealand, and Canada offered forces at once (sixteen other member states, notably Turkey and France, supplied further armed contingents later and in all forty-five powers gave some form of aid), and on 7 July the Security Council resolved that all military forces should be placed under a unified command, and that the U.S.A. should name the Supreme Commander. On 8 July General MacArthur was so appointed.

All this prompt and powerful action met with virtually no opposition in the Security Council, which thus overnight emerged as something surprisingly like the custodian of peace and security which the Charter had envisaged. The U.N. could claim with justice that it had met its first great challenge squarely, and in face of a clear act of aggression had responded, as the League had not, with the collective might of its members. That this was due, above all, to the resolute action of one member, the U.S.A., did not detract from the Organization's credit. Less auspicious, however, was the fact that the U.N.'s response to American leadership had only been possible because of Russia's fortuitous absence from the Security Council and the Council's consequent freedom from the Soviet veto. This was strikingly demonstrated in August, when Mr. Malik announced his intention of returning and assuming the Presidency of the Council (which, by rotation, he was due to do). He then employed his position in the chair to obstruct all further Council business for the entire month. Nor was the position essentially improved in September, since Mr. Malik armed with the veto was almost as obstructive as Mr. Malik in the chair.

This led in October, not merely to the mobilization of the General Assembly by the 'sanctionist' powers, with the passage of resolutions there advocating a 'unified, independent, democratic Korea' and setting up a Korean rehabilitation commission, but also to the advocacy, again by the U.S.A., of new authority for the Assembly to act in a crisis. This was the 'Acheson Plan' or the 'Uniting for Peace Resolution', which passed the Assembly on 2 November 1950 by 52–5–2. Fuller treatment of it will be found in later chapters. Here it is sufficient to note it as the lineal descendant of the aborted 'Little Assembly' scheme, designed, like it, to get round the stultification of the Security Council by the veto. From one point of view it was merely a recognition of the impotence of the Council, from another it was an attempt at a virtual amendment of the Charter—such as would have constituted a major shift of power between the organs of the U.N.

'The Uniting for Peace Resolution' started from a recognition of the factors whose fortunate conjunction had alone made the U.N. action of June possible. They were (in addition to the prompt leadership displayed by the United States):

(1) The presence in the affected area of a U.N. authority (the U.N. Commission on Korea) which was able to provide immediate, unequivocal, and official evidence that aggression had occurred.

(2) The presence, almost on the spot, of American armed forces whose aid, inadequate as it was, yet enabled the South Koreans to avoid being completely submerged by the first wave of invasion.

(3) The absence from the Security Council, not only of the formal aggressor (North Korea was not even a member of the U.N.), but also of her Great Power champion.

To reproduce, so far as possible, this favourable concatenation of circumstances, the Assembly was now empowered to meet within twenty-four hours if the Security Council failed to 'exercise its primary responsibility for the maintenance of peace and security', a Peace Observation Commission was set up 'to observe and report situations anywhere in the world likely to endanger international peace' and (in place of the forces that were to have been put under the Military Staff Committee) member states were asked to hold armed contingents of their services ready for use as a U.N. unit. This made it possible for the Assembly to act when the Security Council was in the grip of a veto; it would have made armed sanctions possible (though admittedly only, as in League days, as a result of *voluntary* action by Assembly members); furthermore it tried to equip the U.N. with a permanent observer corps of its own which could provide it with the plain facts of the case if aggression or a breach of peace was alleged to have occurred.

The Resolution was not equally implemented in all its parts. The Peace Observation Commission, though set up and used on one occasion (in 1952 in the Balkans), did not in fact become that universal and ubiquitous eye which its more optimistic sponsors hoped. Instead it became merely a pre-constituted commission of fourteen member states which might, if enough members of the Security Council or the General Assembly at any time wished it, be dispatched to an area provided that the state whose territory it contemplated entering was willing to receive it. Similarly, a poor response was accorded by member states to the proposal to allocate some of their forces for use as U.N. contingents. The prevalent disposition was to reply in general terms with general promises of aid in vaguely defined circumstances. The one feature of the Resolution, in fact, which did strike root was the machinery providing for the holding of a special emergency session of the Assembly at twenty-four hours' notice. Despite the U.S.S.R.'s refusal to recognize this as legal, it has established itself—less by reference to such Charter loopholes as Article 10 (which enables the Assembly to discuss and make recommendations on 'any question or any matters within the scope of the present Charter') than on the analogy of Abraham Lincoln's defence of his suspension of Habeas Corpus: 'Are all the laws but one to go unexecuted, and the government itself go to pieces lest that one be violated?'

Though the U.N.'s immediate response to the Korean challenge was as vigorous as any friend of the Charter could have wished, it was inevitable that with the whole Military Staff Committee aborted and with the Security Council stalled by the veto, the effective direction of military operations and the co-ordination of member states' assistance could not really be conducted from Turtle Bay. In fact, of course, it was conducted by the United States—reporting indeed to the U.N. but in reality making its own decisions, in greater or lesser degree of concert with the other fifteen nations who were also contributing contingents to the Korean action. Friends of the Organization could and did complain that less emphasis was laid on the U.N. character of the military action in Korea than might have been; in the eyes of public opinion in Korea, in the U.S.A., and in the rest of the world it bore too often the aspect of an American operation. This might be so, yet it was no less true that as long as states sympathizing with North Korean behaviour were members of the U.N. little but the most formal superintendence could be given by the Organization; correlatively, the U.N. in Korea could only be very little stronger than its strongest member there—America's resolve, America's dollars, America's might were 90 per cent. of the Korean war effort.

Moreover, though sanctions had been launched in a Great Power's despite, that Great Power had stopped short of using her full strength (not only military, but also diplomatic) against the operation. It was possible to regard it as an operation against a small state and as such, despite all its threatening overtones, what President Truman always described it, a 'police operation', which could be limited and controlled. However, as the hostilities continued and as it became obvious that Chinese Communist forces were becoming engaged in support of North Korea, U.N. members developed an increasing concern at the risk of a widening of the area of hostilities, and at their being involved in a war against a major power, with all the illimitable hazards that that entailed. Thus, almost insensibly, the Organization (which in any case, for the reasons mentioned, lacked full pride of fatherhood for the conduct of the military operations) began to think less about the imposition of sanctions and more about the termination of hostilities.

As long as General MacArthur remained in command in Korea there was little hope of securing full American co-operation for a policy of 'limited objectives' and a negotiated settlement. But with his removal on 11 April 1951 American opinion gradually changed and eventually even Chinese intransigence thawed sufficiently for the signature of an armistice agreement at Panmunjon on 27 July 1953, although neither through the U.N. nor outside it (e.g. the Foreign Ministers' Conference at Geneva in 1954) has it yet proved possible to translate the armistice agreement into a peace settlement. Thus the latter end of the Korean affair, inevitably, was a good deal less resounding and, from the point of view of the U.N., less heartening than its beginning. Nevertheless, it could be claimed, with reason, that although the war did not result in the full attainment of the U.N.'s objective of a unified, democratic, and independent Korea, it did demonstrate that aggression could be halted and an invader thrown back. Though North Korea remained to fight and, if it chose, to commit aggression another day, it was contained once more on the north side of the 38th parallel and taught that it could not victimize its southern neighbour and go unpunished.

The constitutional implications of the Korean conflict affected other U.N. organs besides the Security Council and the General Assembly. The Russians contended that the behaviour of the Secretary-General throughout had been that of a tool of British and American diplomacy—originally because, as Mr. Lie himself expressed it, 'I [had] anticipated and associated my office and myself with the most determined effort to give reality to the principles of collective security', and subsequently because he had acted as the executive for the anti-North Korean resolutions of the Security Council and the General Assembly. Since the Russians and their satellites never departed from the view that all these resolutions (including the 'Uniting for Peace') were illegal, they regarded the Secretary-General's behaviour as illegal too. As his term approached its expiry in February 1951 the Soviet vetoed his re-nomination in the Security Council. Since the U.S.A., for their part, regarded it as a matter of principle that the Secretary-General should not be penalized for his loyalty to the Organization, they announced that they would veto any other candidate. Thus deadlock threatened, and was only evaded by a constitutional subterfuge. Lie was not re-nominated for another term (which would have required a Security Council recommendation) but was 'continued in office' for another three years, on an Assembly vote of 46-5-8. The principle was saved, but the result was far from happy. The U.S.S.R. insisted, after February 1951, that it would not recognize Mr. Lie as Secretary-General. They insulted him personally, and boycotted him socially and officially. Their conduct, however much it might be deplored, was effective in forcing even Mr. Lie's warmest supporters to realize that in consequence he was largely crippled in his endeavours as Secretary-General to serve the full interests of the Organization and to retain the confidence of all member states. At the same time Mr. Lie's position was further weakened by developments on another front—attacks launched on his Secretariat from inside the United States. In 1952 the high tide of McCarthyite agitation, having flooded Washington, began to lap at the base of the U.N. in New York. In November a federal grand jury claimed to have found evidence of the 'infiltration into the U.N. of an overwhelmingly large group of disloyal United States citizens'. In fact no American member of the staff of the U.N. was, either then or later, even charged (much less convicted) by any American court for espionage or subversion. The Secretary-General, however, came under heavy fire from opposite sides—from those who, believing the charges, blamed him for having tolerated such a state of affairs, and from those who, fearful for the international independence of the Secretariat, blamed him for not putting up a firmer stand against American attacks.

The net result of all these pressures was that on 10 November 1952 Mr. Lie announced his intention to retire before the expiry of his extended term.

At once the search began for an acceptable successor. As in 1946, Mr. Lester Pearson of Canada was a strong candidate—particularly favoured by the Commonwealth and Western European countries. The U.S.A. supported General Romulo of the Philippines. The Communist bloc put forward the Polish Foreign Minister, Mr. Skrzeszewski. In the Security Council voting Mr. Pearson emerged as the generally most popular candidate, but was blocked by the Soviet veto. Negotiations behind the scenes were resumed and a number of other names were considered until, on 31 March, the Great Powers meeting privately agreed on Mr. Dag Hammarskjöld who was Minister of State in the Swedish Foreign Ministry. The nomination won general approval and on 10 April, after an Assembly vote of 57 to 1 in his favour (and one abstention), he was formally installed for a five-year term.

In 1955 a notable shift in the political balance of the U.N. was produced by the admission of sixteen additional states to membership. Since its inception the membership of the Organization had only risen from 51 to 60, largely owing to persistent East-West disagreement and a reluctance on either side to admit each other's candidates 'on their merits'. At last, however, a 'package deal' was worked out—a deal which corresponded to the facts of U.N. politics more than to the letter of the U.N. law (cf. the Advisory Opinion of the International Court in 1948 that a vote for the admission of one state must not be made conditional on the admission of others). By this sixteen states were admitted in December 1955. Four of these—Albania, Bulgaria, Hungary, and Roumania—were obvious members of the Communist bloc. Six were Western European states of varying degrees of 'committedness' but all non-Communist—Austria, Eire, Finland, Italy, Portugal, and Spain. Jordan and Libya added strength to the Middle East, Arabian representation, while Cambodia, Ceylon,

Laos, and Nepal were all Asiatic. In relation to another familiar U.N. alignment it was probable that at least ten of the new members could be counted as 'anti-colonial'.

It was fortunate for Dag Hammarskjöld and his office that it was not until 1956 that the U.N. had to sustain the impact of another major crisis involving the Great Powers. The interval of relative non-contention enabled him to win the confidence of both East and West by the time the simultaneous blasts of Suez and Hungary burst upon the Organization. The controversy arising from President Nasser's nationalization of the Suez Canal Company on 26 July was not brought before the United Nations until it was already far advanced.

On 13 October 1956 the Security Council agreed on a series of six principles which should govern any settlement—but on nothing more. In particular, no agreement could be reached on implementation. In the next fortnight tension steadily mounted, both between Egypt and the Anglo-French front, and between Jordan and Israel, whose complaints the Security Council heard on 19 October, without arriving at any decision. Then on 29 October Israel launched an invasion of Egypt. The Security Council debate the following day was interrupted by news of an ultimatum presented by Britain and France to both combatants, threatening to intervene with force unless they stopped fighting and withdrew their forces to a distance of ten miles from the Canal. The British justified their action by the impotence previously displayed by the Security Council. The United States proposed in the Council a resolution ordering Israel to withdraw, and calling on all U.N. members to refrain from force or the threat of force. The voting on the resolution was 7-2-2; using her veto for the first time in U.N. history, Britain, supported by France, prevented its passage.

Thus for the first time since Korea a situation of the kind envisaged by the 'Uniting for Peace' Resolution confronted the U.N.—a situation created, ironically, by two of the Resolution's original sponsors. Under the Resolution, the Assembly was called into emergency session, and met on 1 November when the Anglo-French attack on Egypt from the air had already been launched.

On 2 November the Assembly by a vote of 64-5-6 adopted a United States resolution urging an immediate cease-fire and the withdrawal of attacking forces. Britain and France neither obeyed nor flouted the resolution *in toto*, but replied they would stop their military action if a U.N. force would keep the peace until settlements between Jews and Arabs and satisfactory arrangements for the Canal were established and guaranteed. On 3 November Canada secured the passage of a resolution asking the Secretary-General to prepare within forty-eight hours a plan for an emergency U.N. Force. Within seven hours the Secretary-General reported with an outline plan. On 5 November the Assembly learnt that Britain and France had agreed to cease hostilities at midnight on 6-7 November and to withdraw, provided a U.N. force could take over. On 7 November the Assembly approved the detailed proposals of the Secretary-General concerning the Force and eight days later, on 15 November, the first contingent of the United Nations Emergency Force (UNEF) landed in Egypt. They could have arrived on the 10th, but Egypt delayed the granting of permission for them to land. The build-up continued until by mid-December 5,000 men were deployed, drawn from ten countries, none of them Great Powers and all 'neutrals' in the dispute. On 3 December, under mounting pressure from the General Assembly, as well as from outside, France and the United Kingdom announced that they would withdraw their troops and on 22 December the last Anglo-French forces left Egypt. It took longer to get the Israelis out of Sinai; not until 1 March 1957 did Israel announce full withdrawal, and then only on condition that UNEF patrol the armistice demarcation line in Gaza and on a rather vague American promise to uphold free navigation in the Gulf of Aqaba. Meanwhile, in response to an Egyptian request, a U.N. salvage force was at work clearing the Canal, a task it completed by the end of April 1957.

Simultaneously with the early stages of the hostilities in Egypt occurred the uprising in Hungary and its brutal suppression by Russian forces. The Western powers originally brought it before the Security Council on 28 October under Chapter VI of the Charter. On 2 November the Hungarian Premier, Mr. Nagy, appealed for the support of the Council in obtaining the withdrawal of Soviet troops. The Council debated the problem inconclusively and adjourned at 6.50 p.m. on 3 November after receiving a Soviet statement that negotiations between Soviet and Hungarian army leaders were in progress. Before midnight Soviet forces had launched an all-out attack, Kadar had formed his puppet government, and Nagy had sought asylum in the Yugoslav Embassy. In the Security Council, recalled in emergency session, an American resolution calling for the immediate withdrawal of Soviet forces was blocked by a Russian veto. Invoking once again the 'Uniting for Peace' procedure, the Council called an emergency session of the General Assembly, where virtually the same American resolution was carried by 50-8-15. Interrupted by the Suez problem, the Assembly allowed four days to elapse before reverting to Hungary and then only to learn of Kadar's refusal to admit U.N. observers. The truth was that the Assembly was in no mood to proceed beyond verbal protest. No stronger resolution was proposed, or would have been carried if it had been. When the U.S.S.R. persisted in its indifference to U.N. requests, it was condemned for 'violation of the Charter'. Finally an Assembly Committee of five—Denmark, Australia, Ceylon, Tunisia, and Uruguay—brought in a report, made public on 20 June 1957, which documented in detail all the charges made against the U.S.S.R. and the Kadar régime. This was made the basis for a resolution passed on 14 September by 60-10-10 condemning Soviet behaviour and calling on the Soviets and the Kadar régime to desist from repressive measures.

The contrast between the U.N. in Egypt and Hungary made a strong impression on contemporary observers. In the one case the Organization appeared to have forced two Great Powers and one small one to reverse their policies and withdraw their forces, leaving their objectives still unrealized. In the other a Great Power successfully defied the Security Council and the General Assembly, persisting in a brutal intervention to the end, and denying to the Organization even the right to send its Secretary-General to observe what was going on. Of the propriety as well as the effectiveness of the U.N.'s reactions to the two crises many different views could be—and were—entertained. What certainly emerged, with a clarity which many observers found painful, was the essentially limited powers of the Organization and the basically voluntary character of the association. The resolutions of the General Assembly had been obeyed, reluctantly but eventually, in relation to Suez because the states concerned had judged it prudent to obey them. Into that judgment many factors had entered, some of which had little or nothing to do with the U.N. and would have been equally operative had the U.N. not existed. The resolutions passed by the U.N., in both cases, though strongly worded, had been entirely recommendatory (no action had been even attempted under Chapter VII of the Charter) and respect had been shown throughout for the sovereignty of all the parties involved. What the U.N. had done was to mobilize world opinion and to provide, in the case of Suez, an agency of local insulation, a *cordon sanitaire*, in varying degrees acceptable to all parties in the dispute. As far as Hungary was concerned no such agency could have been acceptable, but as far as the mobilization of opinion was concerned, the Assembly resolutions were as effective as in the case of Suez; the difference was that the U.S.S.R. had not judged it in her interest to respect them. This left Hungary at her mercy but did not necessarily prove that the U.S.S.R.'s judgment of her own interests had been sound or that the U.N. resolutions had been entirely without effect. It did demonstrate, what the framers of the Charter had always held, that the proper enforcement of the Charter was impossible where a Great Power was determined to defy it—and especially where (owing to the synchronization with Suez) the Great Powers were split three ways. Suez, on the other hand, did suggest that, at least under certain circumstances, even Great Power conduct could be powerfully modified by U.N. pressure—and to that extent it may be evidence of a certain (though limited) growth in the potency of the association in the decade since its inception.

One important legacy of Suez was the experiment of UNEF. UNEF was not a police force; it was a buffer force, best understood as representing one stage further in the evolution of bodies like the Truce Supervision Organization in Palestine. It operated only on territory where states were willing to receive it—thus it was excluded from the Israeli side of the Israel–Egypt armistice line. It was lightly armed and fired only a shot or two when itself attacked. None the less it had great potential significance. It was a substantial size—over 5,000 men. It happily combined units from ten very different national forces. It established itself swiftly and worked with astonishing smoothness—both on the spot in Egypt and in relation to its ultimate superiors in Turtle Bay. Without it, it is hard to see how the Suez crisis could have been resolved. Nor did its usefulness end with the passing of the immediate crisis; until 1967, when Egypt demanded its withdrawal, the physical presence of UNEF kept the peace between the two principal antagonists in the area.

When in June 1958 Lebanon charged Syria with intervention in her affairs the Security Council responded by dispatching an Observation Group which at its peak comprised 214 observers from fifteen countries. In July, at the request of Lebanon and Jordan, American and British troops were landed in support of the existing régimes. The fierce Soviet criticism which this aroused suggested for a moment that a serious Great Power clash might result, but the Lebanese–Syrian tension subsided as quickly as it had arisen and the withdrawal of American troops began even while an emergency session of the General Assembly was debating what to do. The incident turned out to have its principal significance as another example of the Secretary-General in his role as 'trouble-shooter' (see pp. 170 ff.).

Thus far in its history it had been the Middle East whose troubled condition had most engaged the attention of the U.N. But 1960 saw a new focus for U.N. energies and anxieties in the emerging continent of Africa. The rapid emancipation of colonial dependencies led in that year to the addition of seventeen new member states to the Organization, of whom all but one were African. With the admission of Nigeria in October 1960 the membership rose to three figures. This in itself presented considerable problems, in the emergence of so many new and untried actors on to the already fairly crowded U.N. stage. The states which were now appearing were, in most cases, the artificial creations of their previous European administrators, their personalities less formed and their political structures less stable than any previous group of entrants. They leaned heavily on the U.N. for aid of every kind which would be free of all the associations of their old, dependent, colonial status.

None leaned more heavily than the vast territory of the Congo, which in June 1960 arrived at an independence for which Belgian administration had ill prepared it. The almost immediate mutiny of the *Force Publique* created a situation of a kind never envisaged by the authors of the Charter—not an external threat to a state but its internal disintegration, a relapse into a condition of anarchy in which the basic presupposition of U.N. action—that a member state should have a government—was seldom or not at all fulfilled. True, the action of the Belgian government in rushing in troops to defend its own property and nationals might be held to constitute an external threat as well, but what made the Congo problem so peculiarly intractable was the internal anarchy of the Congo itself. The political setting was explosive in the highest degree: to other African states their new-found independence seemed at stake in the fate of the Congo; to the U.S.S.R. this was a heaven-sent opportunity to intervene in the name of anti-colonialism; to Belgium and to a lesser degree other Western states a valuable economico-strategic interest was involved in the big copper mines of the *Union Minière* of the province of Katanga.

The establishment of a United Nations force in the Congo (ONUC) and ensuing developments were so intimately bound up with the functioning of the Secretary-General's office that further treatment of them is postponed to pp. 179 ff. But in every respect—in scale, complexity, and intractability—the Congo operation was a landmark in the development of the Organization. Moreover, it exacted from the U.N. one of the heaviest sacrifices conceivable, when it claimed as a victim the person of Dag Hammarskjöld, killed on active service, if ever a civilian was, when his plane crashed near Ndola in September 1961.

The election of U Thant of Burma as Acting Secretary-General to fill out the remainder of Hammarskjöld's term was a direct reflection of the added prominence of the new Afro-Asian membership in the affairs of the U.N. When Sir Zafrulla Khan became President of the 17th General Assembly it was remarked that for the first time in the history of the Organization three representatives of Asian countries occupied the dais—Khan, Thant, and Mr. C. V. Narasimhan, *Chef de Cabinet*.

One of the shifts in attitudes and standards which this new membership signified was dramatically revealed in December 1961 when India invaded the Portuguese colonial enclave of Goa. The 'liberation' of Goa was complete before there could be any serious possibility of U.N. action, but the failure of the three elected Afro-Asian members of the Security Council to vote for a cease-fire made it clear that in their eyes the Charter's ban on the use of force was very far from being binding. 'Colonialism is permanent aggression' was the justification offered by Krishna Menon, the head of the Indian delegation. Of course India's argument derived additional appeal from Portugal's deplorable colonial record, if not in Goa then in Africa, but it was also true that Mr. Menon's sentiments reflected a widespread conviction that colonialism *per se* was such an enormity as to excuse in-difference to most of the otherwise accepted canons of inter-national behaviour.

If the U.N. failed over Goa, it was, in large measure, bypassed over Cuba. In this, the most direct confrontation between the Super-Powers which the world had seen since the invention of the atom bomb, the U.N. could only hold a watching brief for an anxious world and provide a forum, obtrusive or unobtrusive, whenever anyone wanted to use it. The United States found the Security Council an ideal stage on which to display the irrefutable evidence of Soviet missile sites in Cuba; backstage, the presence of the permanent delegations and the mediation of the Secretary-General often smoothed the negotiations once the crucial man-to-man decisions had been made between Khrushchev and Kennedy. But it was not from the U.N. that the United States sought and obtained validation for the 'quarantine' it imposed on Cuba, but from the Organization of American States. Moreover, when U Thant tried to persuade Castro to allow the U.N. to supervise the dismantling of the rocket sites he met with a complete refusal. The Cuba crisis, in fact, like Berlin, demonstrated anew the familiar truth that in a major confrontation of the U.S.A. and the U.S.S.R. the U.N.'s role is necessarily a marginal one.

U Thant, however, emerged from the testing-ground of this incident, as from the continuing harassments of the Congo, with considerable credit, so that there was no disposition anywhere to challenge his election in November 1962 to a term of office expiring in November 1966, i.e. five years from his appointment as Acting Secretary-General. But although 1963 was a year comparatively free of major crises (save for Vietnam, where the U.N. was virtually inoperative) it was a year marked by a deepening conflict inside the Organization over the constitutional and financial responsibility for peace-keeping.

The Congo operation, like UNEF, had been launched first, to be paid for later. Its cost was considerable. For the first six months it amounted to over $66 million, at a time when the normal annual U.N. budget was only about $70 million gross. Even though, in the early flush of unanimity, this was cut to $48½ million by the willingness of Canada, the U.S.S.R., and the U.S.A. to waive reimbursements due to them for the transport services they provided, it remained a substantial figure. For 1961 the cost was about another $120 million, for 1962 about the same. The General Assembly decided, as it had for UNEF, that this commitment should not be charged to the regular U.N. budget but that members, none the less, should be assessed for it according to a roughly similar scale of contributions. Already in respect of UNEF there was widespread defaulting on payments, the Arab and Soviet bloc countries insisting that only the 'aggressors' should have to pay, while the Latin Americans insisted that the assessments were only Assembly recommendations, not legal obligations. Then as the U.S.S.R.'s hostility to the Congo operation grew so its refusal to contribute became firmer, taking root in far-reaching constitutional objections. Basically the Soviets objected to the General Assembly's taking any action in respect of peace-keeping and contended that both its conduct of ONUC and its assessments for it were *ultra vires*. France, the second most conspicuous defaulter, supported these objections, contending that if the General Assembly were able by a two-thirds majority to impose financial obligations on all members, it would take on the attributes of a 'super-state'.

To meet pressing bills the Secretary-General had to resort to every kind of expedient, including even borrowing from the U.N.'s Children's Fund (UNICEF). If the United States, at crucial stages, had not, by voluntary contributions or payments in kind, contributed up to almost 50 per cent. of the cost of the operation it would certainly have foundered. When as a desperate measure in December 1961 the General Assembly authorized a $200 million bond issue even this would have failed had the U.S.A. not been willing to take up the lion's share.

To buttress their interpretation of the Charter the contributing members sought the opinion of the World Court on the legality of the UNEF and ONUC assessments—specifically as to whether they constituted assessable 'expenses of the Organization' under Article 17. The Court, by a vote of 9 to 5, ruled in July 1962 that they did. The ensuing General Assembly accepted this opinion and thereby committed itself to the consequences laid down in the Charter, where Article 19 specifies that any state which is in arrears to the amount of twice its annual assessment shall lose its vote in the General Assembly.

In retrospect it seems incredible that a majority of member states should have expected two permanent members of the Security Council to knuckle under to this threat, even though believing it to be grounded in a sound interpretation of the Charter. Part of the explanation is undoubtedly to be found in the general reluctance to antagonize the United States who shouldered so much of the burden, part in the pervasive conviction that to allow a 'financial veto' in the General Assembly on top of a Charter veto in the Security Council would be to deprive the Organization of any capacity for peace-keeping at all. So the combatants dug in while the clock ticked away until the two years' arrears piled up.

Meanwhile the Congo debts mounted. By 30 June 1964, when ONUC was terminated, over $381 million had been spent on military operations and over $51 million on the civil aid programme. (An item which did not appear in the financial accounting was the casualty list: 235 dead, of whom 126 were killed in action.) Of this $123 million were still owing to the U.N. from member states, most notably, of course, from the Soviet Union and France. The General Assembly postponed its nineteenth session to enable the search for a 'formula' to continue, such as would bridge the gap between the two interpretations of Articles 17 and 19. The search, however, was vain, and on 1 December 1964 the Assembly opened with the U.S.A.'s insisting that the U.S.S.R. had no right to a vote (France and six other members were not liable until 1 January). However, neither side really wanted a 'confrontation' and so, to avoid it, the Assembly resorted to all the procedural devices that ingenuity could suggest and rather more than the dignity of the 'world's parliament' could support. The President, Mr. Quaison-Sackey, was appointed by acclamation, but no committees could meet because no chairmen or Vice-Presidents could be elected. Three new members were admitted without opposition but the only way in which vacancies in the Security Council could be filled was by an unofficial ballot 'behind the President's chair', the Assembly agreeing to elect by acclamation those countries which the President pronounced successful. (The election, incidentally, of one of these, Malaysia, provoked Indonesia in January 1965 into leaving the Organization as a protest—an added, if temporary, source of dismay.) For three weeks at the turn of the year the Assembly recessed but resumed on 18 January 1965 with no solution in sight and sixteen countries (including France) in arrears.

By 27 January steam had run out of the General Debate, which, extraordinarily prolonged, had so far kept the Assembly harmlessly in being, and resort had to be made to successive adjournments. Meanwhile irritation mounted until at last on 16 February Albania demanded a vote. The President ruled against it and in an undignified vote-which-was-no-vote his ruling was upheld 97-2-13. Two days later, by unanimity, the Assembly

authorized a budget at 1964 levels, urged members to contribute to a voluntary fund to meet the deficit, handed its central
problem over to a Committee of 33 on Peace-Keeping and
adjourned till 1 September.

The Peace-Keeping Committee reported in due course a
failure to agree on any financial solution, but it recommended
that the Assembly should meet without the issue of Article 19
being raised and that the Organization's deficit should be made
up by voluntary contributions. The adjourned Assembly accepted
this and its successor, the twentieth General Assembly, met on
21 September to transact business as usual. This meant, in effect,
that the United States acquiesced in the Soviet refusal rather
than risk breaking up the Organization. There was, however,
more to it than that. The growing strength, within the expanding
membership, of the 'third world' and their disposition to use this
strength in the General Assembly (and in the specialized agencies)
to force through resolutions (e.g. on colonialism or development
programmes) which the West thought doubtfully legal or finan-
cially excessive, had undoubtedly bred in the United States a
certain distrust of the General Assembly's powers which gave
her a sneaking sympathy with the Soviet point of view. The
U.S.A. could not be entirely indifferent to the force of the
argument that a thoroughgoing insistence on Articles 17 and 19
would give to the General Assembly a virtually unlimited taxing
power of which the richest states could be the biggest victims.

This did not mean, however, that the U.S.A. (or the United
Kingdom) wished to abandon the peace-keeping potentialities
of the U.N. Indeed if demonstration were needed of the general
acceptance of this role it was provided by the Security Council's
readiness (with Soviet acquiescence) to mount a new operation
in Cyprus, in March 1964, while ONUC was still in being with
all its attendant problems. It was Britain who sought the U.N.'s
aid in handling the intractable Cyprus situation, and the U.N.
force (UNFICYP) then established was notable as the first to
include a contingent from a permanent member of the Council;
there were 2,700-odd British troops in the first few months,
scaled down to a thousand later when the other component ele-

ments—Canadian, Finns, Irish, Swedes, Danes, and Austrians—came up to strength, making 6,000 in all. UNFICYP bypassed the ONUC deadlock by relying on voluntary contributions, but the Secretary-General often had to complain of the inadequacy of the hand-to-mouth financing that this involved. Moreover, the Security Council kept UNFICYP on a short leash, initially by successive authorizations of only three months at a time, and then from June 1965 for six-month periods. Its strength was also reduced to between 4,000 and 3,000 men. However, no one, not even the Soviet Union, seriously disputed the value of UNFICYP's work in pacifying Cyprus, even though it entailed the peculiarly delicate responsibilities of operating within the boundaries of a member state without 'interfering in internal affairs'. Meanwhile the General Assembly agreed to continue UNEF, though at a reduced level, and with assessments scaled steeply against the richer countries, plus provision for voluntary contributions.

As 1966 wore on without agreement on the financing or future arrangements for peace-keeping, there was widespread concern about what would happen on the expiry of U Thant's first full term as Secretary-General. He himself made clear his own unwillingness to serve again in the absence of support for U.N. peace-keeping or development programmes and a settlement of the Vietnam war. It became apparent, however, that though the Great Powers were unwilling to modify their policies to meet his criticisms, they were nevertheless sufficiently conscious of his merits to be reluctant to embark on the painful search for an acceptable successor. Though several names were bandied about, there is no evidence that any of them was seriously considered by the Security Council. Instead U Thant, after initially agreeing to stay on until the end of the twenty-first Assembly, was unanimously proposed by the Security Council and unanimously accepted by the General Assembly on 2 December, to serve a second term until 31 December 1971.

The year 1967 proved a poor one for the Organization. In May, while a special session of the General Assembly was wrestling with the intractable problem of South-West Africa, Egypt presented the Secretary-General with a sudden demand for the withdrawal of UNEF, by now reduced to a strength of some 3,000 men. The Secretary-General felt he had no choice but to assent, but the institution by the Egyptians of a blockade of Aqaba, following on the Force's withdrawal, precipitated the Israeli attack which in turn produced the catastrophic *bouleverse-ment* of the Six Days' War. The Security Council's calls for a cease-fire went unheeded until the Israelis had achieved their objectives, and the General Assembly, called into emergency session at the U.S.S.R.'s request (but under Article 11, *not* the 'Uniting for Peace' Resolution), adjourned at the end of five weeks without having agreed on any resolution save two aimed at terminating Israel's annexation of Jerusalem.

Once again, however, the deadlock of the Great Powers pointed up the indispensability of the Secretary-General. The Security Council did agree on one thing—the need to restore a U.N. presence, in the form of a substantial observer corps. The Secretary-General, implementing the cease-fire resolution, sent General Odd Bull, at the head of an UNTSO team, to the area and when the U.S.S.R. contended this should have been done under the Security Council's authority, the President of the Council announced a Council 'consensus' in his 'support'. In November, when peace was obviously no nearer, the Council authorized the appointment of the Swedish diplomat, Dr. Gunnar Jarring, as the Secretary-General's special representative in a search for a negotiated settlement. But despite his long and patient endeavours no settlement could be reached. A state of war persisted between Israel and all her Arab neighbours with increasingly frequent acts of violence on both sides. UNTSO suffered serious casualties and the Secretary-General, on more than one occasion, seriously contemplated its withdrawal. The Security Council was seldom able to speak with one voice or, when it did, to enforce it—the Great Powers were too much at odds.

Despite the winding-up of UNEF, the U.N.'s finances continued to be precarious. The long-standing deficit for peace-keeping expenses persisted. The voluntary contributions pledged in 1965 were still not forthcoming, neither the U.S.A. nor the U.S.S.R. being willing to make the first moves. As a consequence there were some $50 million of unpaid debts for peace-keeping. True, this did not directly affect the working budget of the Organization, but it was observable that, by a kind of infection of irresponsibility, member states were becoming increasingly tardy in the payment of their regular assessments, obliging the Secretary-General to resort to makeshift borrowings from trust funds to meet pressing obligations.

The Russian occupation of Czechoslovakia in 1968 damaged both the general fabric of international relations and highlighted the inescapable impotence of the U.N. in face of such Great Power criminality. It was Hungary over again. A resolution condemning the 'armed intervention' and calling for immediate withdrawal was blocked by the Soviet veto. The Czech government which originally joined in the protest was, of course, induced to recant and request the removal of the item from the Council's agenda. The U.N.'s hands were tied.

Meanwhile in Vietnam a merciless, seemingly endless, extraordinarily destructive and inchoate war continued, in relation to which the U.N. was peculiarly impotent. Neither of the local rivals, North Vietnam and South Vietnam, was a member of the Organization; each half of the country claimed to represent the whole. The U.S.A. accorded no role to the U.N. other than as a sounding board for its claims to be an aggrieved party to the conflict and·a tireless seeker after peace. The Secretary-General attempted several initiatives and made his often quite critical opinions known. But so long as Communist China was excluded from representation in the U.N. there could be no effective role for the Organization in this area.

In 1971 the steadily mounting pressures for recognition of the Peking government burst the dykes. The United States, after a vain attempt to hold out for a 'two Chinas' solution—i.e. U.N. membership for both Nationalist Taiwan and Communist Peking—gave way before the pressure. The General Assembly voted decisively (73 for, 35 against, 17 abstentions) to seat Peking in place of Taiwan. This belated victory for realism, by recognizing the government of almost a quarter of the world's population, made the U.N. at last something very close to the universal organization it claimed to be. It was regrettable that the price paid for ending the twenty years of make-believe was the denial of all representation to Taiwan.

Followed swiftly, as it was, by President Nixon's visit to China in February 1972, Peking's admission marked an end to 'bipolarity' inside the U.N. as well as outside. The new member confounded the fears of those who thought this formidable revolutionary recruit might prove unassimilable. The Chinese settled in as unobtrusively as the Western press allowed them. Ideologically the U.S.S.R. was their main target and the 'third world' the main object of their solicitations.

Their arrival contributed to a painful demonstration of U.N. impotence for which, none the less, the basic responsibility lay elsewhere. The India–Pakistan war that developed out of the independence movement in East Pakistan presented the Security Council with a series of dilemmas that defied resolution. The principle of self-determination clashed with the principle of the integrity of frontiers. Russia as protector of India was at odds with China the patron of Pakistan. The U.S.A., with both the *détente* with Moscow and the *rapprochement* with Peking at stake, was reluctant to take a strong stand. In the Council, resolutions and vetoes succeeded each other while the conflict raged, until in recognition of its own impotence the Council agreed to use the Uniting for Peace machinery and pass the problem to the General Assembly. The Assembly called for a cease-fire and withdrawal of forces by a vote of 104–11–10 and it was a fortnight later when the Security Council passed a similar resolution, by which time the Pakistani capitulation was almost complete and the Indian forces had achieved their objectives. It was, altogether, an unedifying episode.

In the midst of these events U Thant's term as Secretary General came to an end and, understandably in view of his very poor health, he discountenanced all efforts (especially Russian) to draft him for a further term. There was not a plethora of candidates; Max Jacobson of Finland probably headed the list in terms of personal distinction, Makonnen of Ethiopia could argue that it was Africa's turn, but the African states could not consolidate behind his candidacy. At the last minute Kurt Waldheim, a frequently mentioned possibility, became the Security Council's unanimous choice. He came from a 'neutral' country, Austria; he had experience both of the U.N., where he was head of Austria's mission, and of world affairs generally, as a previous foreign minister for his country; above all, he had an uncontroversial record. Thus surprisingly in an organization where its influence was otherwise waning, Europe secured its third Secretary-General out of four.

Dr. Waldheim was fortunate in that his first years in office coincided with the development of the East–West *détente*. This made possible a solution to the 'two Germanies' problem such as had not been possible for the 'two Chinas'; in September 1973 both East and West Germany (formally the German Democratic Republic and the Federal Republic of Germany) were admitted to U.N. membership *nem con*. No such immediate resolution of the 'two Koreas' rivalry was practicable but the long-standing U.N. Committee for the Unification and Rehabilitation of Korea was dissolved and the General Assembly adopted a consensus resolution in favour of a North–South Korean 'dialogue'.

In two other areas of persistent conflict the U.N. was not so fortunate. In October 1973 the smouldering Arab–Israeli war burst into flame again, with simultaneous attacks launched against Israel by Egypt, Syria, Jordan, and Iraq, and the U.S.A. committed to keeping Israel armed and in being and the U.S.S.R. equally committed to the Arabs. The Security Council, remarkably, in the light of previous dissension, managed to agree not only on a call for a cease-fire and negotiations but also on the establishment of a second UNEF. China alone declined to support the proposals, but significantly she did not oppose them; she merely abstained. Thus a UNEF, over 5,000 strong, constituted much as before, came back to life with impressive celerity and made possible the supervised disengagement of the opposing forces on the Sinai front, an operation completed by March. On the Syrian front, with less 'no man's land' between the combatants, disengagement proved harder and it was the end of May before a smaller force of about a thousand men, more than an observer group but less than an emergency force, UNDOF (U.N. Disengagement Observer Force), was able to discharge a comparable function.

Ironically, just as U.N. peacekeeping was again demonstrating its indispensable if limited role in the Middle East, in Cyprus, after ten years of beneficial interposition, it was the limitations rather than the value of UNFICYP which were thrown into high relief. In July 1974 the deposition of Archbishop Makarios and the Turkish invasion demonstrated that UNFICYP's presence had postponed, without facilitating, a political solution of the island's problems while the Turkish forces showed scant respect for the U.N. forces that stood between them and the total imposition of their will. This was humiliating, as was the failure, mainly of the Turks, to heed the unanimous resolutions of the Security Council until the call for a cease-fire had been made four times. Perhaps humiliation is an unavoidable experience for peace-makers. Certainly when the fighting stopped it was to the same ill-used and injured UNFICYP (it sustained 36 fatal casualties) that all sides had to turn for aid in the implementation of the cease-fire agreement. Even the U.S.S.R. did not oppose UNFICYP's re-establishment and China was content to abstain.

Cyprus was a good example of the U.N. as the world's fire-brigade bringing its strength to bear on a single trouble spot. But Dr. Waldheim's Secretary-Generalship looked like being just as significant for the U.N.'s preventive role, inducing the world to take heed of problems more diffuse but of universal concern and mounting urgency. In 1972, largely as a result of Swedish efforts, the U.N. sponsored a Conference on the Human Environment at Stockholm with Mr. Maurice Strong of Canada as its secretary-general. 114 countries were represented and despite a fortnight's overcrowded agenda and the predictable displays of national selfishness, the conference produced a surprising degree of agreement on what needs to be done, and even took some initial steps towards action. On its recommendation the General Assembly in December set up a $100m fund to launch, under Mr. Strong, a U.N. environmental programme (UNEP), housed in Nairobi, with its primary task the setting up of a world monitoring system for pollution ('Earthwatch').

Linked with environmental questions—perhaps indeed part of them—are the control of the world's seas and the growth of its population. In 1974 these were singled out for global conference treatment. The Law of the Sea Conference met at Caracas for ten weeks without arriving at much agreement between the 148 countries represented. It was not to be expected that an area so controversial and so little charted could be brought under the control of a generally acceptable system of law at one go. No doubt the follow-up conference held at Geneva in 1975 will be only the second of a series. This would be even truer of the vexed question of population control, and the World Population Conference held at Bucharest in August 1974 was even more clearly only a first stage in a long process of elucidation and education. Nevertheless acceptance without a vote was accorded to a plan of action that recognized the gravity of the problem, suggested population targets and put the problem within the general context of economic development. Thus in its own ragged, hesitant way the U.N. demonstrated its continuing function as the only forum in which the world's conscience and consensus could live side by side.

4 · THE SECURITY COUNCIL

OF all the organs of the U.N. none has shown a greater discrepancy between promise and performance than the Security Council. Upon the improvements introduced by the Charter into the structure and working of the Council most of the high hopes of 1945 depended. Here the weaknesses of the League would be eliminated. Force would be put at the service of law, and even law itself would be obliged to serve and not obstruct the overriding concern of a post-war world with peace and security. As the British official commentary on the Dumbarton Oaks proposals put it, 'The powers to be conferred on the Security Council are greater than have ever before been given to an international body.' This was echoed in the proud comment of the Chairman of the United States delegation at San Francisco when he reported to the President: 'The Security Council is without precedent in international relations; it differs from the traditional alliance and is unlike the Council of the League of Nations.' And the fledgling U.N. itself, speaking through the official voice of its Information Department, summed it up by saying, 'The Security Council's powers are thus equivalent, in substance, to those of a supreme war-making organization.' It was indeed as an armed policeman, quick on the draw and concerned more with peace and order than with rights and wrongs or diplomatic niceties, that most contemporary opinion envisaged it. A writer in *Foreign Affairs* in October 1945 expressed a prevalent expectation when he foresaw the Council moving 'rapidly to the negotiation of the special agreements under which member states are to supply armed forces, assistance and facilities'. In terms no less emphatic of the *security* aspects of the Council's role, he added, 'While Council deliberations will not, of course, be open to the press, the results will be made known and Council reports to the Assembly will be published.'

It is hard now to recapture the hopes and assumptions on which such thinking about the Security Council rested. One's wonder is less that the Council failed to live up to the expectations of its founders than that realistic statesmen should have imagined in 1945 that such a body, equipped with a functioning Military Staff Committee with armed forces at its disposal, could actually operate in the post-war world. Undoubtedly, were the truth known, it would be found that by no means all the allied statesmen who gave public endorsement to the U.N.'s 'Grand Design' really believed it would work. But some did, and while of these a few may be charged with wishful thinking, the great majority endorsed the plan largely from a belief that it conformed to the inner logic of world politics, that only this, or something like this, could provide an adequate basis for peace and security.

The core of the Security Council plan lay in the assumption of Great Power unity. The wars it was to stop were conflicts among the *other* powers (especially, of course, in the thinking of 1945, conflicts launched by ex-enemy states). While experience of working on the Council would, no doubt, lubricate the relations between the Big Five, the Council was never envisaged as an agency for policing the Five themselves. *Quis custodiet ipsos custodes?* was, quite properly, regarded as a nonsense question. Either the Great Powers abstain from war against each other, or their conflict tears the U.N. apart. The Organization which is their creation and instrument cannot, least of all in its infancy, give orders to its most potent progenitors and protectors.

From this follows, again with perfect logic, the so-called Great Power 'veto'. 'So-called' because, so far from according to the Great Powers some exceptional privilege denied to them in the days of the League or in other security associations, it represents only the retention by them of that right which was the perquisite of all sovereign states in the pre-U.N. world, the right *not* to be overruled by other members. In abandoning the unanimity rule the U.N. took a great step forward, but to have exposed *all* states, regardless of size and responsibilities, to dictation at the hands of a possibly incoherent majority would have been unrealistic in the extreme. Not only would it have kept at least the U.S.A. and the U.S.S.R. out of any world organization; it would also have prevented the Great Powers from giving that leadership inside the organization which only they could give. If the unanimity rule was in general to be abandoned, while at the same time special responsibilities were laid upon the Security Council and, within the Security Council, upon its five permanent members, then it was essential that these five should be armed with special powers of control. What in fact is remarkable, in view of the discrepancy in economic and military strength between the Big Five (especially the U.S.A. and the U.S.S.R.) and the other members, is that the giants were content with such limited powers of control as the Charter concedes them. And although from one point of view (and in the light of our experience with the Russian veto) the veto power is a device to *stop* international action, from another point of view (and one which was dominant in the thinking of Dumbarton Oaks and San Francisco) it is a guarantee that only those proposals will be adopted by the Organization which the Great Powers will support. As Dr. Philip Jessup has put it, the veto is 'the safety-valve that prevents the U.N. from undertaking commitments in the political field which it lacks the power to fulfil'.

Had logic continued to dominate the drafting of the Charter, the Security Council would have been constituted only from the Great Powers themselves. Since no important U.N. action could be initiated, much less executed, without them, it would have been logical to have restricted membership in the 'executive' organ of the U.N. to the Big Five. This would have kept the world's policing agency compact in size and proportionately swift in action; power and responsibility would have been precisely correlated. Why was this not done?

The short answer is that the precedent of the League Council stood in the way. Once General Smuts in his 1918 essay, *The League of Nations: A Practical Suggestion*, had aired the idea of diluting the Great Power Concert by the addition of other states with temporary membership, a concession had been made to 'democracy' or 'representativeness' which all the logic in the world could not revoke. It was idle to argue that to admit states to membership merely because they represented some region or bloc would almost certainly violate the central idea of the Council and result in the inclusion, at intervals, of states so impotent as to contribute nothing save their voice and their vote to the preservation of peace. It was equally vain to expose how much confusion inhered in the idea of a non-permanent member of the Council being a 'representative' of some area or group of states. (It is only to a very limited degree that the spokesman of a state can represent anyone other than the state which accredits him. The sentiments he expresses and the votes he casts may be in accord with the views of neighbour states, but who is to guarantee that they are, and who is to impose on him the obligation to see that they are?)

The experience of the League Council exposed no flaws in these theoretical objections. What it did do, however, was to demonstrate the tenacious hold which the illogical system had upon the affections of all states, save perhaps those who enjoyed permanent membership of the Council. It might not be democratic, but it went some way to satisfy the pervasive desire to use the world organization as, amongst other things, a device to control the Gullivers in the interest of the Lilliputians. As such, the smaller powers campaigned continuously to increase their strength on the Council, expanding the number of non-permanent seats from the original four to six in 1922, nine in 1926, ten in 1933, and eleven in 1936. The Council might not in any proper sense be representative, but just as, for League purposes, regional or other blocs came to have a certain validity and effectiveness, so those blocs evinced, by their zeal in supporting their 'candidate' for a seat on the Council, their feeling that this device gave them some collective voice expressive of their interests, real or imagined.

By the time of Dumbarton Oaks the concentration of military and economic power in the hands of a few countries had reached a point that Geneva never knew. Yet by a natural human reaction this very fact strengthened the appeal of the Geneva precedent when it came to the framing of a successor to the League Council.

At Dumbarton Oaks it was accepted as axiomatic that the Security Council should find room for the lesser powers, while at San Francisco pressure was strong (though unavailing) for increasing their allocation of places above the six provisionally allotted. The Charter in its final form did indeed stipulate, as the Covenant had never done, that in the election of non-permanent members 'due regard' should be 'specially paid, in the first instance to the contribution of Members of the U.N. to the maintenance of international peace and security and to the other purposes of the Organization' (Article 23). Strictly applied, this clause, the product largely of Canadian pressure, would have preserved something of the logical correlation of power and responsibility. In fact it has been largely ignored in the election of non-permanent members; indeed there have been years in which not one of them has been a power that would rate inclusion in the 'middle class'. Instead the General Assembly, like the old League Assembly, has persisted in electing members who represented blocs or regions, without worrying too much about whether these were states of straw or not, and finding all the warrant needed for its behaviour in the final five words of the 'due regard' clause—'due regard being paid . . . also to equitable geographical distribution'.

Though this is a constitutional infirmity, it is also a fact of international politics which the tears of purists will deplore in vain. A practice so tenaciously retained ever since 1919 obviously reflects something real, even if it is only, in a great many cases, the reality of group feelings, racial pride or prejudice, regional or cultural tradition. As such it undoubtedly contributes something to the representativeness of Security Council debates that is almost certainly of value on those occasions when the Security Council is called upon to function, not as an agency of collective action, but as a microcosm of world opinion. Nor, when action is called for, should its baneful consequences be exaggerated; it may at times have robbed the Security Council of the services of a useful 'middle power'; it may have swollen unduly the benches of those 'brute voters' whose presence in another assembly Walter Bagehot once satirized; but it has never seriously impeded the work of the Council and has seldom been responsible for aggravating in any significant degree the animosities of the permanent members. If we are concerned about the real weakness of the Security Council our search for causes must be directed elsewhere.

In the inter-war years, it had been the almost unanimous opinion of statesmen and students of the League that one of the greatest weaknesses of the Covenant was its 'sanctions' clause, Article XVI. This in theory obliged members to sever all trade and financial relations with any state which went to war in defiance of the Covenant—in practice it had largely been emasculated by the gloss put on Article X by the League Assembly in 1923—but where military sanctions were concerned it merely laid on the Council the duty 'to recommend . . . what effective military, naval, or air force the members of the League shall severally contribute to the armed forces to be used to protect the covenants of the League'. This procedure was unsatisfactory in two respects: it left it open to member states to respond, or not to respond, to the call for military aid, and it provided no machinery or system for organizing League forces in advance, or indeed even for co-ordinating such responses as members might make.

Both these faults Chapter VII of the Charter was designed to remedy. By Article 42 the Security Council is empowered itself to 'take such action by air, sea, or land forces as may be necessary to maintain or restore international peace and security', and by Article 43 to call on other members of the U.N. to co-operate in such action. In Articles 43–47 advance preparation of such collective military action is envisaged, through a Military Staff Committee. This would consist of the Chiefs of Staff of the permanent members (or their representatives). It would advise the Security Council on all questions relating to its 'military requirements' and if the Council, so to say, 'went to war' it would act as its strategic director. Member states would negotiate 'as soon as possible' with the Security Council agreements stipulating what armed forces they would place at the Council's disposal and what facilities and assistance they would provide it. To this end members would hold 'immediately available national air-force contingents for combined international enforcement action'. All this would be effected 'with the assistance of the Military Staff Committee'. As far as draftsmanship could do it, the gaps that had existed in the Covenant were closed. But obviously in practice everything hinged on the effective operation of the Military Staff Committee and the negotiation of appropriate military agreements.

No time was lost in setting up the Military Staff Committee. Its first meeting was held in London on 4 February 1946; twelve days later on 16 February it was instructed by the Security Council, as its first task, to examine from the military point of view the implications of Article 43—i.e. the Security Council's agreements with member states. But from the outset its prospects of success were poor, since its own membership reflected the most serious of the tensions within the U.N., that between the U.S.S.R. and the West. Nevertheless for over twelve months its military men (and the Committee was well served in the quality of its representatives) worked away in privacy, and in April 1947 produced their report. Disagreement was not total; the twenty-five articles in the report on which the Committee were unanimous included some matters of consequence—e.g. that the permanent members should contribute the bulk of the armed forces. But there was a crucial area of sixteen points on which agreement could not be reached. They included such questions as the size of the forces—the U.S.S.R., United Kingdom, France, and China favoured relatively small contributions, the U.S.A., large ones; the balance of contributions from each member—the U.S.S.R. wanted strict equality, the others only comparability, leaving each state free to fix the exact size of its contingents; the location of the forces in peace-time—the U.S.S.R. insisted that they must remain in their own countries until actually called out by the Council, while the others wanted the Security Council to place them in advance where it thought fit; finally, the question of bases and supplies—the U.S.S.R. could not agree that one state might provide supplies and bases for another. The details of these disagreements are not, however, important, because it was not dissension over these relatively technical issues which really mattered but the political mistrust that lay behind them. When the Security Council itself failed to give its Committee the guidance on general principles necessary to formulate a practicable plan, it became obvious that total deadlock had occurred. On 2 July 1948 the Committee, with a frankness not always characteristic of divided U.N. committees, reported that no further progress could be made, and although the Committee still formally meets every fortnight it has had no real business to transact ever since.

This failure left the Security Council with a central part of its system of peace-enforcement totally inoperative. Yet within two years of the virtual stultification of most of the procedures envisaged in Chapter VII of the Charter for 'Action with respect to Threats to the Peace, Breaches of the Peace, and Acts of Aggression', the U.N. provided in Korea the most signal demonstration of collective action since the inception of the League. The happy and perhaps unique combination of circumstances which made this politically feasible has been described in Chapter 3, and we have seen that the fragility of the Security Council's *modus operandi* on that occasion led to the determination to equip the General Assembly as a substitute organ in case of another impasse in the Council. From 1950 to the early sixties it looked as if the 'Uniting for Peace' procedure, with the transfer from Council to Assembly which it provides, would be the normal U.N. substitute for the application of any of the Articles of Chapter VII. But with the deadlock produced by the Soviet and French 'financial veto', the future of this alternative became cloudy.

The Russians have always insisted that because Article 43 (the negotiation of agreements between members of the Council) has never been implemented, therefore Articles 41 and 42, which give the Council binding authority to take collective enforcement measures, are inoperative. But those who supported the action the U.N. took in Korea have contended that this was valid enforcement action under Chapter VII and have justified it by reference to Article 39. Admittedly this Article only empowers the Security Council to 'make recommendations'; it does not authorize it to *require* members' participation in collective action.

It does, none the less, create a powerful moral presumption in favour of their doing so. However, in 1966, when the tide of U.N. feeling was running so strongly on the colonialist issue in relation to Southern Rhodesia, the Security Council was able to take, for the first time, explicit enforcement action under Chapter VII. In April the United Kingdom secured authority 'to prevent by the use of force if necessary' the arrival of oil tankers at Beira bringing supplies to Southern Rhodesia, on the grounds that the continuance of Rhodesia's illegal independence was a 'threat to peace'. And when, despite all pressures, the Smith regime persisted in its defiance, the Security Council in December 1966 at Britain's instigation, for the first time in the history of the U.N., imposed selective but mandatory economic sanctions. Finding that 'the situation in Southern Rhodesia constitutes a threat to peace and security', it explicitly invoked Articles 39 and 41 and called on all member (and non-member) states to ban the import of a wide range of Southern Rhodesian products and the export to her of oil, aircraft, arms, or equipment, and also to deny her any financial or other economic aid.

In May 1968 the Security Council unanimously made the sanctions both comprehensive and mandatory, an exercise of authority that went beyond anything previously attempted by either the League or the U.N. None the less the total non-compliance of South Africa and Portugal, the inability of dependent and adjacent African states to cut off all trade, and the persistent and cynical evasion by many states which voted for sanctions in the U.N. substantially reduced their effectiveness. The Smith regime was able to consolidate its internal position, proclaim a republic, and impose more restrictive measures on its black majority. So in March 1970 the Security Council went even further, calling upon states to sever all relations, diplomatic and economic, with the regime and also interrupt all transport links. Even this, of course, was less than the African states (abetted by the U.S.S.R.) were demanding. They wanted the United Kingdom to use force to bring down the regime. In the General Assembly they secured easy majorities for such demands, but in the Security Council their persistence provoked a

British veto and, for the first time in history, an American one.

Rhodesia, like many other intractable situations, illustrates the gap between Security Council performance and the aspirations of the Charter. Early in the history of the Organization recognition of this led member states to seek protection outside the United Nations, in regional organizations like NATO. From that time forward all the Great Powers and the great majority of small ones, however much their policies respected the U.N., relied for their security upon alliances and pacts with states like-minded with themselves. In other words something essentially the same as the old balance of power system re-created itself within the U.N. That this would happen was already foreseen by the Charter. Article 51 was, of course, framed to provide for this, with its wide provision that '*Nothing* in the present Charter shall impair the inherent right of individual or collective self-defence . . .'. Thus provision was made for the fact that a collective security system could not fully function in advance of a much stronger sense of international community, or at least could only put out tentative shoots, such as UNEF in the Middle East and ONUC in the Congo, which did not threaten the vital interests of sovereign states.

This enfeeblement of its central function has not, however, left the Council with nothing to do.

The Charter, though it gives the Council exclusive competence in the enforcement field, never regarded this as the only task appropriate to its nature. In the first place, although it gives the Security Council little or nothing to do with the administration of the U.N. Organization, the Charter makes its initiative and consent necessary before the General Assembly can proceed to discharge two of its most essential functions—the election of a Secretary-General and the admission of new members. The Secretary-General has to be 'recommended' by an affirmative vote of nine (originally seven) members of the Security Council (including the five permanent members) before he can be 'appointed' by a majority vote of the General Assembly. This affords a guarantee that the Secretary-General will be someone acceptable to all of the Great Powers—an obviously essential qualification. The General Assembly can, of course, reject the Security Council's nominee for the office, but if it does so, it cannot appoint someone of its own choice instead. The Preparatory Commission thought it desirable that the Security Council should put forward only one candidate for the Assembly's consideration in order that 'debate on the nomination in the General Assembly [should be] avoided'. This practice has been followed in every election so far, though of course the negotiations which preceded each nomination wore the veil of secrecy almost to the point of transparency.

The admission of new members to the Organization has been a constant source of friction in the U.N., as we have seen. Here again a 'recommendation' by the Security Council has to precede a 'decision' by the General Assembly (Article 4)—i.e. an affirmative vote of nine (including the permanent members) of the Security Council has to precede an affirmative vote of two-thirds of the General Assembly. This gives full play to the veto, and in fact about half of the vetoes initially cast by the U.S.S.R. were used to blackball candidates for membership. The dissatisfaction occasioned by this has been freely vented in debates in the General Assembly (which is under no such vow of silence where membership applications are concerned as where candidacy for the Secretary-Generalship is involved) and it has frequently pressed the Security Council to reconsider its rejections and even agitated against the employment of the veto, legal though this undoubtedly is. Two principles, or perhaps one should rather say attitudes, have clashed in the debates on membership. One view, deriving not from any particular article of the Charter, but from the mere fact of the U.N. being a 'world organization', presses for universality of membership; this means, in effect, that all applicants should be admitted unless strong arguments can be adduced to the contrary. The other view is essentially that of the Club; membership in the U.N. is a privilege reserved, as Article 4 says, to the founder members and to 'all other peace-loving states which accept the obligations' of the Charter and are 'able and willing' to carry them out. On this view the onus is on applicants to prove their virtue to the satisfaction of the Club at large and the Club committee in particular, one committee blackball excluding. Without doubt, the wording of the Charter lends support to the 'club-blackball' school; its weakness, however, is that if 'peace-loving' and similar criteria are to be applied the founder members themselves shall scarcely 'scape whipping. In fact, of course, founder members (particularly permanent members of the Security Council) have invoked each set of arguments, without much regard to consistency, having generally been guided in their voting by a cruder set of considerations—namely whether a given applicant, if admitted to membership, would strengthen their 'side' in the U.N. or not. In general, as might be guessed, this has meant that the West has supported new admissions and the Communist bloc has been suspicious of them. Increasingly, however, the concept of universality has gained ground, most conspicuously as the new membership has itself come to dominate the General Assembly. Now the onus is on the exclusionists to show why a state should not be admitted.

A rather different sharing of authority with the General Assembly is implied in the system laid down for electing to the International Court. Here, of course, the election is of individuals, not of states, 'from among persons', as the Statute says, 'of high moral character, who possess the qualifications required in their respective countries for appointment to the highest judicial offices, or are jurisconsults of recognized competence in international law', and who should represent 'the main forms of civilization and the principal legal systems of the world', and to assist in the realization of this an elaborate system of election, carried over from League practice, was adopted. Member states nominate, nominations go to both Council and Assembly, each votes by secret ballot, and those candidates who receive an absolute majority in both organs are considered elected. Balloting goes on until all vacancies have been filled, or—if too many have been filled—until any surplus has been eliminated. Any discrepancy between Security Council and General Assembly elections is resolved by the same methods. The membership of the Court is fifteen, and judges retire in groups of five every three years. Re-election is permissible.

Another function, though of a completely different order, which the Security Council to some extent shares with the General Assembly is 'the regulation of armaments and possible disarmament', as Article 47 puts it. The Charter envisages the General Assembly (as is appropriate to a large debating body) concerning itself with 'the general principles' (Article 11) of disarmament and the Council as producing specific plans. Logically, but alas fruitlessly, the Charter delegates this function, within the Security Council, to the Military Staff Committee on the principle that since the U.N. needs force to police the world, therefore the same organ which plans the police force ought to regulate the levels of national forces other than those dedicated to the U.N. Two things upset this arrangement. The first was the advent of the atomic bomb, which seemed to pose a disarmament problem of a different order of magnitude from that envisaged by the Charter. The second was, of course, the stultification of the Military Staff Committee. As a result, initially, of the atomic problem the first serious U.N. effort to cope with disarmament was lodged not in the Security Council, but in the General Assembly. The Atomic Energy Commission, set up in January 1946, was established by the Assembly, though its membership (apart from Canada) was the same as that of the Council, and it was to report to the Council and be accountable to it 'in matters affecting security'. The melancholy history of the Atomic Energy Commission need not detain us here; only for a brief period did its deliberations hold any promise of success, and by 1948 it had reached total failure. In 1947, as a result of resolutions passed by the General Assembly, the Security Council set up a Commission for Conventional Armaments with membership identical with that of the Council itself. This ran into the sands of East–West disagreement in its turn and in 1952 the two frustrated Commissions were merged, by Assembly resolution, into one Disarmament Commission with the same membership as the Atomic Energy Commission and 'under the Security Council'. Thus, in effect, the main responsibility for the handling of this intractable subject was lodged once again with the Council, though the General Assembly has increasingly shown in its debates its interest and concern in the progress—or rather, to be accurate, the lack of progress—which the Commission has made. In November 1958 the General Assembly, after a Soviet boycott of the Commission, re-composed it to include 'all the members of the U.N.', but this led to no improvement. In 1959 a ten-member committee, outside the formal structure of the U.N., on which NATO and Warsaw Pact countries were equally represented, became the forum for most of the ensuing negotiations. In 1961 it was expanded to eighteen, to include representatives of the 'neutrals'. However, the Assembly's concern remained, continuing prominence being given to the subject in its debates. The conclusion in August 1963 of the test-ban agreement between Britain, the U.S.A., and the U.S.S.R. may, in part at least, be regarded as some reflection of this. On disarmament proper, however, virtually no progress was made. At Soviet urging, the Security Council reconvened the full Disarmament Commission in April 1965, ostensibly in consequence of the deadlock in the eighteen-member committee, but more obviously as a gesture of protest against the immobilization of the nineteenth General Assembly. It proved, of course, practically unproductive and the smaller committee (enlarged in 1969 to twenty-six) continued to be the main forum. Interest increasingly concentrated on control of nuclear weapons, where the signature of the Treaty on Non-Proliferation represented a substantial achievement, while the opening in November 1969 of 'SALT' (the Strategic Arms Limitation Talks) between the U.S.A. and the U.S.S.R. encouraged hopes of further progress in this field. The Committee, like the General Assembly, also gave increasing attention to the problems of chemical and biological warfare, which led in 1972 to a Convention on Bacteriological Weapons.

Just as the Charter shares control between the Security Council and the General Assembly in the field of disarmament, so it permits them both to contribute to 'the pacific settlement of disputes'. (This is the almost technical term the Charter employs for all those operations of pacification which stop short of any form of sanctions and all those disagreements between states which stop short of being outright threats to the peace.) But here too, though the General Assembly is allowed a wide power of inquiry and debate, it is obvious that the Security Council was envisaged as the principal operating organ. Chapter VI of the Charter, which deals with the 'Pacific Settlement of Disputes', makes much more frequent reference to the Security Council in this connexion than to the General Assembly. Furthermore, by Article 12, the Security Council was conceded to have a kind of priority in this role, since the Assembly is forbidden to deal with questions with which the Security Council is dealing. Nor is this out of keeping with the 'Concert' concept of the Security Council which, as we have seen, it inherits from its League predecessor. Most wars, after all, have their inception in disputes; the policeman will only be needed if the quarrel has not previously been otherwise composed.

Paradoxically, however, while the Security Council as police-man has power to *impose* its decision—summon members to its aid and use force against the combatants—the Security Council as settler of disputes can only *recommend*, even if an ignored recommendation means a graver risk of war. This, of course, reflects the basic paradox of the present stage of development of the international community. The nations are sufficiently con-scious of their proximity as mutual menaces to make war *as such* an offence (at least on paper); at the same time they do not feel sufficiently like-minded to accept any agency's compulsory jurisdiction when it is a matter of a dispute between them. They can tolerate a policeman more readily than a judge. In part this reflects a sensible awareness of the peculiar destructiveness of modern war, in part the difficulty of conceiving of a law-court in advance of a law-making and law-changing agency (i.e. a parlia-ment). But also, of course, it reflects the fact that it is only *on paper* that the policeman has yet been accepted; it is no accident that, as we have seen, the enforcement provisions of the Charter have proved inoperative.

Indeed, when it is a matter of the pacific settlement of disputes the Security Council—and for that matter the General Assembly —is much better thought of as an extra diplomatic agency than as anything resembling a court. To adapt Clausewitz, it is engaged on the continuation of diplomacy (traditional diplomacy, that is) by other diplomatic means. This is clearly brought out in Article 33 of the Charter, which requires that international disputants 'shall, first of all, seek a solution by negotiation, enquiry, mediation, conciliation, arbitration, judicial settlement, resort to regional agencies or arrangements, or other peaceful means of their own choice'—i.e. all the techniques of traditional diplomacy. Security Council diplomacy was envisaged as starting where these conventional techniques leave off. In fact this has by no means always happened, and disputes have frequently been brought before the Council long before other procedures have been exhausted. But in either event what the Security Council contributes to the resolution of a dangerous situation or the settlement of a dispute is much the same—in one form or another it is what one might call institutionalized moral pressure.

The techniques which the Security Council has employed for this purpose have been as various as the cases with which it has had to deal. But for convenience they may be broadly classified as investigation, interposition, conciliation, recommendation, and appeal—though it is rare for any one of these techniques to prove adequate by itself; they will normally be employed in some blend or combination.

Investigation is that process of fact-finding, of arriving at some acceptable substratum of evidence, which is the almost essential pre-condition of any recommendation which the Council may wish to make. If a dispute exists, there is almost certain to be disagreement about the sequence of events which led up to it, about who did what, about what the present situation is, about the relevance of the facts to the dispute in question, perhaps even about whether a substantive basis for a dispute exists at all. The Council itself will not usually attempt an investigation, but it will generally appoint a committee of its own membership, or a commission of representatives of its members, sometimes (as in the case of 'The U.N. Commission of Investigation Concerning Greek Frontier Incidents' of 1947) sending it to the scene of the dispute to collect its evidence on the spot. Of course the search for the indisputable fact is liable to prove as difficult as the quest for the rainbow's end, but it is a rare piece of U.N. investigation which does not result in some unravelling of the skein of allegation and counter-allegation.

Interposition. When a situation is potentially explosive, when the problem is not so much Who is to blame? as How to stop matters getting worse? it is often of the greatest value if the Security Council can interpose between the disputants the physical presence of some of its own representatives. Sometimes they can combine with this the business of fact-collecting and reporting, but in a situation where anything is liable to happen at any minute it is their mere presence which is likely to prove of the greatest use, as a shield and a deterrent. Generally they will be formally charged with overseeing the conduct of a truce or an armistice agreement. Such was the Security Council Truce Commission for Palestine, while the U.N. Observation Group in Lebanon, indirectly, through its function of trying to ensure that there was no illegal infiltration of arms or men, had a certain deterrent effect on any disputant who might resort to force. The value of such groups, in any event, will derive not from their own strength but from their function as the symbol of the world authority, the disinterested third parties whom both disputants will be anxious not to offend.

Conciliation in the old diplomacy was the historic role of the benevolent neutral, 'the honest broker', the state whose detached posture made her acceptable to the warring or quarrelling powers. In U.N. diplomacy the Security Council may simply take over this role, though always (unless it violates the Charter) not merely with a due regard for a settlement, any settlement, *per se*, but also for 'the Purposes and Principles of the U.N.' (Article 24). The process of conciliation may be entrusted to a committee or to an individual. Thus the Security Council Committee of Good Offices on the Indonesian question consisted of two members each appointed by one of the disputants (Holland and Indonesia) and a third appointed by the previous two. The U.N. Commission on India and Pakistan followed a similar pattern, but with its three members appointed by the Security Council itself. Often, however, an individual has advantages as a negotiator or conciliator over a committee, especially if he is a man of repute and discretion. Such were Sir Owen Dixon and Dr. Frank Graham, whose services the Security Council also utilized in connexion with the Kashmir dispute, or Dr. Gunnar Jarring, who has been in constant demand in the Arab–Israeli context.

Recommendation. Sometimes a dispute cannot be resolved or a situation adjusted merely by inducing the parties concerned to behave or to compromise. Some constructive changes in the *status quo* may be necessary. This was clearly so in Palestine and in the Suez Canal dispute. In such cases the Security Council may formulate certain principles or courses of action and recommend them to the disputants—or even set up machinery for implementing them itself. Thus, in relation to the Canal dispute the Council laid down that any settlement should meet various requirements, such as freedom for users from all discrimination, respect for the sovereignty of Egypt, and the allocation of a fair proportion of the dues to development. Few tasks are harder for the Council than the framing of such recommendations. They must conform to the Charter's standards of justice and the principles of international law; at the same time, since they depend for their effect primarily on the parties' willingness to implement them, they must be framed either with a realistic eye to their practicability or as a kind of long-term investment in *Fiat justitia, ruat coelum.* The veto generally prevents the Council (by contrast with the General Assembly) from too ready a resort to the latter procedure, but often at the price of the Council's being unable to make any agreed recommendation at all.

Appeal. Sometimes because other methods have failed, sometimes in order to assist fact-finding, fortify a truce, or accelerate a negotiation, the Security Council may simply address a direct appeal to the disputants to abstain from improper behaviour. The appeals have been as diverse as the situations giving rise to them. As a fairly typical example one might quote the Security Council's resolution of 4 July 1969 on the Israeli attempt to change the status of the captured city of Jerusalem. In this the Council

(1) 'censured in the strongest terms' all measures taken to

change the status of the city of Jerusalem and deplored the failure of Israel to show any regard for previous resolutions on this subject;

(2) confirmed that all legislative and administrative measures and actions by Israel which purport to alter the status of Jerusalem are invalid and cannot change that status;

(3) requested Israel to inform the Council of its intentions with regard to implementing the resolution and warned that 'in the event of a negative response or no response' it would reconvene without delay 'to consider what further action should be taken'.

In the issuing of such appeals there are virtually no limits to the Security Council's powers except those imposed by the good sense of its members. But all such resolutions, it must be remembered, have only so much effect upon disputants as these may choose to give to them. They are exhortations, implorations, appeals which the Council has no power to enforce. The nearest the Council has come to trying to enforce such a recommendation was its celebrated resolution of 15 July 1948 (referred to above), provoked by the truce violations in Palestine. This read:

[The Security Council] *Determines* that the situation in Palestine constitutes a threat to the peace within the meaning of Article 39 of the Charter; *Orders* the Governments and authorities concerned, pursuant to Article 40 of the Charter of the U.N., to desist from further military action . . . not later than three days from [this date, and] *Declares* that failure by any of the Governments or authorities concerned to comply . . . would demonstrate the existence of a breach of the peace within the meaning of Article 39 of the Charter, requiring immediate consideration by the Security Council with a view to such further action under Chapter VII of the Charter as may be decided upon by the Council.

This is the only occasion on which the Security Council has found that the ignoring of one of its recommendations under Chapter VI (The Pacific Settlement of Disputes) led it on into the territory of Chapter VII (Action with Respect to Threats to the Peace, Breaches of the Peace, and Acts of Aggression), where its powers of enforcement come into play. In particular the Council has very properly always refused to try to enforce a political decision. In 1948 the General Assembly, having voted in favour of partition in Palestine and set up a Commission to supervise it, found that the plan could not be carried out and asked the Security Council to 'provide the Commission with adequate means . . . for the execution of its authority'. This the Security Council declined to do on the grounds that it would have been *ultra vires*.

Indeed, in this whole field of pacific settlement the Security Council occupies a position which can best be understood as analogous to that occupied by government conciliation machinery in a democratic state, one which leaves labour–management disputes to be settled by the free processes of collective bargaining. So long as the dispute within the industry does not turn to violence, directly or indirectly threatening the order and existence of the community, the government confines itself to fact-finding, conciliation, the making of recommendations, arbitration, and the policing of picket-lines. It may bring moral pressure to bear on one side or the other, but it does not impose any settlement of wages or hours or conditions of work even if the dispute continues and a strike ensues. What a democratic government abstains from doing out of regard for civil liberties, the Security Council abstains from doing out of regard for the rights of sovereign states, duly safeguarded by the provisions of the Charter. And just as the democratic state relies ultimately for the settlement of its industrial disputes upon the play of public opinion on the disputants, together with the disputants' own awareness of where their real interests lie, so the Security Council acts by mobilizing opinion and trying to get the disputants to see reason.

In this connexion the role of the veto has often been misunderstood. At San Francisco most of the hostility to the veto was directed not against its use in connexion with Chapter VII, where it was recognized that for any successful enforcement action Great Power unanimity was virtually essential, but against the employment of it when the Council was merely making recommendations, as under Chapter VI. The standard Great Power reply to such criticism was to deny the validity of the distinction. The 'chain of events' doctrine was invoked, according to which even recommendations under Chapter VI might by a 'chain of events' lead to enforcement action under Chapter VII. On this line of reasoning strict logic would conclude, as the Russians did indeed contend, that since words have been known to lead to blows, the veto should block even discussion of a dispute. However, strict logic was defeated by the pressure of conference opinion, particularly the opinion of the other permanent members, and the distinction between 'procedural' and 'substantive' questions was instituted in its place. By this it was agreed that the veto should apply to *all* substantive issues of whatever kind, but discussion was regarded as a procedural matter and as such not subject to the veto. Consequently the Council is free to discuss any issue that nine out of its fifteen members vote to place on the agenda. It is when a resolution is proposed at the end of the debate that the veto comes alive. (Though of course a Great Power cannot use the veto to stop the peaceful settlement of a dispute to which it is itself a party.) Even here, however, usage has softened strict legality. Following a precedent set, ironically, by the Russian Mr. Gromyko in 1946, it has come to be accepted that abstention on a vote does not constitute a veto, and in fact a substantial number of Council resolutions have since been carried in the face of the abstention of one or more of the permanent members.

Moreover since, outside Chapter VII, even Security Council resolutions have only the force of recommendations, one may ask what is the precise degree of impairment that they suffer through the veto? Presumably a permanent member uses the veto only because it disagrees with a resolution. It is therefore a reasonable corollary that, even deprived of the veto, it would still vote against the resolution. The power, in other words, would still remain to rob any resolution of the moral force that comes of unanimity. Is there any practical difference between a resolution which secures 14 votes out of 15 but fails of passage because the fifteenth is cast by a Great Power, and a resolution which passes by 14 votes to 1? Does not the first represent as significant a mobilization of opinion as the second?

Critics of the veto power in relation to Chapter VII do, however, have a stronger case when the immediate object of a resolution is not to bring moral pressure on a disputant but to set up some piece of the machinery of pacific settlement. It is the vetoes which prevent the appointment of a fact-finding committee, or a truce commission, or an observation team, that seriously hamper the work of the Council, and it is the Soviet Union's persistent use of vetoes such as these which has enfeebled the Council even in its non-enforcement activities. However, since the Laos dispute of 1959 a possibly significant precedent has been established. The ruling given then (see p. 184) by the President and upheld by the Council that the appointment of a sub-committee to conduct inquiries is a procedural, not a substantive, act may have opened the way to breaking the stranglehold of the veto in such circumstances.

Just as the various procedures for pacific settlement differ in the degree to which they depend upon auspicious votes in the Security Council, so they also differ in their dependence upon publicity as a prerequisite for their success. In the same way that the use of the veto has greatly exceeded the expectations of the Charter-makers, so the light of publicity beating on the Council chamber has proved more persistent and more glaring than most people originally imagined. A private meeting of the Security Council is a great rarity—generally confined to occasions when such a matter as the nomination of a Secretary-General is under discussion. At other times the Security Council meets under a public gaze every bit as constant as that directed on the General Assembly—and, because the theatre is smaller and the actors fewer, considerably more intensive. The advantages and drawbacks of this are by now generally recognized—on the one hand the popular interest and sympathy aroused by the ability to see and hear, by radio, press, and television, not only the words but the very features of world statesmen in action; on the other hand the stimulus given to public posturing and 'mere' propaganda, the constant incentive to ignore one's actual colleagues at the committee table in favour of the unseen millions outside, particularly those of one's home country. What is less often realized is that there are, in effect, two Security Councils—the one which meets before the public and the one which meets in the delegates' lounges, dining-rooms, and embassies. Each is necessary to the other; at any given time the blending of their two functions may be imperfect, but neither can function in isolation. The investigation of a dispute may often require weeks or months of patient, unobtrusive fact-gathering and fact-sifting, but for it to have any effect upon the dispute itself it requires at the end the fullest deployment of all the agencies of publicity at the Council's disposal. Much of the work of a truce observation team can be hampered or even wrecked by the playing up of some incident or by the premature disclosure of some informal local agreement whose publication may involve a disputant in a seeming loss of face. At the same time it is because these observers represent the eyes of the world that their presence in the trouble zone has value; they cannot therefore operate in total secrecy. Even the process of conciliation, which is so obviously dependent upon closed doors and unrecorded confidences, may arrive at a point where only the threat or the use of disclosure will crystallize an agreement reached, while a deadlock can sometimes only be resolved by a reference back to the Council chamber and some frank speaking there. Finally, the recommendation or appeal which a Security Council resolution addresses to a disputant, while obviously public in nature and intention, generally assumes its final form only after a great deal of private negotiation to which indeed the disputant may well have been a party.

All this makes it particularly hard to measure accurately the effect produced upon the Security Council's work by the setting and form of its public deliberations. The Council meets in one of the more intimate public rooms of the U.N. building. The effect, not altogether happy, is somewhat that of a well, or a pit. The delegates sit in a horseshoe-shaped ring, the President at the mid-point of the horseshoe, the Secretary-General on his right, the Under-Secretary for Political and Security Council Affairs on his left. Behind each delegate sit two or three of his official subordinates; at a table sunk within the centre of the horseshoe are interpreters, stenographers, and press officers of the Secretariat. Behind the President stretches one of the U.N.'s more garish and crudely symbolic murals, on either side of which are wide windows fronting on the East River. Seldom, however, are the room's occupants allowed a glimpse of what lies outside; the strong light of the North American continent generally makes it desirable to have the curtains drawn. Facing the President are the extensive public galleries. The other two sides of the room close in, as it were, on the deliberations in the centre. They house the glass-fronted booths of the radio, television, and movie camera men, who look down on their prey at such close quarters that it requires only reasonably keen eyesight to read the large type on the nearest delegate's papers.

For all the intimacy of its setting, the Security Council is not a cosy, integrated, or organic body. It seldom—very seldom—develops a corporate personality. Most of the time it stubbornly remains fifteen men (or, with the Secretary-General and his Assistant, seventeen) sitting around a table, with their deputies and subordinates behind them and their national publics behind them. The effect of its intimacy is much more often to add personal rancour to public controversy than to soften political disagreements with private regard. It *has* known moments when common purpose and common fear have fused it into a unity, but most of its life has to be passed at a lower level of integration, where the search for agreement has to be pursued through the slow and painful process of manœuvring fifteen national wills until some point of contact can be established between them. It is, after all, neither an executive nor a legislature, but a diplomatic conference in semi-permanent session. This is reflected in its deliberate tempo and repetitive procedure.

In 1969 Russian and Spanish were added to French and English as working languages of the Council and in 1974 Chinese was made a working language as well. Consecutive interpretations into any or all of these can be demanded as well as the simultaneous interpretations which are always provided. In practice this seems unlikely to become the norm, but it is a reminder that the Security Council is a chamber in which the spontaneity of debate must always take second place to the diplomat's concern over precise forms of wording, the desire to refer back to the home government for instructions, or the wish to reserve comment until a full text has been studied. As a result only a particularly forceful and unconventional individual can rise above these constraints sufficiently to put a strong impress upon the proceedings. That this can be done on occasion was demonstrated by the duels between Mr. Vyshinsky and Sir Gladwyn Jebb, or by the remarkable histrionics of Mr. Krishna Menon. But to any ordinary performer, a Security Council debate by its discontinuity and artificiality is a very taxing art form at which few can hope to excel.

The Council's practice of rotating the Presidency each month amongst its members accentuates rather than diminishes these characteristics. It deprives any presiding officer of much chance of imposing even a fleeting personality upon the proceedings. It is, no doubt, a necessary safeguard against abuse, limiting at least in point of time the damage which a President in a wrecking mood, like Mr. Malik in the August of 1950, can do to its deliberations. For this reason, if for no other, the practice is most unlikely to be modified. None the less, when to this is added the fact that the delegates of the ten non-permanent members are in any case birds of passage, men with only two-year terms, it will be seen how weak the forces making for continuity in the Council are.

The many weaknesses of the Council early led to a decreasing reliance upon its services. In its first three years, 1946, 1947, and 1948, the Council met on an average 132 times a year, but this high rate was not sustained. Figures of meetings by themselves might be misleading, but there was also a decline in the importance of the business transacted. Thanks to the veto, it was the General Assembly and not the Security Council which had the major handling of questions like Hungary and the Suez Canal, just as earlier the Korean conflict and the Greek question were shifted from the Council to the Assembly. There were also certain significant occasions on which, without the question of the veto arising, powers preferred, where a choice was possible, to take their problems to the Assembly for debate and resolution. This reflected, of course, the 'democratizing' trend at work in the U.N. which led an expanding membership to support any aggrandizement of the 'popular' chamber at the expense of the oligarchical one.

However, with the sixties, the decline in the Security Council's role was halted. It was the principal agency employed over the Congo and Cyprus; it had the handling of Cuba and the Santo Domingo and India-Pakistan crises of 1965. It was the main forum for action, as opposed to mere expressions of opinion, over Rhodesia and South Africa. It was the organ that exercised such authority as the U.N. retained in relation to the problems of the Middle East. The deadlock in the General Assembly over the Congo, the humiliations to which it was exposed by the Article 19 controversy, the impotence which it felt in face of the 'financial veto' on the employment of the Uniting for Peace resolution— all these set limits to the 'democratizing' trend mentioned above. Indeed the pressure for the expansion of the Security Council constituted the greatest tribute that the weak members of the General Assembly could pay to its importance. At the same time it represented what might also be regarded as a certain infection of the Council by the 'democratizing' tendency of the Assembly itself. The provisions under Article 31, by which non-member states may be invited to address the Council, and Article 39, which permits similar facilities for other persons, have been sometimes so liberally applied as to make Council meetings as unwieldy and repetitive as a typical Assembly session. The holding of Council meetings away from headquarters, as in Addis Ababa in 1972 and Panama City in 1973, reflected a similar trend towards making the Council a mini-Assembly, designedly exposed to the pressures and propaganda of regional blocs. It is possible to recognize the educational value of such exposure for the permanent members and still doubt whether this constitutes the best employment of a unique agency for peace and security. In the crises of our troubled times a body which is designed to function continuously and which needs to be able to act promptly and decisively has enough to do if it confines itself to its essential tasks.

5 · THE GENERAL ASSEMBLY

IMAGINE a cavernous hall, with floor sloping from front to back and walls sloping inwards from floor to domed ceiling. The forward part of the floor is given over to long rows of green desks and blue chairs arranged in narrowing and concentric arcs to focus on a raised tribune and, behind and above that, a massive rostrum. The rear of the floor is filled with steeply rising rows of seats above which rises a broad cantilevered gallery. Lightness is given to the walls by vertical timbered slats, broken on each side by long, glass-fronted camera booths; further back two huge, gay, abstract but vaguely crab-like murals line the walls by the spectators' gallery. At the centre, above the podium, is set the U.N. emblem, blue and white, a circle on a vast oblong backdrop of gold. Light flows over everything, shining down from cat-walks (startlingly undisguised) in the dome, rising, reflected, from desks and table tops on the floor, seeping imperceptibly from hidden embrasures everywhere.

The galleries are packed with spectators, chirruping, questioning, or passively receptive to the multi-lingual expositions of guides, official and unofficial. The seats in front of them contain a fair sprinkling of the press of the world, old hands renewing acquaintance, new hands learning the ropes. In front of them stretches the floor reserved for delegates and distinguished guests. Here all is animation, as figures move in from the lobbies and lounges on either side. Handshakes, waves, embraces, shoulder clasps are the order of the day. Greetings, recognitions, introductions proceed in a rising hubbub of talk and laughter. Ushers and usherettes show guests and strangers to their seats and dissuade intruders from entering the privileged area. Photographers weave their way from group to group, delighting their victims and dazzling their neighbours with their flashbulb attentions. The hands of the clock have moved on well past the appointed time for the commencement of the proceedings, but few delegates show any desire to exchange their sauntering for their seats. The movement and the hubbub continue undiminished until at last, twenty-five minutes after the hour, the sound is heard of a gavel hammering the meeting to order and suddenly there can be seen, diminutive by reason of the vastness of the hall, three figures upon the President's podium. The hammering is repeated, the groups scatter, and the last straggler finds his seat. There is 'a minute of silence dedicated to prayer and meditation' but in fact filled with the whirr of movie cameras. Another session of the General Assembly has begun.

When the session has been under way for a few days it is a considerably less animated scene that presents itself to the eye. The attendance will have thinned, the distinguished guests around the floor will have given place to the sightseers *de deuxième classe*, or the licensed, patient bearers of briefs for some oppressed minority who are waiting their moment to be heard. The public galleries will still be full, but only half a dozen of the ample press seats will be occupied; a smooth public address system will be piping the entire proceedings of the Assembly into the rooms which most accredited correspondents occupy at the other end of the Secretariat building. Nor will the delegates themselves be in full attendance; their 1,300 odd seats will be less than half filled and their attention will be unevenly divided between the speaker of the moment, the chance acquaintance who pauses for a chat in the aisle, and their colleagues or the secretaries of their own delegation whose brief-cases bulge with the *New York Times* or the morning telegrams from the government at home. Debate— if that is not too indulgent a term—moves more continuously than in the Security Council, thanks to simultaneous translation, but what is gained in continuity is often offset by the greater garrulity and irrelevance of the speeches. Save where some African or Asian delegation appears in native costume, or some Latin American spokesman gives himself up to uninhibited rhetoric, there is little that is colourful or arresting about the proceedings. The tempo is normally lethargic, the language flat. Yet considering the diversity and often the rancour of the opinions expressed there is a surprising orderliness about the proceedings. The President is seldom seen to intervene, except to call upon a new speaker. Like a herd of grazing cattle, that moves as it chews, head down, the Assembly gets through its day (or more often its morning) without any particular drive, yet not without a certain vaguely diffused sense of purpose.

To the British observer this is a far cry from anything at Westminster. It is not merely that the expansive hall violates all the St. Stephen's canons of a debating chamber, nor yet that the speakers, instead of rising in their places, march to the tribune. Such after all are characteristics of continental assemblies. What most baffles outsiders who have lent easy credence to catch-phrases like 'legislature of the world' is the absence of focus, the lack of organization about the Assembly. Where are the parties, where are the whips, where are the usual channels? What takes the place of government and opposition, of front-benchers and back-benchers? Who, in the inescapable phrase of British politics, is 'responsible'?—in this centre, as Zimmern puts it, 'where there are neither hosts nor guests and everyone is equally away from home'. Vainly seeking answers to questions such as these, many have echoed the plaintive cry of the M.P. on the British delegation, '*Where* is the discipline?'

The House of Commons is in fact a peculiarly unsuitable training ground for the General Assembly. In many ways a body like the Trade Union Congress or the Labour Party Conference, with its federal structure, its bloc votes, its discontinuity, its frequent (and deliberate) inconclusiveness, breeds a style of politics that transplants more readily to the U.N. But the fact is that any purely British institution will reflect too nicely the close, compact, orderly, and intimate character of these islands to provide many suggestive analogies for this sprawling assembly that serves the world. Countries with a federal structure like the U.S.A. much more readily throw up the kind of loose, untidy, legalistic yet anarchic institutions which the General Assembly resembles. The American Congress, with its pressure groups and entrenched minorities, its jealousy for states' rights, and its shifting channels of power and control, has much in common with it. But perhaps the quadrennial conventions of the great American parties have more. There the diversity of interests to be harmonized is of course continental, not global; but in kind, if not in scale, comparable clashes of creed, race, interest, and psychology have to be accommodated. Each is more than a forum for action. They are also meeting grounds at which acquaintances are made or maintained and awareness of other styles of thought and behaviour is—however reluctantly—cultivated. Each institution has only a certain amount of control over constituent parts that are frequently older, prouder, and more tenacious than the whole. Problems of credentials, recognition, and voting strength occur in both, and though the rivalries of state delegations in the party conventions necessarily stop short of war they do not balk at walkouts or secessions. In neither, though, can a single unit, however determined, get its way alone; it must seek friends and allies and to do so must trade votes, offer gifts, threaten (but with discretion), and promise (but not much more than it can deliver). The chiaroscuro of publicity and privacy— of appeals to public opinion from the platform and to private interest in the lobbies, and the ensuing discrepancy between outward appearance and political reality—this is a dominant characteristic of each. The party convention, of course, is assisted towards unity by the existence of a permanent and pressing rival; the General Assembly has no enemy but itself; yet both, in varying degrees, work in a common task-master's eye—the public which has put them there and which, for all its partialities and indulgence, expects some result.

The formal organization of the General Assembly is simple enough. Its regular sessions open every year on the third Tuesday in September. Each member state is entitled to a delegation of five, with five deputies (and often trailing an ample phalanx of advisers, specialists, and understudies in the wings). Sessions open under the charge of the President of the previous session (or the chairman of his country's delegation) and the first task of a new Assembly is to elect its own President to hold office for the next twelve months. In the U.N., as in the League, the convention has become firmly established that the President should not be a representative of a Great Power. This has not prevented the office attracting the services of some of the leading figures of the international scene and from the first President, M. Spaak of Belgium, onwards it has been well served by its incumbents. The powers of the President are limited, but an able man can do a good deal by his personal influence to smooth the work of a session and to maintain the interests of the Organization against the sectional pressures of its members. The qualities required are essentially those of any other presiding officer of a large assembly —a refusal to be bored, a memory for faces, a capacity to slough off private and national partialities, a sense of humour coupled with a concern for the dignity of his office, a ready grasp of procedural technicalities, a proper sense of pace, and a quick feeling for the sense of the meeting. Probably no Assembly President has possessed all these virtues in full degree, but fortunately none has had to rely on his own unaided resources. At his side in the Assembly chamber always sits the *Chef de Cabinet* of the Secretary-General who is also the Under-Secretary for General Assembly Affairs and who acts, in this capacity, as a Parliamentary Clerk would to a speaker. From 1946 to 1962 this office, under the title of Executive Assistant to the Secretary-General, was held by Andrew Cordier, whose notable tact, discretion, devotion, and ability contributed greatly to the smooth evolution of the office of President. It is now held by Mr. C. V. Narasimhan of India. The President is elected by secret ballot, and normally everything possible is done before the session opens to find, by private arrangement, a candidate on whom an impressive majority can agree. In the first Assemblies there were some closely contested elections; subsequently the machinery of pre-selection has worked sufficiently smoothly to make these a rarity, and the normal Assembly opens with the identity of its President-to-be one of the worst-kept secrets of the Organization.

The rules of the General Assembly provide in addition for the election of seventeen Vice-Presidents and of Chairmen of the Association's seven standing committees. These unite, under the President, to form a body known as the General Committee, which is a kind of steering committee for each session. No two of its members can be members of the same delegation, and it is to be 'so constituted as to ensure its representative character'. Its business is procedural—determining the agenda and the priorities of debate, allocating items to the seven standing committees and co-ordinating their work, fixing a date for adjournment, and generally assisting the President in the conduct of his duties. It is, of course, advisory only, and its recommendations are not binding on the parent body. Nevertheless, in a context where procedural issues can assume much importance, the fear—so far only too groundless—that the General Committee might become a dictator has made membership of it (and the Vice-Presidencies which confer it) much sought after. The number of Vice-Presidencies was originally fixed at seven and it has always been accepted that five of these would go automatically to the Great Powers. Since Committee Chairmanships, like the Presidency, are recognized small-power perquisites, the Great Powers need some such preserve if they are to be assured of their voice on the General Committee. At the same time the smaller powers have always chafed at this, contending that this did not leave enough open seats on the General Committee to 'ensure its representative character'. As a result, in 1956 the number of Vice-Presidencies was increased to eight, in 1957 to thirteen, and in 1963 to seventeen, on the grounds of the increased membership of the Organization. The seventeen are formally allocated as follows:

(a) seven to Asian and African states;
(b) one to an Eastern European state;
(c) three to Latin American states;
(d) two to Western European and other states;
(e) five to the permanent members of the Security Council.
(An overlap is allowed for between the categories.)

The seven Committee Chairmanships are supposed to be distributed between the blocs on a similar basis. Thus the Assembly formally recognized the existence of some of its most obvious blocs and took a considerable step forward towards the 'democratization' of its steering committee, even at the risk of making it unwieldy and rigid.

One other special committee is important in relation to the Assembly's organization and functioning. This is the Credentials Committee, a body of nine members, elected at each session. Little continuity has been shown in its membership except, significantly, that since 1952 both the U.S.A. and the U.S.S.R. have been members—reflecting their roles as leading spokesmen in the dispute over the recognition of Communist China. This committee, of course, has only advisory powers; important arguments about credentials are always ultimately fought out in the General Assembly itself.

This completes the formal organizing machinery of the Assembly, but mention should also be made of an institution which, ever since 1948, has in fact had as much to do with its smooth operation as anything laid down in the written rules. This is the weekly lunch given by the President and attended by the Chairmen of the seven main committees, the Secretary-General and his assistants, and the Secretaries of the committees. Each Chairman reports on the work of his committee and brings up any problems on which he needs guidance. This is followed by a general discussion of all issues of common concern. The result is the evolution of uniform practices in the standing committees, the easy transference, whenever necessary, of work from committee to committee, and the smooth planning of committee time-tables in relation to the work of the plenary sessions.

The General Assembly is a talking shop, with all the potentialities and disabilities that that implies. What does it talk about? Article 10 permits it 'to discuss any questions or any matters within the scope of the present Charter or relating to the powers and functions of any organs provided for in the present Charter'. The mandate could hardly be wider. How then, with the world as its oratorical oyster, and over a hundred members vying to open it, does it decide on its themes and its spokesmen? The agenda of each Assembly session is, in the first instance, drafted in July by the Secretary-General and the rules prescribe certain items that this must include, e.g. the Secretary-General's own annual report and the reports of the other organs of the U.N., items carried over from a previous session, and—comprehensively—

'all items proposed by any member of the U.N.' This obviously excludes nothing and inhibits no one, and when to this provisional agenda are added such supplementary items as occur to members between July and September, it will be seen that there is always a guaranteed quart to fill the pint pot. A normal provisional agenda now generally runs to over ninety items and, with supplements, may easily exceed the hundred mark.

This agenda is then reviewed in the first instance by the General Committee of the Assembly, meeting in private. It is not common for the Committee to reject an item altogether, but sometimes it will re-formulate it, or subsume it under some existing, broadly phrased item with a view to avoiding overlap and minimizing repetition. The General Committee's recommendations rest on a broad base of custom and precedent and are generally accepted by the Assembly, but there invariably occur certain contentious items. These will form the subject of debate—frequently bitter, sometimes prolonged—in the General Assembly itself. No part of the Assembly's proceedings provides an easier target for the cynic than these debates about the agenda, debates which often run on into the middle of a session (though the Assembly will always be getting on with the agreed items in the meantime). 'Why! They can't even agree on the agenda!' is a natural comment, but one which proceeds from a mistaken concept of the Assembly's nature. The exact reverse of Blackstone's parliament, the General Assembly can only do what sovereign member states will let it. Every argument about an agenda item is an argument about powers—the powers of the Assembly and perhaps of the U.N.—and about the limits of sovereignty. To discuss a state's behaviour in some respect is almost always to criticize it; this involves national pride and may even, where public debate inflames a minority's (or majority's) passions, involve national security. This has been particularly evident where racial and colour questions have been involved, cf. the debates on Algeria and South African 'apartheid' policies. It was concern for such considerations that no doubt prompted the inclusion in the Charter of the ban contained in Article 2, § 7, on intervention 'in matters which are essentially within the domestic jurisdiction of any state'. Of course it can be said, as Mr. Krishna Menon observed (apropos of Algeria, but not of Kashmir), that 'discussion is not intervention', and in one sense this is true. But since the object of raising a disputed issue in the Assembly is almost always to put moral pressure on some state or states, to concede the right to raise the issue is to concede, in some degree, a right to outsiders to have a voice in the way the criticized state conducts itself.

For all this, it is seldom that efforts to keep an item off the agenda are well grounded. This is not only because in the atmosphere of the General Assembly any attempt to ban discussion looks suspicious, looks as if there is something to hide, as if the state which is criticized has a bad case. More than that, the attempt is self-defeating, for the simple reason that the argument about discussion is itself discussion. Although in theory arguments about the composition of the agenda should not deal with points of substance, in fact they do and indeed almost necessarily do. Thus it is a poor critic indeed who cannot make all the substantive criticisms he wishes within the framework of an agenda debate. Consequently a wise defendant will readily accept the inclusion of an item (while making much of waiving the question of legality) and concentrate his efforts on seeing that it appears in an innocuous rather than an offensive form, e.g. 'The question of Ruritania' rather than 'The aggressive attack on Ruritania'.

The agenda once agreed (or at any rate accepted), the Assembly, again advised by the General Committee, proceeds to allocate items to its seven standing committees. Like the chambers of continental parliaments, or like the American Congress, the General Assembly works through specialist committees and readily entrusts to them, as the House of Commons will not, the consideration of a question *ab initio*. The Preparatory Commission originally equipped the Assembly with six committees, following the League precedent:

First (Political and Security) Committee;
Second (Economic and Financial) Committee;
Third (Social, Humanitarian, and Cultural) Committee;

Fourth (Trusteeship) Committee;
Fifth (Administrative and Budgetary) Committee;
Sixth (Legal) Committee.

This made a tidy pattern but underestimated the way that the load of work would fall. Already by the second Assembly it was found that the First Committee had more than it could handle and to relieve it a so-called Ad Hoc Committee was created. The ad hoc became permanent, and eventually its name was changed to the Special Political Committee, though no one has ever got around to providing it with a number as well.

In a sense all these so-called Committees are alternative Assemblies, since every member state is represented on each. This reduces their efficiency whenever they have to turn their hands to the sort of legislative or supervisory work that the committees of an ordinary parliament would do (though they occasionally set up small sub-committees of their own). Such cumbersomeness is, however, the inescapable result of having to cater, not as in a legislature, for parties, but for over a hundred sovereign and unassimilable member states. Moreover, every one is aware that owing to the pressure on the Plenary sessions it is often in the Committees that the most important debates take place. The General Assembly is a circus in which there is no guarantee that the main show will be going on in the centre ring. Foreign Ministers and heads of delegations will move from Plenary to Committee and back again as the importance of the occasion dictates. And when the time comes towards the end of the session for the Committees to report, debate in the Plenary will often be perfunctory and sometimes non-existent.

One item of the agenda the Plenary always keeps for itself. That is the so-called 'General Debate' with which each annual session of the General Assembly opens. Anything less like a debate could hardly be imagined, though its generality is indubitable. The practice dates back to League times when members, basing themselves on the Secretary-General's annual report, raised any issue they wished, either on the grounds that it was mentioned in the report or, with equal speciousness, on the grounds that it was not. But what in Geneva days used to take a week now in New York seldom exhausts itself in less than three, nine out of ten member states availing themselves of the opportunity to conduct a *tour d'horizon* on the logical but chronophagous assumption that the sky's the limit. Thus the Assembly is treated to a series of speeches with little or no connexion between them, prepared well in advance in the foreign offices of member states and released to the press and the delegates in advance of delivery, so that even the faint spice of a first hearing is denied to these effusions. Yet, boring as it often is, the General Debate has its uses. Though the world of 1919 has passed, when it was a daring and wholly admirable innovation for a small state to be given a recognized forum in which to criticize the Great Powers, the small states in particular still prize—and rightly so—the opportunity annually given them to appear before the rest of the world and show their wounds, their medals, and their personalities. The Great Powers, after all, have no lack of opportunities for making their voice heard, but for many of the member states the General Debate is what the Debate on the Address is to the House of Commons back-bencher—a rare moment for seizing the spotlight and putting a point of view that might otherwise be ignored. If one of the advantages of the U.N. is that the world comes flooding in there, making of Turtle Bay a kind of synthesis of the seven seas, the General Debate is, if not an indispensable, at least an established and convenient channel for this. Of course member states present themselves exclusively in the guise in which they wish to be known, but this too is an aspect of reality—one often neglected in ambassadorial dispatches and intelligence reports. And like the Greek generals who voted each for himself first and Themistocles second, even the egocentrics of the General Debate may sometimes cumulatively demonstrate an important consensus of opinion not to be so well displayed in any other way. Thus the world-wide demand for some progress on disarmament was a significant feature of the General Debate at the twelfth Assembly. Apart from this, the time spent on the General Debate is not wholly time lost; elsewhere in the Committees more focused discussions will be going forward, and in any case, since the Debate comes at the beginning of the annual Assembly, delegations often find it a convenient façade behind which they will be busy settling down, taking the measure of friends and rivals, reading the voluminous documents that each year's U.N. activities provide, or merely getting to know who's who in all the other delegations—for the U.N. is, amongst other things, a society of its own, and never the same society two Assemblies running.

The whole concept of the General Debate implies that speakers must be given their heads. But when debate is on specific topics some limits on loquacity and irrelevance are desirable. The record of the Assembly in this respect is not, however, very praiseworthy. It does have a rule permitting itself by a majority vote to impose a time limit on each speaker and to restrict the number of times a representative of a delegation may speak. It has also provision for a closure—though a fairly protracted one. But these rules have been very sparingly invoked and when invoked have saved disappointingly little time. All attempts to formulate an acceptable and effective rule for curtailing debate in the Plenary on matters already fully examined in Committee have broken down. More speakers emulate the practice than the frankness of the speaker in the Plenary who began his remarks by saying:

I do not know whether the subject gains by being the subject of successive debates by the same representatives with the same arguments, open necessarily to repetition, so that I apologize in advance to my colleagues who have already heard me in the Committee, in the Sub-Committee, and again in the Committee, if I now come to the General Assembly . . . .

It is vain, however, to look for drastic remedies for such logorrhoea in a gathering whose members are not M.P.s or Deputies, but spokesmen of sovereign states—many of which, incidentally, have not been conspicuously successful in regulating debate in their own national assemblies. So far from being under the control of the Chair, their relationship to it is well exemplified by the rule which declares, 'The President shall call upon speakers in the order in which they signify their desire to speak'—i.e. he is obliged to call them and no discretion in the interests of balanced or unrepetitious debate is allowed him. M. Spaak undoubtedly spoke for many of his successors when he wistfully declared: 'I must say that, as President, I dream of the day when I might have the same powers as the Speaker of the House of Commons and might refuse the floor to all those who had not "caught my eye"! But we have not yet reached that point.' On paper the President has some of the powers of a Speaker, e.g. to call a delegate to order for irrelevancy, and occasionally strong Presidents have employed them. But, apart from the fact that by no means all Presidents are strong, such employment has to be sparing if it is not to provoke a resentment that might ultimately prove damaging. Experience so far suggests that a President usually gains more by gentler methods, by requesting, suggesting, or appealing to the goodwill of members and by seeking to secure their compliance by intensive consultations before the day's debate begins. At the same time, with its larger membership and increasing agenda, the Assembly will almost certainly have to give some greater authority to its President. When it decides to do so it can fortify its resolution by one notable precedent, demonstrating the availability of one weapon of control most assemblies lack. In the fourth Assembly when the election of Yugoslavia to the Security Council was evoking the protests of Mr. Vyshinsky, protests which the interventions of the Chair had failed to silence, General Romulo of the Philippines eventually secured compliance with his Presidential ruling by threatening to cut off the interpretation system. Fortunately, however, full-blooded filibustering and obstructionism in the General Assembly will always be rare because it offends too many of the audience to too little purpose. Generally, for all the delegates' loquacity, a willingness to compromise and co-operate with the time-keepers becomes increasingly apparent as a session wears on. As one follows a session's debates one sometimes feels that the work of an Assembly is like packing a bag or dressing for dinner—it takes just as long as there is time to do it in. (In the case of a normal Assembly the terminus is fixed by the delegates' desire to get home from New York by Christmas.) As the deadline approaches sittings get longer, but also more businesslike, there is a growing readiness to accept formulae, hairs are left unsplit, votes are allowed to speak for themselves. Yet the Assembly does not make a fetish of adjournment; when a critical situation requires continued watching, as Suez did in 1956–7, or the Congo in 1961–2, the Assembly will prolong its session past Christmas into the New Year, and, of course, emergency sessions in spring, or even New York's torrid summer, have been increasingly frequent.

The General Debate apart, Assembly discussions normally have as their goal the adoption of a resolution. Here, as contrasted with its virtually unlimited freedom of discussion, the Assembly feels the first constraints imposed on it by the Charter. Even so, its present powers mark a considerable development from modest beginnings. To the Soviets, who envisaged the U.N. in its inception exclusively as a security organization of the Great Powers, the Assembly was an unnecessary appendage which ought to be restricted to a minimal role, the Security Council being the only body fit to be entrusted with the really important problems of security. At Dumbarton Oaks the first compromise was effected. The General Assembly was accepted as the central organ in the U.N. system, the body which should receive and consider reports from all the others, the Security Council included, the body which would control the budget and the secretariat, and fix the contributions of member states. Yet this centrality was somewhat formal; the primary responsibility for peace and security was placed on the Council, with the Assembly allowed to share in it only to a very limited—advisory or exhortatory—extent, the emphasis being thrown very heavily on the Assembly's long-range and economic and social functions, functions which the Soviets regarded as unimportant and comparatively harmless. By the time of San Francisco a sizeable body of opinion had come to regard this as inadequate. The smaller powers, by their very nature, wanted a larger role for the Assembly; but elsewhere too, and in the U.S.A. in particular, there was a feeling that reliance on the unanimity of the Big Five might prove mistaken and that it would be just as well to have some method of mobilizing the rest of the world in the protection of peace and security. The result was a fairly considerable enlargement in the final stages of Charter-making of the General Assembly's political role. Out of San Francisco emerged the broad terms, which we have already noticed, of Article 10—'discuss any questions . . .'—the right to call the Security Council's attention to situations 'likely to endanger international peace and security', conferred in Article 11, § 3, and the very wide recommendatory powers of Article 14. These last logically needed no itemization after the sweeping mandate of Article 10. But as we have seen, politics had more to do than logic with the shaping of the Charter and politics dictated the addition of Article 14:

Subject to the provisions of Article 12 [which forbids the Assembly to make recommendations on a subject while the Security Council is exercising its functions with regard to it] the General Assembly may recommend measures for the peaceful adjustment of any situation, regardless of origin, which it deems likely to impair the general welfare of friendly relations among nations, including situations resulting from a violation of the provisions of the present Charter setting forth the Purposes and Principles of the United Nations.

This wordy and cloudy elaboration of Article 10 was designed to give some recognition to the need for peaceful change without mentioning anything like 'revision of treaties', which might encourage flightiness where international obligations were involved.

It still remained true that in 1945-6 these were largely potential grants of authority, grants the Assembly was to draw on only if the Security Council failed to function as intended. This was evident from the fact that these powers were all subject to the important proviso incorporated in Article 12. From the beginning, of course, there was a certain dynamism which, even unaided, would probably have led the Assembly eventually to try and assert itself in the political field. In fact, however, as we have seen, the paralysis of the Security Council set in so early that by 1947 the Great Powers themselves were invoking the General Assembly for the discharge of political functions which the Council was unable to assume.

The Assembly itself has seldom drawn very clear lines of

distinction between its various functions—this indeed has been a frequent source of complaint by critics who would like to see a nicer regard for the letter of the Charter—but it is nevertheless possible to view its activities under a number of convenient, broad headings. The first is what, had the General Assembly been a parliament, Walter Bagehot would have called its 'teaching' function. This is the task of formulating general principles, laid down in Article 11, § 1:

The General Assembly may consider the general principles of co-operation in the maintenance of international peace and security, including the principles governing disarmament and the regulation of armaments, and may make recommendations with regard to such principles to the Members or to the Security Council or to both.

Acting under this authority, the Assembly has repeatedly debated general problems of peace-making and peace-keeping and has adopted various resolutions—e.g. the 'Essentials of Peace' in 1949 or the 'Declaration concerning the Peaceful Co-existence of States' in 1957. Read in cold print many of these resolutions have all the pungency and appeal of manifestoes against sin, this effect being heightened by the fact that their most eloquent promoters are often states whose standards both of domestic and inter-national behaviour are generally based on exclusively Marxist concepts of vice and virtue. Similarly, the debates preceding these resolutions generally display the Assembly at its worst, reaching a higher level of hypocrisy, unctuousness, and flatulence than is healthy for any organization. They have seldom come near to solving the problem that Bagehot described as 'to know the highest truth which the people will bear and to inculcate and preach that'. For all that, they have, upon occasion, been of value, not for the resolutions passed, so much as for the opportunity which the debates have sometimes afforded of registering a con-sensus of opinion, or a direction in which sentiment is moving.

In the more specific exercise of this function, where the prob-lems of disarmament are involved, Assembly debates have been on the whole more constructive. Repeatedly, as we have seen on pp. 88–89 of Chapter 4, the Assembly has served as the conscience and the goad of the Security Council in this matter, not only formulating some general principles but also taking an important hand in the establishment of the actual machinery for negotiations and investigations—e.g. the Atomic Energy Commission in 1946, the Disarmament Commission in 1952, and the scientific Committee on the Effects of Atomic Radiation in 1955. Here the urgency of the theme, the relative disinterestedness of most of the member states (since great armaments are mainly confined to the Big Five), and the comparative concreteness of the issues involved have given to the debates a greater solidity and direction than those concerned merely with 'general principles'. Consequently, in addition to their valuable function of just 'keeping the heat' on the principal parties involved, they have often been productive of serious and practical proposals.

A second General Assembly function is the one which brings it nearest to the law-making activities of a national legislature. This role is conferred upon it by the terms of Article 13, § 1:

The General Assembly shall initiate studies and make recommendations for the purpose of

    (a) . . . encouraging the progressive development of international law and its codification.
    (b) . . . assisting in the realization of human rights and fundamental freedoms for all without distinction as to race, sex, language, or religion.

In functioning under this article the General Assembly is, of course, not making recommendations which have any legally binding effect upon the members of the U.N. One may call its operations 'quasi-legislative', in that it is the form and not the force of law which characterizes any such resolutions as it may pass. The first part of Article 13 owes its inclusion in the Charter to the feeling at San Francisco, particularly strong amongst the smaller states, that the Dumbarton Oaks document did not show enough regard for law as a basis for international organization. The second part derives from the same impulse as led to the establishment of a separate Economic and Social Council, and such respect as has been accorded to it has mainly been through the operations of that body; detailed consideration of it may therefore conveniently be deferred to the following chapter.

The General Assembly has gone about its 'quasi-legislative' functions in three main ways. First of all, in 1948, it set up the International Law Commission, a body originally of fifteen (now twenty-five) experts who serve for five years each in their private capacity and not as representatives of governments. The Commission's task is to undertake studies and prepare draft codes and declarations for submission to the Assembly. On the basis of these the Assembly has, as a second step, affirmed principles of international law to exist—e.g. those embodied in the Charter of the Nuremberg Tribunal and in the judgments of that Tribunal. Thirdly, without necessarily being guided by the International Law Commission, the Assembly may prepare and adopt 'conventions' or 'declarations' which embody a code of proper behaviour by states; these it will ask states to ratify, passing the necessary domestic laws to give effect to them. In this last category come such instruments as the Convention on Genocide, which seeks to make group murder a crime (adopted by the Assembly in 1948), or the Convention on the Elimination of All Forms of Racial Discrimination (adopted in 1965).

In general the results of the Assembly's works in this field have not been impressive; it has certainly achieved less than the Assembly of the League. The reasons for this are not hard to seek. The years since 1945 have not been propitious for the development of international law through any medium. A revolutionary and troubled age gives little encouragement for the steady building up of accepted standards and procedures Geneva, though its lot also lay in troubled times, served a world which was still dominated by Europe and for which European concepts of law had a generally accepted value. Too many members of the U.N. are in revolt against a real or a fancied oppression by 'the West' to consider soberly how far the West's concepts of law may serve to protect their new-found status, as well as to perpetuate that of their erstwhile overlords. Nor have the Great Powers, also jealous of sovereignty and at odds between themselves, given the sort of lead which is indispensable for action along these lines in a body like the General Assembly, whose natural predisposition, left to itself, will always be to think in political and not in legal terms. The result has been that discussions of legal proposals in the Assembly have usually degenerated into crude propagandizing or sterile attempts to apply legal solutions to essentially political problems. The twenty-four year search for a definition of aggression, resulting in repetitious hair-splitting through session after session of the International Law Commission and the Assembly's Sixth Committee, is a pathetic example of this.

Far more important than either of the two foregoing roles of the General Assembly is its function as an organ of political settlement, of peace-making and of peace-saving. Not only is this the role in which the Assembly is best known to the layman the world over; it occupies the central place in its own affections, takes up the most of its time, and has provided it with its most spectacular successes.

This, as we have seen, was no part of the original intentions of the framers of the Charter. Not only was the Security Council given exclusive powers in the field of enforcement; it was given, by Article 12, priority in relation to any 'dispute or situation' which might threaten peace or security; and although, by Article 35, states are free to bring 'disputes or situations' before either the Council or the Assembly, as they prefer, there can be little doubt that the expectation in 1945, at least among the Great Powers, was that serious and urgent issues would go to the Council and that the Assembly would get the rest. The blurring of this division of labour and responsibility began early, with the Security Council's getting bogged down in issues like the Iranian or the Syrian and Lebanese complaints, which were hardly imminent threats to peace or security, and, at the same time, by the abuse of its veto, unfitting itself for handling issues which were. By 1947 it seemed natural to bring to the Assembly issues like the Greek (Balkan) question or the Korean Independence question, because of the foreknowledge that in the Security Council they would run foul of the veto. This process was accelerated in

1947 by the establishment of the Interim Committee or 'Little Assembly', which, had it functioned as intended, would have gone far to rob the Security Council of the advantages it enjoyed by reason of its compact membership and 'continuous' functioning. The 'Little Assembly' came to nothing very much, but the idea of special sessions and (as in 1951-2) continuous Assembly sessions to cope with particular crises has steadily gained ground, so that it is now an exceptional year which sees the General Assembly's activities confined to the period of its regular autumn session. At the same time the effectiveness of the ban imposed by Article 12 began to wear very thin. The convention established itself that to remove an item from the agenda of the Security Council did not require the unanimity of the permanent members—i.e. was not subject to the veto. Again lawyers' ingenuity has been repeatedly invoked to demonstrate that although Assembly and Council might seem to be dealing with the same question, they were in fact (provided it was sufficiently broadly formulated—e.g. 'the Palestine question') dealing with different aspects of it. The practical consequence of this has been to leave the Assembly almost all the freedom it wants in making recommendations without looking over its shoulder at what the Security Council may be doing.

Finally, in 1950, came the 'Uniting for Peace' resolution, seeming to carry the Assembly into a field which the Charter undoubtedly intended to reserve for the Council, 'action with respect to threats to the peace, breaches of the peace and acts of aggression', a field which constitutes the subject-matter of the Charter's Chapter VII. By this the Assembly asserted its competence to act in cases where the Council, 'because of lack of unanimity of the permanent members, fails to exercise its primary responsibility', and to make 'appropriate recommendations' of collective measures to maintain or restore international peace and security, 'including in the case of a breach of the peace or act of aggression the use of armed force when necessary'. For this purpose the General Assembly (if not already in session) can be called together within twenty-four hours if requested either by a vote of any seven (since 1965 nine) members of the Security Council or by a majority of the members of the Assembly. If summoned under this procedure the General Assembly (unless it decides otherwise) meets only in plenary session and proceeds directly to consider the item which has occasioned the calling of the session.

Looking over the substantial history of General Assembly action in the political field—the whole range from what the Charter calls 'the settlement and adjustment of disputes and situations' to 'the preservation of peace and security'—one is struck by the extreme fluidity of the Assembly's procedures and its persistent, and often studied, indifference to the precise legal or Charter basis for its recommendations on any particular occasion. The reason for this is not only that carelessness about legality which we have already observed; it is also rooted in the fact that where the object of a resolution is the maximization of agreement, this is more often gained by imprecision than by clarity. Thus, when during the Lebanon and Jordan crises of 1958 there was a general desire to transfer consideration from the deadlocked Security Council to the General Assembly, no specific mention of the 'Uniting for Peace' procedure occurred in the Council resolution that summoned the Assembly into special session because the Russians, having always denied its legality, would then have been obliged to vote against it. Similarly the General Assembly has used every sort of device for securing settlements without too much regard to consistency or precedent. In particular it has employed all the techniques described in connexion with the Security Council's operations on pp. 91–94 of Chapter 4. *Investigation* is a recurrent activity, e.g. the Assembly's Special Committee on Palestine endowed with 'the widest powers . . . to investigate all questions and issues relevant to the problem of Palestine', or the Committee on Hungary set up in January 1957. Under the heading of *Interposition* one might list many of the Assembly's most successful operations, such as the United Nations Emergency Force in Suez and Sinai. *Conciliation* is a function which the Assembly, by reason of its size, has generally entrusted to some subsidiary organ, like the Good Offices Commission appointed to resolve the dispute over the treatment of Indians in South Africa, or to some outstanding individual like Count Bernadotte (and later Dr. Bunche), who was made U.N. Mediator in the Palestine dispute. Increasingly of late years the services of the Secretary-General have been employed by the General Assembly in this capacity. The *Recommendations* to good behaviour or compromise which the Assembly has addressed to disputing parties have been too numerous to mention and they have shaded into the more imperative *Appeals*, such as those which the Assembly addressed to Britain, France, and Israel over withdrawal from Suez, or to the U.S.S.R. over withdrawal and abstention from brutalities in Hungary. Not even the 'Uniting for Peace' resolution, of course, gives the Assembly power to do more than recommend courses of action to states, and in fact the high-water mark of such strong action was reached in the earliest days of that resolution's life when, in relation to Korea, the General Assembly found Communist China guilty of aggression and called upon 'all states and authorities to lend every assistance to the U.N. action in Korea', following this up with a recommended embargo on the shipment of all munitions of war. Nothing comparable to this was attempted in relation to either the Suez or the Hungarian crises. It required the powerful stimulus of the 'anti-colonialist' issue in the 1960s to bring the General Assembly to another such pitch of imperiousness. Thus, for example, we find the General Assembly in repeated sessions from 1965 onwards calling upon the Government of the United Kingdom to employ military force to correct the Southern Rhodesian situation, and 'urging' states to break diplomatic relations and boycott all trade with Portugal because her treatment of her dependencies constituted a threat to international peace. The legality of such resolutions was, in many members' eyes, debatable, but perhaps an equally serious objection to them was that by urging courses of action which could only become effective with the co-operation of those very members who voted against them, the Assembly ran a serious risk of debasing the political currency of its resolutions.

One constructive function belongs to the Assembly in this field which the Charter has not accorded to the Security Council.

That is its ability to act as an agent of peaceful change by developing new legal and political orders. It was in this capacity that the Assembly worked out the plan of partition for Palestine to take the place of the British mandate, and so, in effect, created the independent state of Israel. Similarly the Assembly has endeavoured to establish an independent Korea, though it has only been able to establish and preserve independence in South Korea. In both Palestine and Korea it has appreciated that political settlements required economic underpinning; relief for Palestinian refugees, mainly through UNRWA (U.N. Relief and Works Agency), has proceeded as far as Arab non-co-operation would permit, while the aftermath of hostilities in South Korea has provided ample scope for the generally successful operations of UNKRA (U.N. Korean Reconstruction Agency).

Unfortunately the General Assembly's attempts to develop new legal and political orders have not always been characterized by a comparable realism. Frustration, provoked by a discovery of its impotence, has led it to exceed its capacity. This, perhaps predictably, has been especially evident on issues of a 'colonialist' kind. The South African refusal to honour its mandate obligations in respect of South West Africa led the Assembly in 1967 to set up an eleven-member Council for South West Africa to take over the mandate; only Portugal and South Africa cast negative votes, but thirty states, including all the major powers, abstained. The territory was renamed Namibia and June 1968 was set as the target date for independence. South Africa, of course, refused the Council admission to the territory and the Council, which proceeded as far as Lusaka, had to make an ignominious return to New York. The Security Council, despite the Assembly's urgings, declined to enforce compliance with the Assembly's resolutions, though it went so far as to demand the withdrawal of South African administration by 4 October 1969. The deadline came and went and South Africa remained in control. All that had been achieved was some publicity, but amongst the conditions publicized was the impotence of the United Nations.

A similar indifference to political realities, as opposed to abstract formulae, characterized the 1967-8 campaign against the status of Gibraltar, where the wishes of the inhabitants expressed in the 1967 referendum were totally ignored and a 'deadline' of 1 October 1969 was set for the United Kingdom to end the 'colonial situation' there.

In all this wide range of political operations the General Assembly has shown a notable inventiveness and flexibility. If the test of the vitality of a political institution is its ability to devise new instruments to assist it in its tasks the Assembly comes out well. Unfortunately this fertility has not been matched by an equivalent faith in the value of its own creations. Instead of using these existing instruments the Assembly has repeatedly, when crises have developed, preferred to meet them with fresh improvisations. Thus at the time of Suez, instead of mobilizing the Peace Observation Commission which the 'Uniting for Peace' resolution had established, or drawing on the services of the Palestine Conciliation Commission, the Assembly sought to act through the Secretary-General and an Advisory Committee of seven member states. No one can doubt that in the context of the events of 1956 this was the most practicable course. None the less it is the behaviour of an institution still largely inchoate, deficient in direction and sustained purpose, lacking confidence in itself and so unable to repose enough trust in its subordinate agencies to enable them to build up continuity and established procedures of their own. This is certainly a weakness, but before censuring the General Assembly too harshly it is worth remembering the brevity of its experience and the diversity of its tasks. The diversity, moreover, is not merely one of situations, for although there is a sense in which no two crises are ever the same, it is also true that almost all can be reduced to a limited number of recognizable categories. It is rather the diversity resulting from the fact that the human components of each situation so seldom recur that makes the main difficulty; both inside the Assembly and in the councils of any disputants with which it has to deal there is enough turnover of participants to place serious obstacles in the way of any ready acceptance of precedent. Add to this the fact that the very idea of precedent may be distasteful, lest it imprison free and sovereign states in either the past or the future, and the Assembly's behaviour becomes more understandable.

At the opposite pole from the foregoing is a fourth function of the General Assembly, that of supervision. In the League it was the Council which supervised the Secretariat, though the Assembly controlled the budget and used this as an often effective device for supervising the administration. There was a comparable division of responsibility over the control of the League's technical organizations. In the U.N., however, in line with the specialization of the Security Council's functions, the whole task of supervising the Organization, not only the Secretariat, but also all the deliberative and political organs, is entrusted to the Assembly. Thus it is to the Assembly that the Security Council, the Economic and Social Council, and the Trusteeship Council make their reports. This, however, does not mean that these three are on the same footing *vis-à-vis* the Assembly. It is true that by Article 11 the Assembly may make recommendations to the Security Council both on general principles (of peace and security and disarmament) and on specific questions; it may also 'call the attention of the Security Council to situations which are likely to endanger international peace and security'. However, it would be a mistake to deduce from this any implication of superiority and inferiority in the relationship of Assembly and and Council. The Charter carefully safeguards the Security Council's autonomy and, as we have seen, endows it in the enforcement field with an authority over Assembly members for which it is answerable to no one. The formalities of 'reporting' on one side, and 'recommending' on the other, do not alter this; in particular nothing could be further from the facts than any language which hints at the Assembly being a 'legislature' and the Council being its 'executive'. The tabling of Security Council reports is generally a formality; they are seldom debated. The recommendations which the General Assembly has made to the Council have been numerous and varied, ranging from exhortations to mend its ways (e.g. over the veto) to requests for specific action on some particular matter. Some have been heeded, many have been ignored, a few have been rejected outright—e.g. the Council's 1947 refusal to enforce the partition plan for Palestine.

The General Assembly's relationship with the other two U.N. Councils is quite different, for all that they are called at one point in the Charter 'principal organs' and listed together (Article 7). Article 60 comes nearer to the facts when it vests responsibility for international social and economic co-operation in the General Assembly and, 'under the authority of the General Assembly, in the Economic and Social Council'. Similarly, where trusteeship functions are concerned, Article 85 speaks of 'the Trusteeship Council, operating under the authority of the General Assembly'. Here we have something much more like that delegation of specialist functions which is a familiar enough feature of state constitutions and which follows naturally from the unsuitability of a large and, in the strict sense, inexpert body to handle topics that require close, detailed, expert, and frequently continuous attention. Unfortunately, as national legislatures have often discovered, the desirability of delegation does not always imply its feasibility. Problems of allocation and definition arise. Though the matters delegated are genuinely technical they often turn out to be also genuinely political. Consequently, though the parent association is ready enough to allow its daughter to swim, it may often be only on condition that she does not go near the water. Exactly these advantages and drawbacks have occurred in the U.N. The Assembly has repeatedly failed to exercise self-restraint and to trust its Councils within the field of their own specializations. In part this is due to faults in the Councils themselves, the inefficiency of ECOSOC and the truant behaviour of the Trusteeship Council. But it has even more been due to the fact that the Assembly holds many more interested parties—interested, that is, in all the problems of the 'underdeveloped' and colonial areas with which so much of both Councils' work deals— than could be represented even on an enlarged ECOSOC and still less on a reduced Trusteeship Council. Moreover, as we have seen, where sovereign states are concerned the concept of representation is liable to be very barren of meaning. From this arises a permanent Assembly pressure to review again in detail the work and the recommendations of these Councils in a setting in which everyone can have a voice, and in which the voting strength of the 'have-nots' is proportionately greater. In consequence the Third and Fourth Committees of the General Assembly always have crowded agendas and long sessions, out of which emerge resolutions instructing the Councils to undertake tasks which are often poorly defined and doubtfully appropriate.

Over the Secretariat the Assembly's control takes a more familiar and, on the whole, satisfactory form. Even here, as we shall see, one must be careful of deceptive analogies drawn from parliamentary practice; thus the Secretary-General, though in a true sense the servant of the Assembly, may also be its conscience and guide. But certainly the Assembly has at its disposal all the instruments of control that it needs. It receives full and regular reports of the Secretariat's work and organization, and has established comprehensive machinery for digesting its information and guiding its deliberations on it. In the Advisory Committee on Administrative and Budgetary Questions it has at its disposal a scrutinizing agency that combines the roles of the Estimates and Public Accounts Committees in the House of Commons, and even aspires to something of the Treasury's control over establishment. The Advisory Committee, as for convenience it is generally known, has a membership of only twelve (originally nine), 'selected on the basis of broad geographical representation, personal qualifications, and experience', and serving for three years, though eligible for reappointment. Two of the twelve must be 'financial experts of recognized standing'. The Committee has in fact maintained considerable continuity of membership; its first chairman, M. Aghnides, not only served the Committee in that capacity from its inception in 1946 until 1964, but also brought to his task a wealth of experience gathered in service on the League. To this body the Secretary-General submits his budget estimates in June for the following financial year. The Advisory Committee scrutinizes these and produces a report on them, with recommendations for possible economies, for revisions in the form of the estimates, or for the organization or deployment of the Secretariat. The two documents are then laid before the General Assembly's Fifth Committee (on which incidentally practically all the members of the Advisory Committee sit as members of their national delegations). There something like a running examination of the work and expenses of the Secretariat ensues, with the Secretary-General or his staff defending themselves and the Committee, assisted and guided by the Chairman of the Advisory Committee (acting almost like the British Comptroller and Auditor General though without the equivalent of his expert staff), passing judgement on the claims and counter-claims of the Secretary-General and the Advisory Committee. Inevitably or not, the deliberations take on some of the character of a tug-of-war, with neither side wholly disdaining any political assistance that comes its way. The Fifth Committee tends to divide along the predictable lines of the poor member states, wishing to increase the scale and scope of U.N. expenditures, and the well-to-do, whose contributions make up the bulk of the U.N. receipts, wishing to curtail them. In this division the Advisory Committee does valuable work in restraining those tendencies to extravagance to which international organizations are prone; unfortunately, in the single-mindedness of its 'Treasury' approach, it sometimes confuses a proper regard for value-for-money with a too-ready acceptance of the view that the less money the U.N. spends the better.

Matching the Advisory Committee on the income side is the Committee on Contributions, recruited on the same basis and serving for equivalent terms, and consisting of twelve members. These twelve must, of course, include representatives of the principal contributing states. The Committee's task is largely, but not wholly, technical in character, involving the fixing of assessments on the basis of two variables, national income and the changing (i.e. expanding) membership of the Organization. There enter, however, into the Committee's recommendations other, less objective, considerations, e.g. the allowance that is to be made for low *per capita* income or the special case of the U.S.A., whose contribution, though much the highest, is well below its capacity to pay, on the grounds that this would give it a grossly preponderant voice in financial matters. The assessments which the Contributions Committee makes remain valid for three-year periods, save where some emergency, like war, upsets some member's capacity to pay. Members are seldom backward in drawing the Committee's attention to any extenuating circumstances in their own finances; they are, however, frequently backward in the payment of their proper contributions.

The General Assembly normally accepts the guidance it receives from its Fifth Committee on the budget and on contributions without too much further review or argument in its own Plenary sessions. This is just as well, because, unwieldy though the Fifth Committee can sometimes be, it has a continuity and semi-professional *esprit de corps* which far better equip it to deal with matters of finance and organization than the entirely political Plenary. The Plenary's self-denial in this matter is, moreover, powerfully assisted by the fact that the Fifth Committee's resolutions generally reach it too late in a session to allow time for much effective reconsideration and debate.

There remains a fifth capacity in which the General Assembly is continually being called upon to act. This is its elective capacity. Some of its responsibilities in this field are shared, as we have seen, with the Security Council—the election of a Secretary-General, elections to the International Court, and the admission of new members (pp. 85–7 Chapter 4). Any hope that the General Assembly might recapture for itself the exclusive control over admissions to membership which its League counterpart enjoyed was dashed in 1950, when the International Court ruled that however frustrated the Assembly might be by Security Council vetoes it could not effect an admission without a Security Council recommendation. There remain, however, a number of elections which the Assembly is empowered by the Charter to make single-handed. The first, and in some ways the most eagerly contested, are those to the non-permanent places on the Security Council. Every year half of these seats come up and retiring members are not eligible to stand again. Initially the filling of the three annual vacancies was accomplished peacefully enough by private consultations that paved the way well before the actual votes, but a sharp wrangle occurred in 1955 which was the forerunner of many more. In that year the failure to acquiesce in the Soviet claim to a seat for Yugoslavia (the U.S.A. sponsoring the Philippines) led to a deadlock, thirty-five ballots failing to produce a two-thirds majority for either candidate. The deadlock was eventually broken only by an understanding that Yugoslavia would resign after one year and be replaced by her rival. With the increase of Afro-Asian membership in the Assembly, competition for Security Council seats became keener, with the result that similar deadlocks developed year after year, and only a similar device, of splitting a two-year term between two members, proved adequate to resolve them. An increase in the number of elective seats was the obvious solution, but action had to wait until 1965 when the number was raised to ten.

None of the seats of ECOSOC is formally reserved or allocated. In practice, however, the Big Four (i.e. the Permanent Members of the Security Council minus China) have been invariably elected, while states of the second rank like Australia or India have been frequently returned. (The term is for three years and there is no ban on re-election.) The remaining thirteen places were not enough to satisfy the claims of other states, especially the 'underdevelopeds', and pressure to enlarge the Council mounted. In 1965 the Council was increased to twenty-seven members and again in 1971 to fifty-four.

Initially there were fourteen seats on the Trusteeship Council, only seven of which were held by non-administering members. Then, as the number of trust territories declined, the number of administering members declined too, until the Council's numbers fell to six. Of these two are administering states, the U.S.A. and Australia. Permanent Security Council members are entitled to seats in their own right; this adds China, France, the U.K., and the U.S.S.R.

It is in elections such as these (as well, of course, as those to the hundred and one *ad hoc* Assembly commissions) that the General Assembly displays most clearly its own equivalent of the party system. This is, of course, the bloc—a group of states united by geography, history, race, or ideology. Much has been heard, and

more will be heard, of the bloc vote in the U.N. It is certainly a
fact of international life. It is also frequently a figment of over-
excited imaginations, a U.N. version of the nineteenth-century
cauchemar des coalitions, on which all that goes wrong in international councils can be blamed. On the identity of the principal
blocs there is general agreement. The Organization itself has lent
them a kind of official recognition, as is evidenced, for example,
in the allocation of seats on the Assembly's General Committee
(see p. 107).

In a total membership of 138 the principal groupings are:

The Arabs, seventeen.

The Africans, including Arab states in Africa, but excluding
South Africa, forty-two.

The Asians, including the Asiatic Arabs but excluding Israel,
thirty-one.

The Latin-Americans, twenty if, as is doubtfully realistic, Cuba
is included.

The West Europeans (excluding Yugoslavia), nineteen (of
whom, however, four are a distinctive group, the European
neutrals).

The East Europeans, eleven.

The Commonwealth countries, reduced by one since the depar-
ture of South Africa, but including several member states
who also feature in other groupings, total thirty.

These groupings however, vary greatly in unity and coherence.
Even the East Europeans, most nearly monolithic of all, show
some raggedness at the edges, with Roumania showing some
deviation on the right and Albania practically isolated on the
left, as an open partisan of Peking. The Arab League which,
with a permanent organization and regular caucusing, seems
to bear the closest resemblance to such a disciplined ideological group, is in fact a voting unit only on certain subjects and
in response to certain pressures. The Afro-Asians, with whom
it may or may not combine, are an even looser agglomeration,
caucusing at the U.N. for a limited number of purposes but also
embracing within themselves some of the bitterest disputants
known to the Assembly or the Security Council. The British

Commonwealth, though not organized in the U.N. as a caucusing unit, holds meetings for exchange of views and information. It undoubtedly exercises some influence on the loyalties and sympathies of its Afro-Asian members; equally, however, even its most intimate members, the older dominions, do not always see eye to eye. Most of the Western Europeans meet to discuss common problems in Assembly sessions, but closer co-ordination is preserved in their sub-groupings, such as the European Economic Community and the Nordic Group. The Latin-Americans, already combined in the Organization of American States, have a long tradition of mutual aid in international voting lobbies, but there are also many issues on which they may dissent from their own caucus or from that Pan-American giant, the U.S.A., who excites such *odi et amo* reactions in every Latin-American heart.

Not only are these blocs natural growths, reflecting the state of world politics as it is today. They are also almost certainly indispensable to the functioning of any kind of world-wide political organization. It is impossible to imagine how the U.N. could work if there were no groupings of member states to provide elements of stability and predictability in an Assembly of over a hundred members. As well imagine a parliament consisting entirely of back-benchers with no party affiliation and every division a free vote. Indeed the Charter, with its frequent references to 'equitable geographical representation' and the like, very sensibly recognizes the need—or perhaps it would be truer to say, accepts as axiomatic the fact—of a world organization resting on a number of closer, pre-existing associations of member states. And it is precisely in relation to the elective functions of the Assembly, where the Charter explicitly recognizes a group function, that the bloc is seen at its most consistent and most disciplined.

Yet there is an ineradicable Rousseau in all of us who is loath to abandon the ideal of individuals' arriving at their vote on all issues independently, each man or state having regard only to what he regards the general good to be. Although an assembly of sovereign states is the last kind of body to incarnate this ideal, yet paradoxically we feel a peculiar shock when departures from it are manifested in the U.N. Nor is it difficult to observe instances when blocs have distorted the 'natural' pattern of Assembly voting with demonstrably harmful results. On one occasion it is known that votes were traded in elections to the International Court and to the Security Council, with the result that undoubtedly the legitimate criteria for the Court were ignored and exclusively political considerations governed the election of at least one judge. Again, it can be demonstrated that in 1948 Spanish was fastened on the General Assembly as a working language (despite the opposition of the Fifth Committee, the Advisory Committee, and the Secretary-General) by a combination of Latin-Americans, Arab Leaguers, and a few other countries. In smaller matters, involving items in the U.N. budget, the staffing of the Secretariat, the extension or inflation of some U.N. operation, log-rolling tactics of a kind familiar in almost all countries not blessed with the peculiar beauties of the British constitution may be demonstrated—or, more often, reasonably suspected—to be in operation.

All this must be granted and the ammunition it furnishes to the gleeful cynic cannot be gainsaid. The main fact, however, remains—that no U.N. caucus has been able to distort the voting of member states so as to produce a significantly different result on any major issue. Elections, jobs, budget—yes, on all these a state may be willing to 'go along' in return for some actual or expected *quid pro quo*. But where an important political question is at stake a state casts its vote the way that its government's assessment of the national interest dictates. This is not to say there is never any constraint, but if so it is an extra-U.N. constraint, not something which proceeds from membership of the U.N. and access to its committee or caucus rooms.

Of course, it is easy to demonstrate how, in an Assembly of 138, where a two-thirds majority requires ninety-two positive votes, the Afro-Asians alone could operate a virtual veto, or how a group of states embracing a handful of the world's population, or a tithe of the world's wealth, could thwart the demands of an overwhelming majority or vote themselves favours that their richer neighbours would have to pay for. From such calculations, and from observation of the artificial and even arbitrary character of such voting entities as Ruritania or Eldorado, spring all those proposals for 'weighted' voting which have exercised the ingenuity of so many reformers. It is safe to predict that no such proposals will ever win acceptance. They are bound to be unpopular; after all, as Dr. Jessup has remarked, states do have feelings, like individuals. No such proposal can claim objectivity —or is it seriously proposed to base votes on population? After all 'one state one vote', for all its 'unreality', does represent an important reality, the sovereignty of member states; any move towards weighted voting would be an encroachment on that, for it would inevitably sanctify the new majorities it would create and thus endow the U.N. with more power at the expense of its member states. Advocates of world government should logically welcome such a step; supporters of the U.N. as its founders conceived of it cannot.

Much of the exaggerated concern over bloc voting proceeds from an exaggerated respect for voting as such. The mesmerism of voting figures has had a harmful effect on delegations to the U.N. Substitution of the two-thirds majority for the unanimity rule of the League has encouraged a tendency to pay more attention to the size of majorities than to their composition and to prefer the winning of a victory to the maximization of agreement. The resolutions of the General Assembly are after all recommendations only, and majorities have moral force only in so far as they represent a real consensus of opinion and not a merely manufactured 67 per cent. in the Assembly chamber. Of course, there can be short-term advantages accruing from manufactured majorities (or, inversely, from contrived vetoes). The setting up of a commission, the settling of some dispute about the organization of the Secretariat—resolutions providing for action of this kind, resolutions which may be said to be self-operating in that they do not depend directly on the further co-operation of members for their realization—these are verdicts which, superficially, a two-thirds majority pronounces once for all. Only superficially, however, for unless the proposal wins acceptance by its intrinsic merits, it may well come to nothing in the long run, or else arouse a resentment which will seek to pay off scores in some other form at a later date. In any case these are the minor matters of U.N. life. For the bigger issues—Hungary or Suez or the Congo, for example—what has mattered has not been the size of the vote but the weight of world opinion and world power that has lain behind it. As Mr. Hammarskjöld once reminded his masters,

If it is accepted that the primary value of the U.N. is to serve as an instrument for negotiation among Governments and for concerting action by Governments in support of the goals of the Charter, it is also necessary, I believe, to use the legislative procedures of the U.N. consistently in ways which will promote these ends. In an organization of sovereign States, voting victories are likely to be illusory unless they are steps in the direction of winning lasting consent to a peaceful and just settlement of the questions at issue.

There is, in fact, a bundle of paradoxes at the heart of the General Assembly. Like a legislature it proceeds by debate and vote, but it must always remember that by themselves debating and voting settle nothing. It is designed for publicity, but it depends continuously on the processes of private negotiation and consultation. It rests on law; it lives by politics. Into its making and functioning have gone the experiences of all sorts of institutions the world over, but it is not exactly comparable to any of them. It is *sui generis*.

For this reason the Assembly demands of its members a distinctive set of accomplishments and attitudes. As a debating chamber it calls for much of the orthodox equipment of the orator and the parliamentarian. At the same time it is like no parliament in the world, least of all the intimate, tradition-ordered chamber of St. Stephen's. Its scale is the most expansive imaginable; it plays always to two audiences, the visible watchers and the invisible. Though the smallest gesture will not go unobserved, it is not a stage which is suited to underplaying. Every actor has to appear in two characters at once—in the national character which he has been chosen to represent, and yet in an international character without which his case, be it the best in the world, will be misunderstood and resented. Debate, however, as we have seen, is only a part of the Assembly's life. Negotiation, incessant and multilateral, is an even more important part. 'Multilateral diplomacy' is the label which many observers have fastened on it, and indeed a certain amount of what goes on in every Assembly is diplomat's work of a familiar kind, even if in an unfamiliar setting. The concept of the Assembly as a world conference in annual and protracted session is certainly valid as far as it goes. Far more, however, of what occurs in an average Assembly session is a kind of collective bargaining operation that has little in common with what traditionally goes on around green baize tables. It much more nearly resembles the kind of building up of a majority out of heterogeneous and floating elements which an American political manager so frequently has to undertake. 'Parliamentary diplomacy' is the term Dr. Jessup has coined to describe the blend of negotiation and legislative debate and manœuvre which makes up so much of Assembly activity. Whether it is indulging in the sort of quasi-legislative activities on behalf of the international community which we have described, or whether it is setting up a piece of machinery or evolving a *modus vivendi* in relation to some situation or dispute affecting many interested parties—in any of these characteristic operations the task of the Assembly is essentially political. It is to maximize agreement, to accommodate a diversity of interests. To do this calls for *all* the arts of management, not only those of traditional diplomacy. Publicity is a weapon for success in it, as well as privacy, a capacity for friendship is needed as well as a nice judgment of foibles, a genuine faith in the goals of the Organization must go hand in hand with loyalty to the national interest.

6 · ECOSOC, THE TRUSTEESHIP COUNCIL, THE SPECIALIZED AGENCIES, AND THE COURT

To treat in one and the same chapter of so many diverse manifestations of the U.N. system as the Economic and Social Council, the Trusteeship Council, the Specialized Agencies, and the International Court may well appear surprising. There is not one of them whose operations would not merit, by their scale and importance, a volume to itself. Here, however, our primary concern is with a limited aspect which they all present in common, their character as political institutions. We shall have little to say about their substantive functions save in so far as these affect their place and movement in the U.N. political system. To do this is not necessarily to pass any judgement on the value or success of their distinctive contributions, but to view them in relation to the central function of the Organization of which they all form a part.

Contemplation of the processes by which the U.N. transacts its economic and social business irresistibly calls to mind Bagehot's comment on the mid-Victorian parliament: 'The manner of our legislation is indeed detestable and the machinery for settling that manner odious.' In the U.N. as in parliament the products of these processes are often commendable, but such successes as are won have to be gained in the teeth of the very instruments designed to obtain them. The Charter references to the economic and social functions of the Organization are ominously verbose, repetitive, and diffuse; largely because so many countries in 1945 refused to take these aspects of the U.N. seriously, nothing like as much care and attention was devoted to these clauses as to those which dealt with the purely political side of the Organization. Thus from the beginning the Economic and Social Council was blurred in conception. Because by historical accident there already existed certain independent specialized agencies, ECOSOC was given the task of acting as a link with them; because these same agencies fell very short of covering all the topics appropriate for U.N. treatment, ECOSOC was made into a kind of hold-all for the residue of specialist activities in the economic and social fields—as well as of some more properly to be regarded as political, e.g. 'the promotion of human rights'. Thus it suffered, as Dr. Loveday has pointed out, from having to be both co-ordinator and part of the co-ordinated. This dual nature of ECOSOC, part specialist agency, part 'super-agency', has made it much more difficult to establish a satisfactory relationship between it and the General Assembly. Though explicitly said to be 'under the authority of the Assembly', it has neither been given a free hand within a limited and subordinate sphere, nor obliged to confine itself to clear and manageable jobs in pursuance of an Assembly directive. In consequence the Second (Economic and Financial) and Third (Social) Committees of the Assembly have functioned more often as rivals to or duplicates of ECOSOC than as the broad policy-framers which (presumably) they were intended to be.

It is arguable that the Economic and Social Council first went off the rails in 1946 when it decided (the Charter gave no prescription) that the members of its functional commissions should be government representatives and not, as the members of the League's technical committees had been, independent experts. If, however, there was substance in the contention that the growing importance of social and economic issues in international politics made it impossible for governments to yield up advisory, planning, and supervisory functions to persons they did not control, then greater care should have been taken to appoint official representatives of ability, especially of administrative ability, with an eye for the distinction between the practicable and the vain and between wordy abstractions and concrete achievements. As it was, encouraged by the loose language of the Charter, the infant ECOSOC began by pursuing every social and economic objective in sight, with an extravagant faith in the virtue of words and resolutions and in the value of proliferating committees and commissions. In 1947 there were twenty-two committees, sub-committees and agencies reporting to the Council; by 1967 the number had risen to thirty-eight. This 'spawning of more and more committees and meetings', as the most objective recent student of ECOSOC, Dr. Sharp, has observed, 'has given rise to frustration and repeated but thus far ineffectual efforts to reduce the volume of documentation'. By 1971 awareness of this had combined with two other factors, the pressure of the developing states for a more representative ECOSOC and the wish of the major contributing countries to make of ECOSOC an effective overseer of the Strategy for the U.N. Development Decade. The result of this was the agreement to expand ECOSOC again in 1974 from twenty-seven members to fifty-four. Whether this will recover for ECOSOC the oversight which it had largely lost to the General Assembly (cf. the way in which the crisis in oil and other raw materials was made a reason for a special Assembly session in April 1974) or whether it will merely make ECOSOC into a kind of mini-Assembly of its own, remains to be seen.

The Council, whose members serve, each of them, for three years, has two sessions a year, the first in New York, April to May, the second opening in Geneva in July and resuming in New York in October or November. As in the Assembly, a president is elected for the year from a member state which is not a great power. Unlike the Assembly, a bare majority of those present and voting suffices for all decisions.

The Charter, in Articles 57, 58, and 63, laid on the Council the first of its duties, that of bringing the various specialized agencies 'into relationship with the U.N.' by means of 'agreements . . . defining the terms'. Seldom have co-ordinating functions been described in more modest or tentative language: 'the Economic and Social Council . . . *may* co-ordinate the activities of the specialized agencies through *consultation* . . . and *recommendations*' (Article 63); 'the Economic and Social Council *may* take appropriate steps to obtain regular reports from the specialized agencies. . . . It *may* make arrangements . . .' (Article 64) (my italics). The phrases of the Charter reflect a continuously tender regard for the sovereignty and susceptibilities of international organizations, some of which, as we have noted, antedate the U.N. and all of which have their own independent political organs, budgets, and secretariats. In consonance with this the Charter evaded the delicate task of defining the terms of the co-ordination and left this to be done in a series of subsequently negotiated agreements.

The agreements, though differing in detail, follow a common general pattern. There are reciprocal undertakings about attendance at meetings, and exchange of documents and information. The specialized agency concerned undertakes to assist the Security and Trusteeship Councils if required, to submit reports to ECOSOC on its activities, and (this does not apply to the International Bank or the Fund) to transmit its administrative budget to the General Assembly for examination and recommendation. It might be supposed that it would be with the negotiation of these agreements that ECOSOC's activities as co-ordinator would begin. But not only is the scope of co-ordination sharply limited, as we have seen, but paradoxically most of the co-ordination that does ensue is entrusted not to ECOSOC but to the General Assembly and the Secretariat. Thus the examination of the agencies' budgets is done by that Assembly watchdog, the Advisory Committee on Administrative and Budgetary Questions (ACABQ) (see pp. 128–9, Chapter 5), which reports its findings and recommendations (it can *only* recommend) to the Assembly's Fifth Committee. But the day-to-day co-ordination, not of grand policy directives, but of the ordinary administrative decisions out of which, as everyone knows, 90 per cent. of policy is made, is entrusted to a body of international civil servants. This is the Administrative Committee on Co-ordination (ACC), which consists of the Secretary-General of the U.N. as Chairman and his opposite numbers in the agencies. It is a kind of international cabinet, but with the peculiar characteristic that each minister is responsible to a different parliament. It was set up in 1946 in response to a recommendation by ECOSOC itself, reflecting a wise awareness of how impotent a remote, intermittently functioning, overloaded Council was to keep a close and continuous watch over a dozen independent and international entities. Not that the ACC has any power to coerce or control; it is an instrument of persuasion, and its recommendations (made to ECOSOC and to the specialized agencies to which it reports) must be unanimous. Nor are its functions and powers as clear as they might be. In particular, the line separating it from the IACB (see p. 170), which co-ordinates aid and development, is a very blurred one.

As to ECOSOC's own work of co-ordination, this is mainly done through its enlarged Committee for Programme and Co-ordination (CPC). Before enlargement this was a body of eighteen members, so-called 'government experts', representing as many member states. In 1970 it was enlarged by the addition of five additional members. These are appointed, not by ECOSOC, but by the General Assembly. The logic of the arrangement is obscure. A possible division of co-ordinating functions could have taken the form of the Assembly's ACABQ concentrating on budgetary co-ordination and ECOSOC's CPC concentrating on the co-ordination of programmes. To some extent this is the way the emphasis falls, but the failure to make the CPC truly expert (its 'governmental experts' are far more governmental than expert) and the intrusion of an Assembly political element into what ought to be a specialist job have combined to limit the esteem and effectiveness which the CPC enjoys.

One other organizational committee of ECOSOC deserves mention, its Committee on Non-Governmental Organization. This body, thirteen members strong, is the Council's liaison with (or should one say buffer against?) the thousand and one associations, philanthropic, disinterested, and interested, which seek to take advantage of the facilities of Article 71 of the Charter. Article 71 permits the Council to 'make suitable arrangements for consultation with non-governmental organizations . . . [either] international . . .[or], where appropriate, national'. Its insertion at San Francisco reflected directly that solicitude for interest groups which is such a marked feature of American government and in particular the indebtedness felt by the United States State

Department to the various private bodies which had conspicuously co-operated with it to recommend the U.N. to a public hitherto isolationist. The gate thus opened might, however, easily have admitted a flood had the Council not established categories of intimacy and set up this committee to handle applications and petitions. As it is, about a dozen organizations have been admitted to category A, well over a hundred are in category B, and almost twice as many on a mere 'register' for *ad hoc* consultations.

While the main work of these standing committees is, as we have seen, concerned with the co-ordinating business of the Council, ECOSOC's own substantive duties are mainly discharged through a series of functional commissions, set up in pursuance of Article 68 of the Charter. These are six in number, as follows:

Statistical Commission (twenty-four members);
Population Commission (twenty-seven members);
Commission for Social Development (thirty-two members);
Commission on Human Rights (thirty-two members) and
Sub-Commission on Prevention of Discrimination and
Protection of Minorities (twenty-six members);
Commission on the Status of Women (thirty-two members);
Commission on Narcotic Drugs (thirty members).

With the exception of Human Rights and the Status of Women (three years) membership of all these commissions is for a four-year term.

Membership need not be and indeed generally is not restricted to those countries which are at the time members of ECOSOC, but the members are in all cases government representatives—they may or may not be expert authorities as well. With the expansion of the Council the expert element has been further reduced by the requirement that the commissions should, like the Council, equitably reflect the regional composition of the U.N. It will be apparent from a glance at the list that the commissions vary greatly in character. Some are almost wholly technical and factual, like the Statistical Commission. Some have a clear and non-controversial objective, like the Commission on Narcotic Drugs. Others are extremely broad, like the Social Commission, and one is almost entirely political, the Commission on Human Rights. As far as ECOSOC is concerned they are all advisory, but the advice they have tendered has been most diverse in character, ranging from the business-like convention on narcotic drugs produced by the Narcotics Commission in 1958 to the kind of all-inclusive, unfocused reports of the Commission on the Status of Women which point the way to no practical action by the Council at all.

Analogous in certain respects to the functional commissions, but having no roots in the Charter, are three standing committees of the Council. They all owe their existence to pressure from the expanded membership of the U.N. in the 1960s for more action in the development field. Ideally the new membership would have liked to see new specialized agencies created to meet its needs; these committees represented compromises conceded by the developed states. The first, set up in 1962, is the Committee on Housing, Building, and Planning, which deals in effect with the world-wide problems of urban development. It has twenty-seven members. The second, set up in 1963, is the Advisory Committee on the Application of Science and Technology to Development. This too was in lieu of a new specialized agency which, apart from anything else, would have cut across the areas of UNESCO and FAO. It is exclusively a committee of experts, twenty-four strong, and enjoys a deserved esteem. However the demand for a more political body remained, in true ECOSOC manner, unabated, until in 1974, a further Committee on Science and Technology for Development was created, governmental rather than political, drawn from the entire enlarged membership and, by a strange piece of hybridization indicative of its political motivation, reporting to ECOSOC through the General Assembly.

A further reflection of the developing countries' desire to see science applied for their betterment was provided in 1970 by the establishment of another standing committee, also representative of the enlarged membership, the Committee on Natural Resources, drawn as far as possible from experts in the field. An even more genuinely expert body is the Committee for Development Planning, nominated by the Secretary-General, whose twenty-four members are drawn from their national ministries or research institutes of Development. A similar body is the fifteen-man Committee on Crime Prevention and Control.

Finally as part of the 'package deal' which led to the doubling of the Council's membership in 1971 there was set up a fifty-four-member Committee of Review and Appraisal, with the specific responsibility of overseeing the Strategy of the Second Development Decade.

Among the most successful of ECOSOC's offshoots have been its regional commissions. The first of these, the Economic Commission for Europe (ECE), was set up in 1947 and has thirty-four members, including the United States and Canada. It usually meets at Geneva, once a year, but in addition to its plenary meeting committees operate on problems of agriculture, coal, power, housing, industry, transport, steel, timber, and trade. A permanent secretariat at Geneva, for many years headed with distinction by Dr. Gunnar Myrdal, services the meetings, undertakes research, and produces such useful documents as the annual *Economic Survey for Europe*. Although in some respects overshadowed by the potent Organization for Economic Cooperation (OECD), an extra-U.N. creation based in Paris, ECE has filled with success a unique role as a mediator between countries with totally opposed economic systems, those of East and West Europe (and the North Atlantic).

ECE has provided the pattern for four more such bodies. The Economic Commission for Asia and the Far East (ECAFE) was established in 1947. It has a membership of thirty-one (plus eight associates), the U.N. members in the area and those outside it, like France, the U.S.S.R., the U.S.A., and the U.K., which have special interests in the area. Its headquarters are at Bangkok but its annual meetings have been held at different centres throughout Asia. In 1974 it changed its name to Economic and Social Commission for Asia and the Pacific. 1948 saw the setting up of the Economic Commission for Latin America (ECLA). It has twenty-nine members plus two associates, and its headquarters are at Santiago, though, like ECAFE, its annual meetings rotate amongst the principal cities of the area. In 1958 an Economic Commission for Africa (ECA) was established with an initial membership of nine independent U.N. members on that continent and six countries administering territories there, also a considerable associate membership of dependent territories. ECA has grown rapidly; it now has forty-two full members as well as four associates. Addis Ababa is the seat of the Commission and its first executive secretary was Mr. Abbas, the Sudanese head of the Gezira project. Finally in 1973, as a result of Arab pressure, there was established an Economic Commission for Western Asia, based in Beirut and conspicuously and exclusively Arab in membership. It has twelve members, and its secretariat is headed by Yemen's representative at the U.N. The regional character of these commissions has given them a unity and coherence which their parent body has lacked; their problems have in the main been real, not propagandistic, their studies and recommendations rooted in the needs of their area. They all deal directly with their member governments, though they report their activities to ECOSOC. This, however natural and proper, has inevitably created a further problem of co-ordination which a natural tendency to act as pressure groups for their region, magnifying claims and pressing priorities (e.g. in relation to the technical assistance programme), has done nothing to diminish.

There remains a further group of institutional emanations from ECOSOC less easy to classify than the foregoing. They range from merely *ad hoc* committees to the so-called 'special bodies' which enjoy a certain independence from ECOSOC control. Of these the most notable is probably the philanthropic U.N. Children's Emergency Fund (UNICEF), financed independently by donations from governments and private sources, operating under an Executive Director of its own, and doing valuable work for children's welfare all over the world. Another type of body is the eleven-member International Narcotics Control Board which in 1964 replaced the Permanent Central Narcotics Board and the Drug Supervisory Body, both inherited virtually unchanged from the League.

Of the functioning of so diverse a range of bodies and of the discharge of such a multiplicity of functions, no generalization can possibly be wholly accurate. Nevertheless a few broad trends can be observed and a few broad judgements passed. The inadequacies of ECOSOC as a co-ordinating instrument have been sufficiently displayed, but fairness obliges one to add that much of the criticism of the Council on this score proceeds from governments who tolerate a degree of overlap and rivalry in their domestic establishments which cast the U.N.'s shortcomings into the shade, while their concern for the smooth dovetailing of U.N. projects and organizations is frequently animated by a desire to save money and reduce their contributions. Some, at any rate, of the proliferation of commissions and sub-organizations is an expression of frustration on the part of poor nations who, having failed to interest the rich in directly ameliorating their plight, have had recourse to these forums as devices for publicizing, however incoherently, their problems and their poverty.

A good deal of ECOSOC's time is taken up with supervisory functions. A sizeable proportion of the U.N.'s activities and of the secretariat's time is devoted to work like technical assistance, narcotics control, or the safeguarding of human rights which ECOSOC promotes or supervises. In general it may be said that its efficiency in the discharge of this function is proportionate to the concreteness and practicality of the job to be done. It is perhaps better on its economic than on its social side, better at a regional than at a global level, better—naturally—when there is a universally recognized need to be filled than when there are priorities to be determined in the allocation of scarce dollars or resources.

For much of its labours ECOSOC has nothing to show except a collection and an ordering of information. Upon occasion this exercise may simply provide an escape from a political impasse; if a committee cannot agree upon action, it can always recommend a piece of research, a survey, the dispatch of a questionnaire to member governments. In fact, however, when disagreements cannot be resolved by frontal attacks, the silent persuasion of a factual report or a statistical return may yield results. In any case over the long haul—and agencies trafficking in social and economic matters have no right to expect quick results—what John Stuart Mill called the 'centralizing of knowledge' is one of the major civilizing influences of government at both the international and the national level, and the activities of ECOSOC and its ancillaries in this field, not only by the information assembled but by the collective self-consciousness bred in its assembling, may prove to be its best claim to respect.

ECOSOC itself and many of its subordinate bodies proceed, of course, by way of debate. Few harsher punishments could be devised for a modern Prometheus than to read through the verbatim records of these talkfests; it would certainly cure him of any pride in the collective wisdom of mankind. Some of the tedium, of course, derives from the inescapable *longueurs* of international intercourse at governmental level; much of it is remediable. Too much of the debate—e.g. on a report from an agency or a functional commission—is devoted exclusively to an airing of views, the compilation of 'an international Hansard on economic and social questions', as Loveday puts it, and is unrelated to any course of action. Too much is unrestricted by any regard for the terms of the Charter or the facts of international politics; thus the ban on interference in domestic politics is continually ignored. Repeated failure to distinguish between resolutions which may produce results and those which are mere utopian verbiage has brought even the serious debates of ECOSOC into disrepute. In this connexion nothing has done more harm to the Organization in general and ECOSOC in particular than the great wild goose chase after human rights. No country is innocent in this matter, neither the United States, which pressed at San Francisco for human rights provisions in the Charter, nor the Soviet bloc, which exploited them with a magnificent indifference to the beams in their own eyes, nor the Latin-Americans, who found here ideal nourishment for their rhetorical appetites, nor the Anglo-Saxons, who, false to their tradition of realism in things liberal and humanitarian, joined with the rest in the collective admiration for the Emperor's new clothes. Thus a cowardly conspiracy developed to gloss over the inherent absurdity of an organization of governments dedicating itself to protect human rights when, in all ages and climes, it is governments which have been their principal violators. Logic and experience were thrown to the winds in extending the concept far beyond anything any court could enforce to cover anything which any state (particularly those with least respect for human dignity) happened to think desirable. When in 1948 the General Assembly gave endorsement without dissentient voice to the Declaration of Human Rights, words came as near to being emptied of meaning as at any time in the history of the Organization. When verbal promissory notes had to be changed into the harder legal currency of conventions some healthy misgivings appeared, but too late to save years of verbiage to which no end is in sight. This was not ECOSOC's crime alone; it was indeed only the middle term between the Commission and the Assembly. It was, however, the principal victim both in fact and in public esteem. Recently the Council has shown some disposition to deal more in realities and less in illusions and the result, for all the inescapable handicaps of its structure and status, is an improvement.

If ECOSOC is primarily a forum, UNCTAD is primarily a pressure group. Its role can best be understood through its history. Despite the existence of GATT (see p. 163) there persisted amongst the developing countries a growing unease about their role in world trade and their relatively increasing impoverishment. To give expression to these concerns a U.N. Conference on Trade and Development was called in Geneva in 1964. The moving spirit in organizing it and directing its deliberations was Raúl Prebisch of Argentina (previously Executive Secretary of ECLA), but its membership of 2,000 delegates was drawn from 120 countries. What emerged from the conference was a virtual 'trade union' of seventy-seven under-developed countries who constituted themselves into a negotiating bloc *vis-à-vis* the industrial economies—a North–South, or more precisely, a West–South confrontation. To consolidate their unity and maintain their pressure they induced the General

Assembly in 1965 to institutionalize the Geneva Conference by setting up, as an organ of the Assembly, what, by a characteristic U.N. employment of language, is still called the U.N. Conference on Trade and Development (UNCTAD) even though it is no longer a conference in the ordinary sense of the word.

Structurally, UNCTAD is a kind of a cross between ECOSOC and a specialized agency. It is located at Geneva (after a belated and unsuccessful bid by the U.K. to site it in London). The Conference itself meets every three years and it consists of all the members of the U.N. or of any of its agencies (144 in all). Between meetings of the full Conference a Trade and Development Board meets twice a year, alternately in New York and Geneva; it consists of sixty-eight members, elected by the full membership. It reports direct to the Conference and, via ECOSOC, to the General Assembly. The Board has established four subsidiary organs whose labels give a fair idea of the topics that worry the membership; they are the Committee on Commodities (the problem for raw material producers of securing acceptable terms of trade), the Committee on Manufactures (industrial development and manufactured exports), the Committee on Invisibles and Financing related to Trade (services for which the poor find themselves dependent on the rich), and the Committee on Shipping (an analogous matter of concern). All this is serviced by a substantial secretariat. Its first head was Raúl Prebisch as Secretary-General.

UNCTAD is a reminder that administrative untidiness in an international organization generally reflects frustration and division in its membership. UNCTAD exists less in order to do something than as an expression of the failure of the under-developed states to get something done. UNIDO (the U.N. Industrial Development Organization) tells the same story. The desire for development stimulated a demand for industrialization. As the demand mounted it sought expression in a distinctive organization. The conflict between developing countries who wanted a pressure group agency which would extort aid for industrial development and developed countries which wanted only a market research organization was reflected in characteristically vague terms of reference when the organization was set up by the General Assembly in 1966. With very limited resources it is supposed to 'co-ordinate' U.N. activities in the industrial area when they include such potent bodies as the I.L.O. and the World Bank. But it is also a co-ordinatee, since in addition to research it also engages in technical assistance projects financed by the U.N. Development Programme.

The principal organ of UNIDO is a forty-five-member Industrial Development Board elected by the General Assembly which is supposed to frame general policy and supervise the Organization's work. It is, of course, dominated by representatives of the developing countries, though its headquarters are in Vienna. The Board, whose members serve a three-year term, meets once a year in April–May.

The complex of ideas and pressures which went into the establishment of the Trusteeship Council has already been outlined on pp. 17–18 and 28–30. Originally there were eleven trust territories with which the Council was concerned: New Guinea and Nauru under Australian administration; Ruanda-Urundi under Belgium; Cameroons and Togoland, under France; Somaliland under Italy; Western Samoa under New Zealand; Cameroons, Togoland, and Tanganyika under the U.K.; the Pacific Islands, consisting of the Marianas, the Marshalls, and the Carolinas, under the U.S.A. All of these, except Somaliland, were previously administered as mandates under the League of Nations. One League mandatory, South Africa, refused to place her territory, South-West Africa, under the U.N. system. Much dispute raged as to whether she was acting illegally in so doing, and in 1950 the International Court ruled that she was not obliged to do so, though she was obliged to present to the U.N. the same reports and petitions which she had to render to the League. (She has not done so despite an Assembly resolution 'terminating' her mandate, a Security Council demand for her withdrawal and a hostile ruling from the World Court.)

Of the eleven trust territories four (British Togoland, French Cameroons, French Togoland, and Italian Somaliland) attained independence by the end of 1960, two, Tanganyika and Western Samoa, by the end of 1961, while Ruanda-Urundi and the Southern Cameroons were hot on their heels. Nauru won independence in 1968. These changes affected the composition of the Council, as described on p. 131. With this went, naturally, a decline in its activities. It now meets, not twice, but once a year, in New York, usually in May or June.

Each territory is held under a Trusteeship Agreement. This is not, as might be supposed, an agreement between the administering power and the U.N. It is, says Article 79, an agreement whose 'terms . . . shall be agreed upon by the states directly concerned'. This has been variously interpreted, at one extreme by the U.S.A., which regarded itself as the sole power directly concerned in the future of the old Japanese mandates in the Pacific, at the other by the U.S.S.R., which insisted it meant all members of the Security Council (and in protest boycotted all Trusteeship Council meetings until April 1948). Most administering authorities interpreted it to mean 'neighbouring powers', which of course were almost always colonial powers. The Somaliland agreement was unique in being drafted by the Trusteeship Council and the General Assembly. The terms of the Trusteeship Agreements vary, but they must all conform to the objectives or code of behaviour prescribed in Article 76. They confer powers of administration on the administering authority and supervisory powers on the U.N. Agreements must be approved by the General Assembly or, in the case of a 'strategic trust territory', by the Security Council. The only such territory is the U.S.A.'s Pacific Islands, and the main advantage conferred by so labelling it is the right to exclude U.N. observers from such unhealthy areas as Eniwetok Atoll.

The powers of the Trusteeship Council are threefold (Articles 87 and 88). The first is the right to submit questionnaires and receive reports from the administering power. The second is the right to accept petitions from the area and examine them in consultation with the power concerned. The third is the right periodically to visit the territories at times agreed upon with the administering authority. And, of course, there is implicit in all of

these the right to debate matters which arise in any of these connexions and to pass resolutions of a recommendatory character.
Since it began to operate in 1946 the Trusteeship Council has been
highly successful in maximizing its powers and making the best
use of its opportunities. Its questionnaires became formidably
elaborate; in 1947 it approved a standard form which involved
247 questions, was divided into twelve sections, and was followed
by a statistical annex in thirteen parts. The replies of administering powers were then made the subject of cross-examination,
written and oral. All this furnished material for a general debate,
upon which was drawn up the annual report to the Assembly.
The petitions from trust territories do not have to come via the
administering authority, but can be submitted direct, and visiting
Trusteeship Council missions can also receive petitioners. The
visiting missions began in 1947 with a mission to Western
Samoa, to be followed in 1948 by missions to Ruanda-Urundi
and Tanganyika. The normal practice is for a visiting mission
to consist of three or four members and for its report to contain
not only an account of its findings but also recommendations to
the administering authority. Sometimes, as in the case of
Tanganyika in 1954, visiting missions have seemed to cross the
narrow line that divides supervision from administration, and
administering powers have dissented vigorously from courses
of action which have been pressed upon them.

In general, however, the tensions within the Trusteeship
Council between administrators and their critics have been
fruitful ones, producing on the one side many real improvements
and on the other a gradual but perceptible shift away from mere
'anti-colonialism' to acceptance of a positive responsibility for
the welfare and development of the territories concerned. The
Council has gained enormously by the fact that although, of
course, political considerations enter into its operations, it has
had a definite piece of work to do which has imposed on all its
members a sense of purpose and responsibility. But this is not the
whole story. The Trusteeship Council, like ECOSOC, is 'under
the authority' of the General Assembly, and from that quarter
there has come a stream of pressures and complaints which

reflects the growing self-consciousness of all those states which have been variously termed 'underdeveloped', 'ex-colonial', and 'anti-colonial'. In the Assembly these states enjoy a preponderance of numbers which the constitution of the Trusteeship Council denies them, and in the Fourth Committee in particular they have conducted what is virtually a continuous review of the Council's policies. The Assembly has itself sent visiting commissions to trust territories, heard and questioned petitioners (through the Fourth Committee), and sent observers to watch elections in a territory such as Togoland in 1958.

The Assembly has also exerted pressure on a much broader front, beyond though related to the field of the Trusteeship Council. The Charter in Chapter XI sets out a 'Declaration Regarding Non-Self-Governing Territories', which applies to the whole range of colonial territories and obliges member states under Article 73e to supply regularly to the Organization information on the territories (other than trust territories) which they control. From the outset disagreement existed on the status of this Declaration and on the obligations it entails. The colonial powers claimed it was merely a 'Charter', a signpost, a set of moral precepts. They would not accept the view that it rendered them accountable to anyone but their own parliaments, and regarded Article 73e simply as constituting the U.N. as a clearing house for non-political information, not as conferring on it powers of discussion in relation to it, much less of recommendation. The anti-colonialists, on the other hand, sought to establish under Chapter XI the same degree of U.N. power and authority in respect of colonial areas as the Trusteeship system established for trust areas, and made of Article 73e an instrument for doing so. The battle was fought out mainly in relation to the Committee on Information from Non-Self-Governing Territories. This body, which grew by degrees out of an *ad hoc* committee of the Assembly set up in 1946 and a three-year 'Special Committee' set up in 1947, came to establish itself as a potent and continuing Assembly organ. It paralleled the Trusteeship Council in its style of composition, equal numbers of administering (i.e. colonial) and non-administering states, and in the questionnaire in standard form that was adopted for the collection of information. It repeatedly sought to extend its authority to require the provision of information on political as well as other matters, to make recommendations with regard to individual colonies, and to determine for itself when a territory ceases to be 'non-self-governing'. On all these points it met with the stout resistance of the colonial powers, who repeatedly threatened to withdraw from the Committee if the Assembly endowed it with (what they would regard as) illegal powers. (An objection of an opposite type was that made by Portugal, which refused to take up a newly created seat in 1961 on the grounds that its overseas territories were merely 'provinces' of a unitary state and not colonies at all.)

All in all the Committee's rise as a parallel body to the Trusteeship Council constituted a forceful instance of the Assembly's capacity to respond to novel demands. Nor did the development stop here. In 1960, the year of the great influx of new African states, the Assembly adopted unanimously (but with the colonial powers abstaining) the Declaration on the Granting of Independence to Colonial Countries and Peoples. This made colonialism *per se* improper, by denying that inadequacy of preparation could ever be a pretext for delaying independence and requiring 'immediate steps' to be taken to transfer powers of government to dependent peoples. The Declaration, almost an amendment to the Charter, provided a platform for further pressure. Alleging that it was being ignored, the activists established a new committee with one of the longest labels that even the U.N. could show, the Special Committee on the Situation with Regard to the Implementation of the Declaration on the Granting of Independence to Colonial Countries and Peoples, the 'Committee of 24', for short. This abandoned the earlier idea of a balanced membership, half administering and half non-administering members. Instead, of its twenty-four members only five represented the 'West', the rest being either from the Soviet bloc or 'the third world'. Thus composed, it was directed by the General Assembly to employ 'all means' to do its job and, in 1963, to this end was authorized to take over all previous committees' work, including that of the Committee on Information. It produced, as an implicit indictment, a list of sixty-four territories to which the Declaration had not been applied, for the most part small or scattered island possessions of the United Kingdom. It kept up particular pressure on the issue of Southern Rhodesia. By going 'on progress' in Africa and holding open 'hearings' in propinquant territory it effectively publicized its case although, of course, in practical terms it could do no more. It also put particular pressure on the United Kingdom in relation to Aden, persuading the General Assembly to set up a special visiting mission. However, the total hostility of the mission to the South Arabian federation which had been set up by Britain as a preparation for independence made the visit abortive, indeed counter-productive. The independence target date of 1 January 1968, set up and adhered to by the United Kingdom, owed little to the Committee's pressure. However, pre-independence visits to Botswana, Lesotho, and Swaziland passed off more happily. In relation to one territory, Gibraltar, attitudes were reversed, the United Kingdom inviting a U.N. mission to observe the referendum of 1967 which so emphatically repudiated transfer to Spain and the United Nations declining the invitation. Elsewhere, in territories such as Fiji, the United Kingdom (as also the United States) has refused to admit Committee visitations which it considers unnecessary and improper. This has not prevented the Committee keeping up a drum-fire of demands, on all and every aspect of surviving colonialism and securing their endorsement and amplification in the Fourth Committee. As a consequence of this Britain and the U.S.A. left the Committee in 1971 and have not returned.

The specialized agencies are all expressions of that 'functional internationalism' on which we have remarked in earlier pages. The philosophy which animates them is the belief that there are international jobs to be done, international interests to be fostered, which can be detached from politics and find their natural expression in separate, if related, associations of member states. It was a corollary of this philosophy that the institutions of these agencies should not conform to any rigid common pattern; the topic should dictate the structure. None the less, certain similarities can be observed. All have a permanent secretariat, all a deliberative body or assembly, and all an executive council or board. The assembly represents the full membership, the council a proportion of it. Decisions are generally reached by majority vote.

The International Telecommunication Union (ITU) can claim to be the oldest of the specialized agencies, deriving from the International Telegraph Union, set up in Paris in 1865, and established in a bureau at Berne in 1868. It now has its headquarters in Geneva. A Plenipotentiary Conference of all members meets every five years; interim supervision is maintained by the Administrative Council of twenty-nine members elected by the Conference and meeting annually; the Administrative Council approves the budget and appoints the Secretary-General. It recommends (unfortunately with only moderate success) the allocation of radio frequencies, circulates information, and provides technical assistance.

Hardly less venerable is the Universal Postal Union (UPU), which grew out of the first International Postal Congress, which met in 1874 and created the General Postal Union. At its second meeting in 1878 the name was changed to the Universal Postal Union. The UPU's plenary assembly meets every five years, making decisions by simple majority vote except for changes in the Convention, fixing maximum rates for mail, etc., which require a majority of two-thirds. An Executive and Liaison Committee of thirty-one elected states functions between sessions and the secretariat takes the form of an International Bureau at Berne. Hardly less technical and non-controversial is the World Meteorological Organization (WMO), dating back to the semi-governmental International Meteorological Organization established in 1878. A world congress meets every four years, an executive committee meets annually. A Secretary-General is appointed by the congress and has his headquarters at Geneva.

With the International Labour Organization (ILO) we enter on an altogether larger scale of operations. This body, the only

'Geneva' creation, save the Opium Board, to have kept a continuous identity from League days, has been a potent influence in the development of international organization. Established in 1919, with the same membership as the League, the ILO flourished as the League declined. It was the only League organization which the U.S.A. would join, it was given exceptional leadership by its first Director, Albert Thomas, it obtained much success in raising labour standards over the world, and it survived the shock of World War II with its structure still intact. It has two policy-making organs, the General Conference of all members held every year and the Governing Body of forty-eight, which meets quarterly as an executive council. A unique tripartite system of representation operates; in the Conference every state has two government representatives and one each for employers and workers; of the Governing Body twenty come from governments, ten from employers, and ten from workers. Without doubt this stimulates a strong institutional and international sense, with divisions reflecting lines of interest rather than of nationality. Voting in the Conference is by a two-thirds majority — the origin, doubtless, of U.N. Assembly practice. The field of ILO activity, while still dominated by the traditional concern for hours, wages, and conditions of labour, has broadened since the war to include such objectives as social security, full employment, and economic planning. This has brought it into a more frequent and intimate relationship with other international organizations, both the U.N. and other specialized agencies, and the provision of technical assistance, either directly or in conjunction with other bodies, has now become a major responsibility of the Organization. David Morse, Director-General from 1948 to 1970, set a record as head of an international agency. His successor, Wilfred Jenks, came from the United Kingdom, but his distinguished tenure was cut short by his untimely death in 1973. The Deputy Director, Francis Blanshard, of France, succeeded him.

During World War II itself the Food and Agriculture Organization (FAO) was floated in the U.S.A., not only in response to the evangelism of such League veterans as F. L.

McDougall, but also with Roosevelt's encouragement as a trial run in United Nations post-war collaboration. Its purposes are to improve food production and distribution and raise living and nutritional standards. Its weapons are the provision of an intelligence service and technical assistance, and the negotiation of international commodity agreements. Perhaps its biggest impact to date has been as the co-ordinator of the Freedom from Hunger Campaign and the World Food Programme. Its headquarters are in Rome, but it has regional offices in eight other capitals across the globe. Its plenary assembly, the Conference, meets biennially, each member state having one vote and decisions being made by simple or two-thirds majorities according to the subject-matter. Its Council of thirty-four elected members meets twice a year and operates by simple majority.

Two financial bodies sprang from a common root, the Bretton Woods Conference of 1944, and came into being in the same year — 1946. They are the International Bank for Reconstruction and Development and the International Monetary Fund. The Bank is a lending agency whose business is the making and encouragement of productive investment, its own capital stock being held by member states in proportion to their wealth and trade. The Fund, similarly financed by members' subscriptions based on a quota, is devoted to the promotion of exchange stability and international trade by making needed currencies available to members and by providing financial technical assistance. Bank and Fund have similar structures; each member state appoints a Governor, the Board of Governors meeting annually; voting power is proportionate to the 'quota' of the member, exactly in the case of the Fund, roughly in the case of the Bank. Executive Directors (twenty-one for the Bank, twenty for the Fund) handle general operations. Each Director wields the votes of the countries which elect him. Simple majorities decide. The Directors select the President (of the Bank) and the Managing Director (of the Fund). Both bodies sit in Washington, D.C.

From the loins of the Bank has sprung the International Finance Corporation (IFC), established in 1956 to stimulate private investment in backward countries mainly by investing itself in private enterprises (usually not on more than a 50:50 basis) in these areas. It works closely with the Bank, has an analogous structure, and in fact shares the same Governors and Directors.

A similar body, the International Development Association (IDA), became a U.N. specialized agency in March 1961. Its object is to promote economic development primarily through long-term low-interest loans.

The United Nations Educational, Scientific and Cultural Organization (UNESCO), established in 1946, is the scarcely recognizable descendant of the old International Institute of Intellectual Co-operation. It suffered at its inception from a confusion of aims. Should it concentrate on practical tasks, like helping to rebuild bombed schools? Should it try to 'sell' to the world a vaguely Dewey-ish concept of 'democratic education'? Should it, in conformity with the muddled slogan at its mast-head, be a psychiatrist-cum-missionary for peace—'Since wars begin in the minds of men, it is in the minds of men that the defences of peace must be constructed'? Unable to decide on its own priorities and cursed by its honey-pot appeal for all buzzing brains, UNESCO suffered more than any other agency from the ills that international organizations are heir to. Its follies robbed it even of the credit for its genuine achievements, and the association with it of many able minds has failed to give it the working efficiency of many more plodding organizations.

However, with the establishment of a permanent head-quarters in Paris in 1958 there came about a rationalizing of its activities and a greater emphasis on concrete objectives, such as the elimination of illiteracy, mass-teaching techniques, teacher-training and school building, the preservation of cultural monuments (e.g. the Abu Simbel rock temples), and international exchange programmes. Its General Conference meets biennially. The five delegates which each state is entitled to send are supposed to be selected after consultation with a national UNESCO commission or, if no such body has been created, with national organizations in UNESCO's fields. An Executive Board of thirty-four members meets twice a year.

Although not established until 1947 the International Civil Aviation Organization (ICAO) also had its origins in a conference organized in the U.S.A. during the war. It is basically a technical organization, if only because the divergent interests of members have prevented it becoming a real regulatory body. It administers a Convention on conditions of civil aviation and serves as a clearing house for information. An assembly of the full membership meets annually for administrative purposes and triennially for broad policy-making, but a Council of twenty-seven elected states is in virtually continuous session and appoints the Secretary-General. Its headquarters are at Montreal.

The World Health Organization (WHO) was the first specialized agency to be created by the U.N. Organization itself. The success of the League's health services and the universal need for international co-operation in fighting against disease led ECOSOC, at its first session, to appoint a Committee which held an International Health Conference of all interested states. WHO's Constitution was signed on 22 July 1946, but a surprising degree of political suspicion and national jealousy retarded ratification until 1948. The Organization, whose headquarters are at Geneva, has carried regionalism further than any other international agency, having separate organizations for South-East Asia, Eastern Mediterranean, Western Pacific, the Americas, Africa south of the Sahara, and Europe. This has created considerable internal administrative problems, while externally WHO has encountered continuous frontier trouble with FAO. Policy and budget (by far the largest of any specialized agency) are controlled by an Assembly meeting annually, and an Executive Board of twenty-four, elected by the Assembly, meets twice a year. The Executive Board nominates and the Assembly appoints the Director-General for a five-year term.

The International Atomic Energy Agency (IAEA), whose draft statute was approved by a conference at U.N. headquarters in 1956, came into being with a considerable membership (including the Communist bloc) in July 1957. The Agency, which sits at Vienna, is designed to encourage and research into the peaceful uses of atomic energy. Its status represents a compromise between those who desired full autonomy for it and those who wanted it brought under U.N. control. Thus it is not, strictly speaking, a specialized agency, though it has most of the attributes of one and has concluded an agreement with the U.N. providing for mutual co-operation. A General Conference of member states meeting annually has broad powers of discussion, recommendation, and budget control, but it is with the Board of Governors, on which the atomic powers are virtually guaranteed permanent membership, that direction of the Agency resides. The Board, with a membership of twenty-five, is elected roughly half by the Conference and half by each outgoing Board. The Director-General is elected by the Conference on the nomination of the Board.

The latest specialized agency to come into existence is the Intergovernmental Maritime Consultative Organization (IMCO). In 1948 a conference summoned by ECOSOC drew up an IMCO Convention which was to come into effect as soon as twenty-one states, seven with more than a million tons of ship-ping apiece, ratified it. Ratification, however, was slow and it was not until 1958 that Japan's signature made up the requisite total. IMCO sets out to do for shipping what ICAO does for aviation; consultative and advisory, it formulates safety rules, fights restrictive and discriminatory practices, and seeks international co-operation in all shipping matters. London is its headquarters. Its Assembly meets every two years, but a Council of sixteen states (half primarily consumers of shipping, half primarily pro-viders) handles all interim business.

Between them these agencies constitute a world of international organization which, as we have seen, is half within, half without the U.N. proper. The scale of their operations is impressive; their total budgets are the equivalent of the whole sum available to the U.N.'s Secretary-General; their total staffs exceed those at his disposal. They can often claim a larger and more co-operative membership; they deal direct with independent states and with each other. The result is not a tidy picture and many observers have succumbed to the temptation to wish it were all neatly ordered under the aegis of the U.N. and its General

Assembly. But its defenders can claim that it has grown in its jungle-like style for perfectly good reasons, that its untidy diversity is a response to real needs, and that to fuse its functional operations with the basically political labours of the U.N. would harm the first without assisting the second.

There remains one other body, which might be described as an aborted specialized agency. This is GATT, the General Agreement on Tariffs and Trade. The Bretton Woods structure of international economic co-operation at the end of World War II was to have been completed by a third organization, alongside the Bank and the Fund, to deal comprehensively with trade, foreign investment, commodity agreements, restrictive practices, and full employment. In 1947-8 at a conference in Havana a Charter for a proposed International Trade Organization (ITO) was in fact hammered out. But it soon became apparent that ITO was not going to materialize as long as the U.S. Congress remained so largely protectionist or the U.K. government so restrictionist— to say nothing of the attitudes of other developed countries. Instead the decision was taken to make permanent what had previously been regarded as purely a stop-gap, the multilateral tariff treaty negotiated in Geneva in 1947, known as GATT. On this was grafted a secretariat, made permanent in 1955, an annual conference, a council to meet between times—five or six times a year, and, above all, a code of rights and obligations applicable to international trade. Its foundation-stones were the twin principles of non-discrimination and reciprocity. On these was built the phenomenal expansion of world trade during the first quarter-century after the war. Its culmination was the signing of the Kennedy Round agreements in June 1967. So far almost eighty countries have acceded to GATT, observing its rules and using it as a forum for negotiations.

In 1946 the International Court of Justice, the principal judicial organ of the U.N., succeeded the Permanent Court of League days. The continuity was as little broken as possible. The Statutes governing the two courts are almost identical. The new court meets at the Hague in the same building as the old one and cites the judgments and opinions of its predecessor as readily as its own. Indeed two of the Judges of the Permanent Court were elected to the new one. We have already described on p. 87, Chapter 4, the process of election of Judges and the part played in it by the regional and political groupings in the Assembly. Though some of the theory (e.g. that no two Judges should be of the same nationality) and a good deal of the practice of the elections runs counter to the concept of a Court whose members rise above all national allegiance and serve only the law, the Court's membership has in the main been of a high level. It is as premature to expect its composition to ignore 'equitable geographical representation' as to expect the American Supreme Court to ignore the claims of states south of the Mason–Dixon line or west of the Mississippi. At the present time the Court's fifteen members include one citizen of each of the Great Powers, excluding China. There are three further Europeans (one a Soviet satellite), three Asiatics, three Africans, and two Latin Americans. Decisions, of course, are by majority vote, but separate and dissenting opinions are recorded and, since the Court is not bound by its own precedents, may exercise an influence upon future decisions.

Despite the Court's acknowledged merits it has been so far from fulfilling the high hopes entertained for it in some quarters at San Francisco and afterwards that its record to date is actually less impressive than that of its predecessor. The volume of business has been smaller and the cases that have been brought seem on the whole to have been less important than those brought before the Permanent Court. Some disabilities it shares with the old Court, e.g. the statutory provision that only states may be parties to suits; this debars all international organizations, including the U.N. More serious, of course, is the fact that even states which are members of the U.N. and by that very fact members of the Court are not thereby obliged to accept the jurisdiction of the Court. Far from it. There is, of course, in the new Statute, as in the old, the (to the layman) confusingly titled 'optional clause'. This (Article 36) gives states the opportunity of signing a declaration whereby they recognize 'as compulsory, *ipso facto* and without special agreement, in relation to any other state accepting the same obligation, the jurisdiction of the Court in all legal disputes' concerning certain specified matters. This would suggest that states who 'opt' for this yield themselves wholly up to the Court's jurisdiction, subject only to the proviso that other states do likewise. Unfortunately for the Court this is not what has happened. Repeatedly, states have accepted the optional clause with reservations of their own making, either about specific topics which they will not allow the Court to handle or, more sweepingly, with some phrase about excluding 'matters essentially within their domestic jurisdiction'—i.e. which *they* consider to be within their domestic jurisdiction. The latter type of reservation has been adopted by the U.S.A., while the United Kingdom has reserved the right to introduce new reservations at any time by simple notification to the Secretary-General. Undoubtedly the introduction of such reservations has weakened the Court as it weakened its forerunner. But perhaps an even more significant index of the decline of faith in the international legal process is the fact that whereas forty-five states signed the optional clause for the old Court the number now adhering to it in respect of the present Court in a greatly enlarged world community is only forty-six.

Perhaps the basic cause of the Court's neglect can be deduced from the attitude of the U.N. itself towards it. Although debarred from seeking judgments at the Court's hands, the U.N. is not debarred from getting advisory opinions from the Court on legal disputes between itself and any of the specialized agencies, or on any of the numerous questions which have arisen regarding the interpretation of the Charter. In fact, however, the U.N. has not availed itself of this facility nearly as often as it might. Some of the cases it has raised have been important for the internal workings of the Organization, e.g. the *Reparation for Injuries* case (1949) arising out of the death of Count Bernadotte, which settled that when an agent of the U.N. is injured or killed in the course of his duties the U.N. is entitled to bring a claim against the state responsible. Of those involving political questions, two dealt with admission to membership of the U.N. (and were completely overridden by the 'package deal' of 1955) and four referred to the status of South-West Africa (and have not yet moved the Union of South Africa from its refusal to deal with the Trusteeship Council). The advisory opinion on Article 17, § 2, given in 1962, which ruled that the expenses of ONUC and UNEF were 'expenses of the United Nations' and as such assessable to members, clarified without in any way resolving the dispute over payments (see pp. 65-69). The Security Council, faced with the dispute between Albania and the United Kingdom over the firing on British warships in the Corfu Channel, recommended resort to the Court. (The Court decided in Britain's favour, but Albania, under Soviet pressure, has not yet paid the damages awarded.) The Council also, faced with the dispute over the nationalization of the Anglo-Iranian Company, postponed action until the Court had decided whether it had jurisdiction. (It finally decided it had not.) These and a few other cases add up to a rather slender record of U.N.-Court relations. Although governed by a legal document, the Charter, the U.N. has preferred time and time again to arrive at its decisions by political rather than legal processes. This may not accord with the disposition of all its members; there are no doubt many, especially among the Europeans, who would prefer to see greater use of the Court, especially where intra-regional disputes are concerned or where they feel the Court would ward off a threat to the *status quo*. But the majority of members, in the majority of their dissensions, do not feel themselves to be so much members of a community as to regard law as a natural and satisfactory way of settling disputes. Furthermore, even where they shrink from war to change it, they are not enamoured of the *status quo* which, by and large, law exists to uphold. Thus less than half a dozen of the new states have so far signed the optional clause. Such members have joined the U.N., less to preserve, by mechanisms of law and order, an existing state of affairs, than to effect, by the pressure of their votes and their voices, a change not only in their own circumstances but often in their relation with the rest of the world. For the disputes that inevitably arise from such a changing world a Court is not the appropriate agency of arbitrament. Indeed if it did get too much involved in what are essentially political quarrels, the Court might run the risk of appearing merely the judicial instrument of the General Assembly. At the same time recent cases involving, not new and restless nations, but well-established and traditionally 'law-abiding' states, painfully demonstrate the decline in the Court's authority. In 1973 it granted interim injunctions to Australia and New Zealand, ordering France not to carry out its planned nuclear tests in the Pacific. In 1974 the Court found for Britain and Germany in their suit against Iceland's extension of its fishing limits to 200 miles. In each case the offending party flouted the distasteful ruling. They may, or may not, have sustained some moral embarrassment, but the Court too has lost face before a cynical world.

7 · THE SECRETARIAT

THE thirty-eight floors and three basements that make up the Secretariat Building have often been regarded as the Whitehall to the Assembly Building's Westminster. There is enough truth in the analogy to make it dangerous. The 10,000 or so members of the Secretariat (of whom about half are in New York itself) do indeed constitute a U.N. civil service, but the nature of their work and the conditions under which they operate are in many respects so distinctive as to invalidate most comparisons with national bureaucracies.

There are, broadly speaking, six different types of function discharged by the Secretariat. The first is what might be called the role of the parliamentary clerk, but vastly extended as befits a polyglot parliament which demands a wide range of servicing—interpretation, translation, minuting, drafting, reproduction of documents, and provision of library facilities—in addition to the high-level legal and procedural assistance which bodies drawing their authority from written documents require. Numerically speaking by far the largest proportion of this 'parliamentary' staff is engaged on the work of interpretation and translation, an intensive and, when the Assembly is sitting, often a round-the-clock operation. In all, more than a quarter of the Secretariat is engaged in servicing, in one way or another, the conference activities of the U.N.

It is a narrow, often invisible, line that distinguishes this first function from the second, what one might call the information function of the Secretariat. The successful operation of all the deliberative activities of the U.N. requires that delegates, committees, and commissions have available to them a whole range of data, technical and otherwise; this is obviously true of specialist bodies like ECOSOC or the Trusteeship Council, but it also holds for a great deal of the work of the General Assembly.

Moreover, as we have seen, it is by 'the centralizing of information', and by giving it every kind of publicity, that the U.N. makes much of its deepest impression upon the mind of the world outside its own conference chambers. The collection, ordering, and providing of information at the points where it is most needed and can produce its greatest effect is one of the most important services that U.N. officials discharge. It is much more than an archivist's or statistician's function; it is political in the highest degree, calling for qualities of political judgement and forethought no less than of accuracy and integrity. No single department of the Secretariat is exclusively concerned with it, but it is a predominant activity of such departments as Trusteeship and Economic and Social Affairs, and of the Office of Legal Affairs.

Executive tasks proper occupy a much smaller percentage of the Secretariat than of any national civil service, for the obvious reason that the U.N. is not a government. It does, however, administer certain services, of which those providing technical assistance and pre-investment aid are the largest. Beginning as a small operation, technical assistance grew in 1949 under the stimulus of President Truman's 'Point Four' programme into a sizeable scheme for providing expert advice and assistance to the underdeveloped countries. Formally, the U.N. always maintained the distinction between the original technical assistance and what it called the Expanded Programme for Technical Assistance (EPTA). In fact it was the latter which constituted the effective programme, whose rates of expenditure rose to $50 million a year—a sum incidentally not chargeable to U.N. members as part of the Organization's budget, but met out of supplementary voluntary contributions, with the United States providing the lion's share. The U.N. itself does not spend more than a fifth to a quarter of the funds involved; the rest is shared out amongst the specialized agencies.

In 1959, in partial response to a long-pressed demand for U.N. aid for capital development, the Special Fund (full title, 'U.N. Special Fund for Economic Development') was set up. Its object was not to provide funds for capital investment but to provide 'pre-investment' aid—i.e. to assist in research projects, surveys, or the provision of training facilities which would make substantial investment from other sources attractive. Led by the dynamic Mr. Paul Hoffman until he retired in 1972 at the age of 80, it unashamedly insisted on the principle of decision by experts as to where and how its funds should be spent; its eighteen-member Governing Council, elected by ECOSOC and composed half of representatives of the 'underdevelopeds' and half of industrialized states, had a right of veto but not of initiative. Like EPTA it got its funds, which rose to over $90 million a year, from voluntary contributors, of whom the U.S.A. was much the largest, giving about 40 per cent. of the whole.

At the beginning of 1966 the two programmes, EPTA and the Special Fund, were combined over a five-year period into one United Nations Development Programme (UNDP), of which Mr. Hoffman was made Administrator. The Programme is directed by a Governing Council of forty-eight, elected by ECOSOC, on which 'developing' and 'developed' countries have roughly equal representation. The Council meets twice a year. One of the major problems in the administration of the now very considerable programme—it runs at over $300 million a year— is that of co-ordination, the efficient harmonizing of the efforts of all the international agencies through which the Fund's resources are channelled. At present principal reliance is placed upon the Inter-Agency Consultative Board (IACB) which is composed of the Administrator, the Secretary-General and the heads of the various agencies—some twenty bodies in all—who are involved in the execution of the Fund's projects.

This structure has come in for heavy criticism—most notably in the Jackson Report of 1969. The IACB is, alas, only one co-ordinating instrument amongst many—e.g. ECOSOC or the Industrial Development Board of UNIDO. It has no powers of compulsion and few of persuasion, since each agency head is responsible to his own governing body, has his own budget, his own 'clients', and his own pressure group. At the local level there is a Resident Representative of the UNDP in each country which has a 'project', but he too has no powers to compel or induce efficiency. With such a structure it is surprising that the whole development operation has worked as well as it has, but the cost of inefficiency becomes increasingly apparent as both the problem of underdevelopment and the effort to cope with it increase. The Jackson Report thought it might be 'the most complicated organization in the world' and estimated that there was about 20 per cent. of 'deadwood' in the operation. The cost of this is reflected in the fact that the First Development Decade ended in 1969 with a widening gap between rich and poor. Although it met its target of a 5 per cent. rate of growth for the developing countries as a whole, only twenty-seven of them actually achieved this level, while those most in need lagged furthest behind. If, as is highly desirable, a much larger contribution is made by richer countries to the development programme in the 1970s, there will have to be an improvement in the U.N.'s development machinery to avoid a repetition, on a larger scale, of the short-comings of the 1960s.

A quasi-executive function of a quite different kind is discharged by the U.N. Field Service. This body, set up in 1949, is limited by Assembly resolution to a maximum of 300 men. It is a uniformed but unarmed force (save that its members may carry side arms on special occasions) whose function is to provide transport, maintain communications, look after security, etc., for U.N. commissions in the field. It does not itself undertake any functions of observation, truce supervision, or the like, but is in permanent being to assist any U.N. bodies who are so engaged.

Even national administrations, headed by politicians whose primary concern is to expound their policies, have not scorned the assistance of information services. The U.N., with no ministerial cabinet to plead its cause and with a world-wide electorate to reach, wisely decided from the first that it should have a substantial information department of its own. In the days when it engrossed 18 per cent. of the U.N.'s budget it was undoubtedly too substantial, but only a hanging judge (there are such) will hold that its present $10 million budget is excessive, bearing in mind the size of its constituency and the diversity of its clientele. Moreover, when so much of what it has to report is necessarily unpalatable to certain member states and may even be virtually banned there—e.g. the 1957 report on Hungary— it is hardly possible to apply to all its operations the criteria of efficiency appropriate to an information service operating in a democracy. This error marred many of the recommendations of the 1958 expert 'economy' committee, on which of course the U.S.S.R. was represented. One may more readily sympathize with the complaint that too much of the information office's efforts are geared to the exacting demands of its customers at headquarters, though against this it must be remembered that no other country's press approaches that of the United States in the seriousness and comprehensiveness of its U.N. coverage. The greatest need still is to induce the rest of the world's press and public to treat the U.N. with comparable seriousness. As a step towards this the establishment of fifty regional information centres is welcome, though in an organization of over a hundred members the number is by no means excessive—nor their scale and staffing unduly elaborate.

Administering the administrators constitutes in the U.N., as in all bureaucracies, an additional and indispensable function. By British standards, the size of the U.N. is no greater than that of many government departments, nor would its dispersion at various overseas centres (particularly the large Geneva office) create any particular administrative difficulties. Such administrative difficulties as the U.N. presents—and they are real ones— proceed much more from the circumstances of its creation and its character as an international organization. The Secretariat had to be fashioned, in 1945 and 1946, out of nothing, at a time when in every country the demand for competent administrators vastly exceeded the supply. Necessity, zeal, and hustle combined to foster a recruitment rate so rapid that some quality was inevitably sacrificed to quantity. Simultaneously there was fastened on the Organization an American system of narrow job specification which led to appointments being made in relation to narrow (and sometimes bogus) specialisms and discouraged the recruitment of all-round administrators. Although the drawbacks of this were not quite as severely felt in the U.N. itself as in some of the specialized agencies, they were harmful enough to give the U.N. bureaucracy a bad name by comparison with that of the League. To correct these initial disabilities took time and the task was considerably aggravated by the battering of staff morale under the McCarthyite pressures of 1950–3. By now, however, it would be true to say that the most serious consequences of these early errors have been removed by reformed administrative procedures and the effluxion of time. The U.N. bureaucracy certainly remains capable of further improvement; administrative standards have always come lower in the scale of U.N. values than the duties of the Secretariat warrant. The Secretariat probably embraces a wider range of quality than any other bureaucracy in the world, from incompetent passengers at one end of the scale to devoted diplomats and administrators of outstanding talents at the other. The staff's adaptability in the face of sudden challenges, like the mounting of the Congo operation in 1960, strikingly demonstrates its potentialities. Unfortunately, at its upper levels the Secretariat has relied disproportionately upon a limited number of outstanding individuals recruited at its inception. As the first generation of U.N. civil servants retires one is conscious of certain vacuums of responsibility and competence, because neither promotion nor recruitment has so far made good the exceptional talent which is being lost.

Article 101 of the Charter stipulates:

The paramount consideration in the employment of the staff and in the determination of the conditions of service shall be the necessity of securing the highest standards of efficiency, competence, and integrity. Due regard shall be paid to the importance of recruiting the staff on as wide a geographical basis as possible.

The wording of the Article glosses over what can obviously be a serious clash in the principles governing recruitment of officials—merit versus geography. Some easement has been provided by acceptance of the principle that clerical and secretarial staffs are recruited, wherever possible, on the spot and language posts filled on the basis of technical qualifications. This leaves open for international recruitment the equivalent of the administrative and executive classes of the British civil service—something over

3,500 posts. As some protection against the pressures which bear in on him for jobs the Secretary-General has been guided by a formula which distributes posts roughly in accordance with states' contributions to the U.N. budget—with a permitted latitude of 25 per cent. each way, save that the largest contributors cannot rise above their precise percentage nor the smallest ones be denied the one representative to which their fractional contribution would scarcely entitle them. Sometimes the result of this has been the inclusion of persons who cannot pull their weight and for whom positions must be found in which they can coast along, with the minimum of drag on the team. Fortunately, attempts to extend the principle of the geographic share-out to promotion as well as recruitment have been resisted; this would obviously spell death to the whole idea of a truly international civil service, and riddle it with national politics, besides being ruinous to staff morale. This does not mean that all officials should necessarily have life tenure; indeed, though the majority ought always to serve on this basis, it may be desirable, partly to avoid blockage of promotion in a small and slowly expanding service, that a proportion of posts should be filled by short-term contracts. This the U.N. certainly does and by so doing is often able to attract able men who could not come on a permanent basis—and so, incidentally, to secure such regional or national representation as may be desired in a certain context at a certain time. For though 'mere' geography is a harmful criterion, an international civil service cannot and should not be indifferent to considerations of nationality. The U.N. official has, after all, to be two men, the dedicated international servant thinking only of the interests of the Organization and the citizen of his homeland able to contribute distinctive national skills, experience—and connexions, for it is through member governments that the U.N. must work and one of the most important functions of an official may be to act as liaison and interpreter with his native country. The *déraciné* international man (by which, of course, I do not mean the refugee or the expellee) is very little use in any secretariat and the international civil servant must indeed learn to recognize as one of the hazards of his occupation that moral rootlessness which may come from being cut off from an organic society. From this point of view the location of U.N. Head-quarters in New York, a city famous for its comprehensiveness and conspicuous for its capacity to involve even the stranger in its strenuous crusadings, may well have advantages which out-weigh certain obvious drawbacks.

In treating of these intangibles we have begun to touch on the sixth and last function of the U.N. official, the diplomatic or the political. The civil servant in every democracy must, of course, be something of a politician—he must persuade, nego-tiate, debate, gauge the movement of opinion, sense pressures before they become explosions. But he need do this only at one remove; his minister, the politician *pur sang*, is in the front line. The U.N. civil servant not only works in a demo-cracy where minorities may refuse to accept majority decisions; unlike his national counterpart he has no minister to act as his front line—or else, what is worse, he has a hundred ministers competing to instruct and order him about. This last may easily result in a vacuum of decision which, if the purposes of the Organization are to be realized, the official may have to fill himself, by practising that most delicate of arts, making policy without appearing to do so. Of course there will be levels and hideaways in the Secretariat where the winds of international politics will hardly be felt to blow, but for most of its thousand-odd administrators the complex politics of a hundred inter-locking states are, in greater or lesser degree, both the context and the content of their labours. It is the Secretary-General himself, of course, for whom this holds most completely, but there is a sense in which, for this purpose, the rest of the Secre-tariat are just his emanation, as the officials of a Whitehall department are all just emanations of the Minister, and they will each, at one time or another, find themselves in situations where he speaks through them.

The office of Secretary-General dates back, of course, to League days. The Covenant left his role obscure, but Sir Eric Drummond, the first incumbent, had a crystal-clear conception of what it ought to be. He was a British civil servant with a

Foreign Office background, clear in his mind that he should interfere only when his advice was sought or in defence of the principles of the Covenant. (As a result his advice was increasingly sought.) As an administrator, he was bold. He made his Secretariat truly international, he kept it efficient and small, and he made the minimum of concessions to the pressure groups of Geneva. He was an energetic diplomat, but always behind the scenes. He never addressed the Assembly, only addressed the Council in public session as a secretary of a committee, and his annual reports were always models of factual statement.

For the U.N. an office on altogether broader lines was envisaged from the start. Roosevelt wanted it to be filled by someone called the 'World's Moderator', and although the modest Geneva title was wisely retained, the new Secretary-General emerged with significantly greater powers and responsibilities than his predecessor. In addition to being (Article 97) 'the chief administrative officer of the Organization', he is endowed, by Article 99, with a specifically political role:

The Secretary-General may bring to the attention of the Security Council any matter which in his opinion may threaten the maintenance of international peace and security.

i.e. in matters of the highest importance for the U.N. the Secretary-General is given a status equivalent to that of a member state and enjoys, as the Report of the Preparatory Commission in 1945 put it, 'a quite special right which goes beyond any power previously accorded to the head of an international organization'. In fact he is made a kind of conscience for the world; to quote the Report again, 'The Secretary-General more than anyone else will stand for the U.N. as a whole. In the eyes of the world, no less than in the eyes of his own staff, he must embody the principles and ideals of the Charter.'

That Article 99 provides for interventions only in the Security Council is largely explicable by the founders' expectation that it would be that organ which would handle the life and death matters of U.N. business. Less urgent and less crucial topics could be raised before the General Assembly through the provision of Article 98 that 'The Secretary-General shall make an annual report to the General Assembly on the work of the Organization'. In fact not only has the annual report been used by the Secretary-General to make the widest possible range of recommendations to the Assembly, but he has also acquired, by the Assembly's Rules of Procedure, the right to put an item on the Assembly's draft agenda and, since 1947, the right 'at any time [to] make either oral or written statements to the General Assembly concerning any question under consideration by it'. In short, the Secretary-General has acquired almost the same political powers *vis-à-vis* the General Assembly as those which the Charter gave him in respect of the Security Council.

Article 99, in its precise and full meaning, was never explicitly invoked by a Secretary-General until the Congo crisis of 1960 (though Mr. Trygve Lie subsequently described himself as having invoked it in the Korean crisis of 1950 and Mr. Hammarskjöld announced that he would have used it in the Suez crisis of 1956 had the U.S.A. not taken the necessary initiative). What, however, has repeatedly happened—so characteristic of the U.N.'s treatment of its Charter—is that it has been interpreted as providing the Secretary-General with a reservoir of political authority on which he can draw or not as his judgement, courage, and patience may suggest. Over the years a body of precedents, some good, some not so good, have been accumulated to guide the Secretary-General in the use of this power, each successful employment facilitating the next—and vice versa.

Mr. Lie, it seems now to be agreed, used his political powers with more exuberance than discretion. In the first months of the Security Council's life he advocated (unsuccessfully) the dropping of the Iranian question from the Council's agenda after Soviet troops had left the country. He was active in support of partition for Palestine in 1947 and of action to stop Arab intervention in 1948. He publicly advocated the seating of the Chinese Communist representative in 1950 and soon afterwards toured the major capitals to gain support for his much-publicized 'ten-point' peace plan. Finally, in the same year he took a clear and strong line over Korea. Though it was American initiative which summoned the Security Council emergency meeting of 25 June, it was Mr. Lie who first took the floor to label the North Koreans as aggressors, to certify that their action was 'a threat to the international peace', and to insist that the Security Council was both competent and obliged to act to restore peace in the area. This done, he aligned himself consistently with the policy of resistance to aggression which the Organization then adopted under the leadership of the United States. His reward for this final stand was, as we have seen (pp. 55–57, Chapter 3), the implacable hostility of the Soviet bloc. This had the effect, quite irrespective of the propriety of his stand, of impairing his usefulness as Secretary-General once the task of peacemaking again took priority in U.N. councils. No Secretary-General, placed in such a situation, could have escaped such a fate. The nature of the office presupposes that its incumbent will be able to serve both the Charter and the membership. If the action of one or more of the members violates the Charter, the Secretary-General's duty is clear, but when the time comes, as it must, for healing the breach (unless there is to be world war *à outrance*), the Secretary-General's partiality, though it be the partiality of righteousness, is likely to be an offence in the nostrils of the returned prodigal.

Mr. Lie's successor was initially more fortunate. He was also more wise. He rightly conceived it as his primary duty in the years immediately following his election to re-establish confidence in his office—internally, by restoring the standards and morale of the Secretariat by guaranteeing to it a security against national and political pressure which Mr. Lie had notably failed to provide in the dark days of 1952; externally, by abstaining from premature initiatives and presenting himself as the apostle of 'quiet diplomacy'. In this he was assisted by his earlier training and background as a civil servant rather than, like Lie, as a politician. An economist by trade, Dag Hammarskjöld had served as under-secretary in the department of finance in Sweden before becoming chairman of the Swedish National Bank and subsequently Director-General of the Swedish Foreign Ministry. His brief period as minister without portfolio in a Social Democratic administration did not affect this tradition of nonpartisanship, since he was not a member of the party and never campaigned for any elective office. With this propitious background Hammarskjöld also enjoyed the good fortune of a couple of initial years at the U.N. free from major East–West clashes. Thus he was able to build up a store of confidence from both sides before circumstances forced on him a more active role.

Hammarskjöld's first venture into public diplomacy was, characteristically, in response to a request from the General Assembly in December 1954 that he seek the release from China of fifteen imprisoned United States airmen. Equally characteristically, practically nothing was made public about the processes of the mission, but in August 1955 the airmen were released. After this success an ever-increasing reliance came to be placed on the Secretary-General's diplomatic capacity. With the aggravation in 1956 of the Middle East disorders, Hammarskjöld became the active instrument of an almost continuous U.N. concern with that area and of course with the disputes between East and West which the Middle East crises stimulated. As subtle in his processes as his predecessor was crude, Hammarskjöld made it a settled principle of conduct that wherever possible he should have authorization in a decision of the Assembly or the Security Council for any action undertaken by him, while at the same time couching his drafts and his public pronouncements in language whose sibyllic ambiguity both did justice to the complexity of the many-faceted interests he served and incidentally enhanced his own freedom of action.

Thus, when in November 1956 the General Assembly had to cope with a situation in which two pillars of the Organization, Britain and France, had taken the law into their own hands and by their vetoes blocked any remedial action by the Security Council, it was on the Secretary-General that its action pivoted. A proper understanding of his role can only be obtained by seeing it in the context of events, which reveal how his initiative, as well as his negotiating skill and administrative efficiency, were vital to the functioning of the Organization in this crisis. He was indispensable to the Assembly and the Assembly, recognizing this, delegated authority to him on a scale which matched his burdens. The situation confronting him was one of peculiar danger and delicacy. Not only were two Great Powers (and one minor one, Israel) at odds with the Organization; a third permanent member of the Security Council, the U.S.S.R., also appeared to be more interested in fomenting dissension than in effecting pacification; finally a large range of the membership, from the Arab League outwards, was in a state of hyper-sensitiveness and quivering apprehension at what they regarded as 'a revival of colonialism'. A U.N. force was needed, to get Britain and France 'off the hook' on which their ill-judged venture had landed them, to deprive the U.S.S.R. of any grounds for military intervention, and to keep Egypt and Israel away from each other's throats. Yet such a body was without precedent; in Soviet eyes it was even illegal; in Egyptian and Israeli eyes it could easily arouse the hostility which both bruiser and bruised feel for the man who stops the fight. Above all, to serve its purpose, it had to be created quickly.

It was in the small hours of the night of 1-2 November that Mr. Lester Pearson, head of the Canadian delegation, first aired the UNEF idea to an exhausted General Assembly and secured the encouragement of the U.S.A. in the person of Mr. Dulles. By midday on 2 November a threefold consultation between Mr. Pearson, the Secretary-General, and his Executive Assistant, Mr. Cordier, had hammered out the broad principles of a force which might be both practicable and legal within the terms of the Charter. Late on 3-4 November the Assembly passed the necessary resolution, 57-0, but the abstention of Egypt and the whole Soviet bloc was disquieting. The resolution asked the Secretary-General to produce within forty-eight hours a plan for UNEF.

Early on 4 November Hammarskjöld invited the representatives of Canada, Norway, Colombia, and India to an informal planning meeting. They saw eye to eye on the establishment of a 'United Nations Command' to be headed by the Canadian Major-General E. L. M. Burns, the U.N. official who was then Chief of Staff of the Truce Supervision Organization in Palestine; initially he would draw a limited number of officers from the Supervision Organization and would then, in consultation with the Secretary-General, recruit personnel from member states who were not permanent members of the Security Council. This first plan was presented to the Assembly that same night and was passed by the same vote, 57-0, as the previous resolution. (The following day, however, Egypt announced her 'acceptance' of the resolution.) The resolution concluded by inviting the Secretary-General to take 'such administrative measures as may be necessary'. These were quickly put into operation. Burns was mobilized. Dr. Ralph Bunche, the Under-Secretary whose experience as U.N. Mediator in Palestine had already made him a veteran of Middle East crises, was appointed to receive and coordinate the offers of troops for UNEF which immediately began to flow in. Handling these was not the least delicate of the diplomatic tasks laid on the Secretariat. Twenty-four countries volunteered, but obviously only certain countries could meet all the criteria that the tricky situation imposed. Both the selection of these (ten were accepted) and the rejection of the rest called for discrimination and a sensitive treatment of national susceptibilities.

Little more than twenty-four hours later Hammarskjöld's second report was ready. It was presented to the Assembly in the early hours of 6 November. It contained a set of far-reaching principles such as, in constitutional theory, the Assembly itself might have been expected to lay down; in fact, for the Assembly to have argued its way through to a consensus of this kind would have taken days that could not be spared and engendered so much ill feeling as to be self-defeating. As it was, presented by the Secretary-General, they were accepted with astonishingly little demur by a vote of 64-0 within twenty-four hours. The main points of political principle were that UNEF should not be used as a means of exerting pressure on Egypt; it should enter Egyptian territory only with Egyptian consent; it should have no military objective or functions but would be, in effect, a buffer force. To meet the costs of the Force, Hammarskjöld suggested that each of the ten component countries should pay for equipment and salaries and that the other costs should be met by the U.N. through a special levy on all members. Finally, Hammarskjöld suggested the appointment by the Assembly of a small committee which should serve as an Advisory Committee to him throughout the whole operation.

The Assembly's 7 November resolution concluded, like its earlier ones, with a sweeping delegation of power to the Secretary-General 'to issue all regulations and instructions which may be essential to the effective functioning of the Force, following consultation with the Advisory Committee . . . and to take all necessary administrative and executive action'.

The application of the resolution proved far from simple. It involved Hammarskjöld in a visit to Cairo and much delicate negotiation before the way was clear for Egyptian acceptance of the Force. *In toto* it constituted a remarkable demonstration of his new legal *persona*; the Assembly's continuing use of his services 'to report compliance' with its resolutions about Anglo-French–Israeli troop withdrawals constituted a singularly effective combination of political pressure and negotiating efforts. Throughout, the Assembly showed striking confidence in the Secretary-General; at the height of the crisis a fortnight elapsed, between 10 November and 23 November, without the Assembly's giving any collective consideration to the Suez problem. In operating on so long a leash the Secretary-General was undoubtedly assisted by the existence of the Advisory Committee set up on 7 November. It consisted of seven members, the original four whom Hammarskjöld had called in to informal consultation on 4 November, plus Brazil, Ceylon and Pakistan—i.e. no permanent members of the Security Council and no Western Europeans. Its meetings were then—and have since remained—informal and private. English served as a lingua franca, dispensing with the clumsy apparatus of interpretation; stenographic records were kept where needed but the committee was free to go off the record. It did not seek to take votes, but to arrive at a sense of the meeting. Similarly, it did not present its conclusions as such to the Assembly (though the Secretary-General incorporated them in his reports), nor did it father collective draft resolutions. What it did was to protect the Secretary-General from the risks and temptations of solitary responsibility, to provide a middle term between his isolation and the Assembly's Babel, and, for an executive who is not an executive, and a legislature which is not a legislature, to discharge some of the services of a cabinet, without being one. It was, in fact, *sui generis* in an institution which is *sui generis*.

The credit which was generally judged to have accrued to the Secretary-General for his handling of the 1956 crises undoubtedly strengthened his position and emboldened him to accept a more positive and public political role than his previous emphasis on 'quiet diplomacy' might suggest. Within twelve months of his having to act against the policies of three permanent members of the Security Council he was being elected unanimously to a second five-year term of office. In his 'acceptance speech' Dag Hammarskjöld told the General Assembly that he believed it 'to be his duty to use his office and, indeed, the machinery of the Organization to its utmost capacity and to the full extent permitted at each stage by practical circumstances', and warned it that though he thought he ought if possible always to be 'instructed' he also believed that the Charter authorized him to act without guidance, 'should this appear to him necessary in order to help in filling any vacuum that may appear in the systems which the Charter and traditional diplomacy provide'. Dag Hammarskjöld's restraint and intelligence were a guarantee that this was not intended to be taken as a self-written authorization of indiscriminate intervention. At the same time it served notice on the great disputants, from an unusually exalted, if frail, position, that if they did not live by the Charter he might feel it his duty to draw the world's attention to the fact. Thus in July 1958, when the Security Council was deadlocked over the crisis in Lebanon and Jordan, Hammarskjöld intervened to say that despite the Council's failure to act, the U.N.'s responsibility remained and he proposed to act in the capacity set out in his 'acceptance speech' and strengthen the U.N. observer group in Lebanon, although the U.S.S.R. had just vetoed a Japanese proposal to that effect. In the assumption of a more conventional but still highly personal responsibility, the Secretary-General took the lead when the continuing dispute was transferred to the emergency Assembly, and set forth at its opening session the plan which subsequently won the Assembly's unanimous approval; in the form eventually adopted, the Assembly's resolution requested the Secretary-General to make 'such practical arrangements as would adequately help in upholding the purposes and principles of the Charter . . . and thereby facilitate the early withdrawal of foreign troops'.

A year later, in September 1959, when Laos alleged that foreign troops had infringed her border, it was the Secretary-General who drew the attention of the Security Council to it. When, in defiance of a Soviet veto (see p. 97), a Security Council sub-committee visited Laos and reported somewhat indeterminedly on the situation, it was the Secretary-General himself who perpetuated the U.N. 'presence' there, first by a personal visit despite Soviet disapproval and later by leaving behind Mr. Tuomioja, executive secretary of ECE. Mr. Tuomioja remained ostensibly in a technical aid capacity, but in fact he was also an advertisement of U.N. concern for the integrity of the country and an observation post for the Organization.

Increasingly as 1960 approached Hammarskjöld interested himself in and directed members' attention to the increased responsibilities which the U.N. would have to assume in Africa. He was thus not unprepared when the Congo troubles burst about his head; in addition, he had at his disposal a substantial fund of trust and goodwill on the part of the U.N.'s African members. He, more than anyone else, recognized the dangerous potentialities for the entire world of a Congo debacle and of an ensuing power scramble in the heart of Africa. This led him to assert and maintain from first to last a responsibility for U.N. action whatever the difficulties or hazards existing either in New York or in the Congo itself. As he himself said, 'the Congo crisis . . . put the Secretariat under the heaviest strain which it has ever had to face'. But on no one was the strain as heavy as on the Secretary-General, who had to operate simultaneously in administrative, military, diplomatic and political capacities.

At the outset the initiative was his. It was he who requested the 13 July meeting of the Security Council, for the first time invoking explicitly and to the full his powers under Article 99.

He himself recommended the creation of what came to be known for convenience as ONUC (from the French title, 'Organisation des Nations Unies au Congo') and it was he who proposed that it should consist predominantly of troops from African states and should not contain any from the forces of the permanent members of the Security Council. Equally explicitly he identified the presence of Belgian troops as a 'source of tension' and recommended their withdrawal. Not only did the Security Council accept these views, either explicitly or implicitly; the resolution which it passed gave him, as at Suez, a wide, loosely-worded mandate—'to provide . . . such military assistance as may be necessary' and 'to report as appropriate'. As he himself said later, 'the only additional guidance was provided by a set of principles . . . which had been evolved during the experience of the United Nations Emergency Force' and which he had told the Security Council he would again adopt.

On this basis the Secretary-General acted with his customary decision and dispatch. Immediately after the Security Council meeting he sent off appeals to all African member states north of the Congo. The first to respond was Ghana. On 15 July General Alexander, the chief of Ghana's defence forces, arrived with four Ghanaian soldiers as the advance guard of the U.N. force. By 17 July about 3,500 troops had arrived from Tunis, Ghana, Morocco, and Ethiopia, aided by an airlift provided by Britain, the U.S.S.R. and the U.S. As Commander-in-Chief Hammarskjöld made one of his less successful appointments in General von Horn, who had had some U.N. experience in Palestine. Close on his heels came the Swedish battalion serving in UNEF, which was switched to the Congo to provide a valuable cadre of troops with U.N. experience. At the U.N. headquarters Brigadier Rikhye of India, a former chief of staff of UNEF, was appointed as the Secretary-General's military adviser.

Thus by 18 July a measure of calm and order had been restored to the Congolese capital and both the Congo government and the U.S.S.R. had been deprived of immediate justification for authorizing extra-U.N. intervention. As the U.N. forces multiplied they took over from the Belgians, who returned to their bases and evacuated Leopoldville by 23 July. By 28 July, the day the Secretary-General himself arrived in the Congo, ONUC had risen to 10,000 men, with Guinea, Liberia, and Ireland as additional contributing countries. However, the tardiness which the Belgians showed in effecting further withdrawals evoked fresh threats, notably from the U.S.S.R., to intervene independently as champions of Congo rights, and Hammarskjöld had to warn the Security Council on 8 August that 'peace or war—and not only in the Congo' were the alternatives confronting it if the Belgians did not withdraw. Reluctantly Belgium accepted the Security Council's ruling, but it was the end of August or later before the withdrawal was accomplished.

All this time Hammarskjöld continued to operate under his wide mandate of 13/14 July adapted only on 8 August by the additional explicit authorization to send ONUC into Katanga. This was granted on his own request and in relation to the problem of applying his own principle that ONUC could not take the initiative in the use of armed force.

In the initial stages of the Congo operation the Secretary-General did not seek the services, as over Suez, of an advisory committee—no doubt for the good reason that he was operating under the aegis of the Security Council and not of the General Assembly. However, before the crisis developed, when the Congo appeared likely to be merely a technical aid problem, he had initiated consultations with nine African states and he maintained informal contact with them in all the ensuing stages of the crisis. But when Lumumba pressed for a team of Afro-Asian observers who would oversee operations in the Congo and when in the Security Council meeting of 21 August the Soviet government supported this in terms clearly designed to curb the Secretary-General's authority, Hammarskjöld himself proposed an advisory committee of the Suez type. So a committee of fifteen was set up not by the Council but by Hammarskjöld himself, representing member states contributing units to ONUC, and including, besides Afro-Asians, representatives of Canada, Ireland, and Sweden. It was later expanded to nineteen, when Malaya, Nigeria, Ceylon, and Senegal also contributed forces to ONUC.

By this time the military force in ONUC had risen to 15,000 men. (At its peak it numbered almost 20,000.) This force had to control an area more than four times the size of France, with very inadequate communications and a virtual breakdown of an ordinary machinery of government. Its composition, dictated by ineluctable political considerations, meant that, even when assisted by technicians from more developed countries, it was still deficient in signalling and supply services. It lacked a common language and was scattered, in small units, over a great many posts. Few of the contingents had had any experience of the distinctive kind of policing operation which they were called upon to conduct. As the irrational passions of Congolese factional politics and lawlessness swirled around them, they found themselves in a series of situations which would have taxed the restraint and assurance of any normal army to breaking-point. Their assignment was one in which complete success was impossible and the slightest mistake might entail sweeping consequences. Repeatedly the Secretary-General's agents had to take decisions on the spot without any prior consultation which might have far-reaching consequences. Not the least of his difficulties was the maintenance of effective contact with a scattered team. He freely admitted that in these circumstances mistakes might have been made, but he never let any of his subordinates down and always insisted on shouldering full responsibility himself.

In addition to the military operation, the Secretariat had to conduct a civilian salvage operation which was almost more urgent and difficult. The Congo found itself, on the withdrawal of the Belgians, with virtually none of the indispensable administrative apparatus of a modern state. There were less than a score of university graduates of any kind and hardly any competent technicians; there was a breakdown in food distribution, and serious threats to water supply and sanitation. To meet these problems the U.N. had to assemble its own teams of technical and administrative experts and become responsible, in the midst of an anarchy which it had no authority forcibly to control, for getting the economy and the administration going again.

A Swedish business man, Dr. Sture Linner, was put in local

control of these operations, first under Dr. Bunche and then as Chief of U.N. Civilian Operations in the Congo—opposite number to General von Horn. The immediate task of reopening the vital, silted port of Matadi was entrusted to General Wheeler, the American veteran of the Suez Canal clearance. All the specialized agencies were invoked: the WHO, in collaboration with the Red Cross, to avert plagues and restore essential health services, the ICAO to organize the essential air transport, the ITU to get radio and telephones going again, the WMO to provide necessary weather forecasting. When a breathing-space had been obtained and essential services were provided again, other problems had to be faced—the collapse of the finances, of the judiciary, of even the legal system. A training programme in the main essential skills and an emergency public works pro-gramme to cope with rising unemployment were put in hand. As months succeeded weeks and as the first year of the whole Congo operation was succeeded by the next the needs increased rather than diminished. The total international civilian team grew at one point to over 500 officials from almost 30 nations, as well as over 500 secondary school teachers.

In doing all this the Organization, as its critics were quick to point out, was taking on a task for which it had never been intended and for which it was very inadequately equipped. But the task was none of its seeking; it had fallen into its lap. The Congo was not, in the first instance, a problem for the inter-national lawyer or for the expert in public administration. It was a critical situation, a crying need. Someone had to respond to it and if the U.N. failed to do so interested parties, in the crudest sense of 'interested', from East and West, would turn it into a battleground.

It was his insistence upon this fact and upon the obligations it imposed that brought the Secretary-General into frequent dis-agreement with the colonial powers, including Britain, who at various times resented his espousal of the Congo cause. Belgium and France in particular refused to accept the dilemma which he posed, while from one Great Power he very soon encountered the most determined opposition. The U.S.S.R.'s designs of gaining a foothold in central Africa were so directly thwarted by his policy that open hostility was inevitable. The Congo soon became Dag Hammarskjöld's Korea.

In the very first Security Council meeting the Soviet delegate accused Dr. Bunche of being utilized by the U.S.A. to further Western intervention. A week later he attacked the Secretary-General for his use of 'units from European and American nations' in ONUC. By the first week in August Hammarskjöld was becoming the target of a Soviet press campaign, in which he was accused of being 'pro-American' and 'perfidious' and of 'capitulating before the colonizers'. At the Security Council on 8 August he was criticized for refusing to send U.N. forces into Katanga. On 22 August the U.S.S.R. tried to impose on him an all-African committee to which he would have to report daily; its failure to carry this in the Security Council was however more than compensated for by the Soviet success in supplying its own 'aid' with the connivance of the Lumumba government. Simultaneously came Lumumba's demand that the U.N. withdraw and Hammarskjöld's request for a further 'clarification' of his mandate and a prohibition of 'outside intervention'. The U.S.S.R. endorsed Lumumba's demand and its attacks on Hammarskjöld quickly mounted to a climax when Mr. Khrushchev in the General Assembly on 23 September accused Hammarskjöld of abusing his position, demanded his resignation, and urged the appointment of a three-man directorate in the Secretary-General's place.

This was an even more serious challenge to the U.N. than the attacks which nine years before Russia had launched at Trygve Lie. Now as then it was aimed at a man whose devotion to the Charter had made him anathema to a Great Power. But it was more than this. As Dag Hammarskjöld said in his reply, 'This is a question not of a man but of an institution . . . I would rather see that office [the Secretary-Generalship] break on strict adherence to the principle of independence, impartiality, and objectivity than drift on the basis of compromise.' The 'troika' proposal, as it soon came to be known, would substitute for an independent, international Secretary-General a triumvirate each of whom would owe loyalty to the bloc that elected him. It would make hay of Articles 99 and 100 and would rob the U.N. of its most distinctive, dynamic, and creative organ, reducing the Secretariat to the level of a service agency for a conference organization.

From this time onwards, the conduct of the Congo operation became inextricably bound up with the future of the Secretary-Generalship. Replying to Mr. Khrushchev's further attack on 2 October, Dag Hammarskjöld made it clear where he looked for support. 'By resigning I would . . . throw the Organization to the winds. . . . It is not the Soviet Union or indeed any other big powers who need the U.N. for their protection; it is all the others . . . I shall remain in my post in the interest of all those other nations, as long as they wish me to do so.' In general 'those others' amply endorsed his stand, but the Congo 'snake-pit', as it was not undeservedly called, continued to present the Organization with problems which in any final sense were insoluble; in particular it obliged the Secretary-General to make invidious choices about how ONUC should behave and whom it should support. The African states themselves lost their solidarity in face of the competing appeals of Congolese factions. In consequence, for the first time, on 16 December, the General Assembly, no less than the Security Council, became deadlocked in face of the Secretary-General's appeal for a wider and more explicit mandate. As far as the deliberative organs of the U.N. were concerned this was the low point of the Congo operation. Fortunately for the Organization, Dag Hammarskjöld responded to the challenge by a quiet reaffirmation of his powers and obligations which is entitled to be regarded as perhaps the supreme assertion of the potencies of the Secretary-General's office: 'Naturally', he said, 'the operation will be continued under the previous decisions of the Assembly and the Security Council . . . with an adjustment—to the best of our understanding—of the implementation of our mandate to the needs and with aims . . . common, at least to the vast majority of member states.'

The death of Lumumba exposed Hammarskjöld to fresh Soviet attacks. They refused to have any further dealings with him and in a draft resolution presented to the Security Council on 15 February 1961 they demanded the discontinuance of the Congo operation within a month and Hammarskjöld's dismissal 'from the post of Secretary-General . . . as a participant in and organizer of the violence committed against the leading statesmen of the Republic of the Congo'. They were decisively defeated (8 to 1) on this and on 21 February Hammarskjöld secured some of the authority necessary to 'reorganize' the Congo national army and to 'take immediately all appropriate measures to prevent the occurrence of civil war in the Congo, including . . . the use of force, if necessary, in the last resort'—an unprecedented licence to interfere in internal affairs. When the General Assembly debated the Congo in the spring, and Hammarskjöld announced on 5 April that it could consider that it had before it his 'standing offer of resignation', the Assembly gave tangible evidence of its basic confidence in the Secretary-General's course by appropriating $100 million dollars to finance the Congo operation until the following October. Gradually the situation in the Congo relaxed and in July a nearly all-faction meeting of the Congolese parliament was held under U.N. protection and established an 'all-Congo' government under Mr. Adoula. But Katanga refused to be 'integrated' and persisted in the use of white mercenaries; the U.N. forces then executed a virtual *coup d'état*, taking over the province to enforce the removal of foreign troops and to protect themselves from repeated attacks. Though almost certainly legal under the resolution of 21 February, the action, which involved heavy casualties and ended in a setback for U.N. forces, was open to criticism and certainly received it. Whether or not local officials had acted on their own initiative and blundered, the Secretary-General did not say. But he flew out to Africa immediately to take personal control. On the night of 17–18 September, when he was *en route* to meet Mr. Tshombe, the President of Katanga, for talks on a cease-fire, his plane crashed ten miles outside Ndola airport. Dag Hammarskjöld and all the other occupants were killed.

The crisis which Hammarskjöld's death precipitated for the Secretary-Generalship and for the whole Organization cast into the shade even the problems of the Congo operation. For almost six weeks the U.S.S.R. held out against the appointment of a successor to fill out his unexpired term. It was comparatively easy to get agreement on a generally acceptable individual; he was found in U Thant, the chief delegate of Burma to the U.N. The dissension was over his powers and status. The Soviets pressed several variants of the 'troika' scheme, designed to win support amongst the Afro-Asians. The essence of all the schemes was the same: to surround the Secretary-General with Assistant Secretaries whom he would have to consult and who would be chosen by the principal voting blocs of the U.N. Fortunately the Afro-Asians were not seduced. The U.S.A. stood firm and at last the Soviets gave way. On 3 November 1961 U Thant was unanimously elected Acting Secretary-General without any commitments other than that he should consult with his Under-Secretaries 'in a spirit of mutual understanding'.

Immediately U Thant found himself plunged into a Congo crisis worse than that which had confronted his predecessor. The cease-fire negotiated with Mr. Tshombe did not last. Violence broke out in Elizabethville, reducing the U.N. forces to a condition of harassment and impotence. The Security Council, by nine votes to none (Britain and France abstaining), on 24 November authorized the Secretary-General to use force to complete the removal of mercenaries. His authority strengthened by this, U Thant ordered vigorous action to 're-establish law and order and to protect life and property' as well as to obtain 'complete freedom of movement' for U.N. forces. On 5 December the U.N. forces attacked and by the 18th resistance virtually ended. A certain sense of shock ran through many Western supporters of the U.N. at the spectacle of a U.N. army actually fighting, complete with armour and air strikes (Swedish jet fighters were employed). Britain and France, critical and sceptical, urged a cease-fire, but the U.S.A. gave unswerving support to an operation which, if ONUC was to serve any purpose at all, was surely unavoidable. U Thant emphasized, with justice, to his critics the strictly limited and basically defensive character of the operation, both permitted and necessitated by ONUC's need to defend itself.

From the Russians an opposite criticism arose, that the U.N. had stopped military operations while leaving the mercenaries still in Katanga. But the meeting of the Security Council called to discuss this in effect accepted U Thant's contention that this problem could be resolved by peaceful means and adjourned without taking a decision. Throughout the next six months negotiations between Mr. Adoula and Mr. Tshombe continued inconclusively until in August 1962 U Thant himself proposed a 'plan of national reconstruction' providing for a federal constitution and a reconstruction of the central administration to provide representation for all groups.

Mr. Tshombe, however, revealed himself a master of delay and prevarication until in December the Secretary-General took the initiative of asking member states to bring economic pressure to bear on him. Before the efficacy of such measures could be tested a further breakdown of the always shaky relationships between ONUC and the Katangan forces occurred and once again, on Christmas Eve, ONUC had to assert itself in order to secure minimal freedom of movement. This time its action, largely conducted by Indian troops, was decisive. Resistance soon collapsed and on 13 January 1963 Mr. Tshombe announced the end of Katangan secession and his acceptance of the U Thant plan for the Congo. With this, organized resistance to ONUC, particularly of the kind which was assisted, openly or covertly, by foreign powers, ended throughout the Congo. However, indiscriminate disorder and bloodshed remained widespread pending the training of a Congolese national army and so, at the request both of the Congo and of most African states, ONUC remained in being. Its numbers, however, were reduced to 5,000 and a terminus was fixed for its stay, the end of June 1964. Its final withdrawal was due more to lack of funds than to a completion of its pacificatory task, but it was perhaps true that the time had also come when the Congo, willy-nilly, had to fend for itself.

The crisis in peace-keeping which was a backwash of the Congo operation was, particularly as far as the Russians were concerned, part of a sustained campaign to curb the initiatives and powers of the Secretary-General. The Russians objected not only to the General Assembly involving itself in what they contended was an exclusively Security Council area but also to the Secretary-General having any discretionary authority in this connexion at all. Partly in consequence of this the most striking demonstration of the Secretary-General's discretionary powers in the remainder of the sixties was a negative one, the withdrawal of UNEF in 1967.

The Egyptians, impatient to launch their blockade of Aqaba, tried initially to secure withdrawal by local pressure upon General Rikhye, the Commander of UNEF. He insisted that he took his orders exclusively from the Secretary-General and two days later the Egyptians presented a formal request to the Secretary-General himself. They rested their case, of course, on the indisputable clause in the initial agreement between Hammarskjöld and President Nasser providing that UNEF should enter Egypt only with Egypt's consent. So when Egypt demanded removal she was within her rights.

But was it for the Secretary-General to grant her request? There were those who insisted that the Assembly (then sitting in special session on the question of South West Africa) should have been consulted. The Advisory Committee (see pp. 182–3) was consulted and informed of the Secretary-General's intention to accede to Egypt's request; it gave him divided advice. But India and Yugoslavia, two of the largest contributors to UNEF, favoured withdrawal. Within the day the Secretary-General gave orders for withdrawal. He was, most authorities agree, entirely within his rights. If, as appears, the contributing states were anxious to escape being caught in Arab–Israeli hostilities, he was also probably left with little or no alternative. He *might* have finessed, brought it to the Assembly, attempted a Hammarskjöldian exercise in creating a new consensus or evolving a new formula. But for U Thant this would have been acting out of character. It would also have been flying in the face of the prevailing winds of U.N. opinion in the middle sixties, as well as against the whirlwind of Middle Eastern passions and prejudices.

The truth was, as the prolonged wrangle over the U.N.'s peacekeeping costs most clearly demonstrated, there was a deep-seated reluctance on the part of all the permanent members, in varying degrees, to allow a reassertion of the wide discretionary powers which Hammarskjöld had enjoyed in 1956–7 and 1960–1. First U Thant and then Kurt Waldheim had to preside over an Organization kept in tight leading strings by its financial difficulties and the inability to formulate any agreed principles of peacekeeping. In such circumstances the only possible policy for any Secretary-General was, while keeping the Hammarskjöldian precedents intact, to be circumspect in his political initiatives. Yet the basic soundness of these precedents was repeatedly demonstrated by the U.N.'s inability, despite the reluctance of its members, to get along without its peacekeeping capacities. For ten years, by six-monthly renewals, UNFICYP kept the peace in Cyprus. In the Middle East the Arab–Israeli war of 1973 which was the predictable consequence of the collapse of UNEF in the hostilities of 1967 led, equally predictably, to the re-establishment of UNEF in the autumn of 1973. With minor modifications it was the 1956–7 model that was revived. The U.S.A. and the U.S.S.R. found that the only mutually acceptable instrument to cope with a conflict which neither wished to see escalate was a force, not supplied by themselves as Egypt originally requested, but one supplied by the U.N. from which the two rivals were excluded. The Secretary-General, in response to the Security Council's resolution of 25 October, came up with a plan which the Council approved on the 27th and which led by 1 November to the deployment on the Sinai front of over 800 troops flown in from UNFICYP. By the end of November their numbers had risen to 3,000 and by the end of January they had reached their target strength of 7,000.

UNEF Model Two reflects a certain tightening of the members' control over the Secretary-General. The force was to be 'under the command of the U.N. vested in the Secretary-General, under the authority of the Security Council'. The commander in the field was to be appointed 'by the Secretary-General with the consent of the Security Council'. But he was 'responsible to the Secretary-General'. (He was in fact General Siilasvuo of Finland, already familiar and acceptable as the head of UNTSO, which had remained in being even when UNEF collapsed.) The Secretary-General was to 'keep the Council fully informed of developments regarding the force and all matters which may affect its nature or effective functioning are to be referred by him to the Council for its decision'. Nor had he a free discretion over the force's composition; contingents must be selected 'in consultation with the Security Council' '. . . bearing in mind the accepted principle of equitable geographic representation'—which in particular meant the first representation of the East European bloc, achieved by the inclusion of a Polish contingent.

Yet despite these repeated reminders of the Council's authority what was most striking was the dependence, in the last resort, of the membership upon the enterprise and diplomatic skills of the Secretary-General. Even the financing of the force did not prove an insuperable obstacle, when it came to the point. The Council accepted that the expenses of the operation were a legitimate charge on the membership and the Assembly devised an apportionment which laid almost two-thirds of the burden on the Big Five and one-third on the other developed states, leaving the rest virtually unscathed. Experience suggested that there would still be haggling and arrears and that the Secretary-General would not escape in this connection any more than in any other the dual fate of being the world's mendicant as well as its fireman. But of his continued indispensability there could be no doubt.

8 · THE U.N. AND ITS MEMBERS

THE portrait of the U.N. which we have so far been presenting has been drawn, as it were, from within. Our study of its character and behaviour has been conducted, so far as possible, from the point of view of the Organization itself, examining how the Charter has worked in practice and how the institutions created by it have responded to the demands made upon them. But since the U.N. is an association of states this can never give us the whole picture. The U.N. is never, so to say, merely what it is in itself; it is also what member states think it is. Its full understanding requires an awareness of the attitudes of at least some of the states towards the Organization they have combined to create and maintain.

For most purposes it is through the so-called 'permanent delegations' that member states have contact with the Organization. The permanent delegation had already established itself to some extent as a feature of international life under the League, but the greater size, complexity, and continuity of U.N. operations have induced governments to establish larger and on the whole more impressively staffed embassies at New York than Geneva ever knew. In this matter the pace was set by the host country. Although with its capital only a few hours' train ride distant it might have been thought to need a U.N. embassy least of all, the U.S.A. not only maintains the largest delegation, between 100 and 200, or even more, according to whether the Assembly is in session or not; its mission's status is also symbolized by the fact that many of its heads of mission, such as Mr. Adlai Stevenson and Mr. Arthur Goldberg, have been not only eminent in their own right, but have also enjoyed membership of the President's Cabinet. No other country maintains such state, but especially at Assembly times almost all permanent delegations will be of the scale and importance of embassies at major capitals and will be headed by senior diplomats of distinction. Thus in the *cursus honorum* of the British Foreign Service the U.N. mission would rank amongst the half-dozen top overseas postings, even when it is not headed, as under the Labour governments of 1964–70, by a Minister of State, Lord Caradon.

Over and above the regular staff of the delegations, most states mobilize a special team to represent them during Assembly sessions. More and more often Foreign Ministers attend—at least for the first few days—just as they do for important meetings of the Security Council. States have also developed the habit of using their Assembly delegation as a kind of animated advertisement of the national genius. The U.S.A. will generally find room for someone with a reputation outside the narrowly political field; if they find someone who, like Miss Marion Anderson in 1958, is both feminine and coloured, so much the better; international respect for two powerful interest groups is thus demonstrated in one and the same person. The French have often included a coloured colonial administrator, like M. Houphouet-Boigny, the Indians an eminent Jesuit, like the Revd. J. D'Souza, and most countries, including the United Kingdom, make a steady practice of including a representative women's leader. Membership of a delegation can also be used to educate opinion at home; the frequent practice of including M.P.s, or their equivalent, from both government and opposition parties, has the effect of mobilizing support for a government's U.N. policies and may also, one hopes, help to spread understanding of U.N. problems and processes. This can be particularly important in a country like the U.S.A., where the separation of powers may impede congressional co-operation in foreign affairs. The so-called 'alumni club' in Congress, of representatives and senators with experience on the U.N. delegation, has exercised a valuable educative function amongst the membership of both parties.

In addition to its expert advisers in all the main fields of U.N. operations—political, economic, social, trusteeship, etc.—a fully equipped mission will have its regional experts who can maintain contact with other delegations, advise on the reactions of individual states and regional voting blocs; in short, act as the liaison men of the U.N.'s 'parliamentary diplomacy'. Perhaps the only mission with a staff large enough to provide continuous and complete liaison of this kind is the American, but within the limits of their resources all the larger powers will allocate staff for this purpose. The U.N. diplomatic world thus becomes a microcosm of a full foreign service, with national delegations taking the place of national governments and liaison men taking the place of ministers and ambassadors.

Inevitably, especially where smaller and poorer countries are concerned, the inflation of delegation staffs runs ahead of the production of brains, and many delegations, particularly on their economic and financial side, have a conspicuously weak tail. Though New York City no longer provides an environment of much attraction, the U.N. itself continues to enjoy a privileged and relatively insulated position, and none of the usual incentives to the full operation of Parkinson's Law is lacking. The result is not always beneficial to the U.N. itself. Delegation members with a vested interest in their jobs may be more concerned to expand or prolong some operation of the Organization than to bring it to a successful and brisk conclusion. Appointed as a channel between their home governments and the U.N., they may complicate communications by putting their own gloss on what passes. To a certain extent it is probably even true that the growth of the delegations has meant a 'down-grading' of the Secretariat; whereas in Geneva days it was accustomed to negotiate with member governments direct, it now almost invariably has to proceed through the New York missions. Yet this can work both ways: in each delegation the U.N. has a friend at court, an ambassador and staff whose concern it is to see that U.N. considerations are given their full weight in the shaping of their country's policy. In any case, of course, there can be no going back on the system; no member state could dispense with a permanent expert delegation and the U.N. itself would find existence intolerable if it had to be continually teaching its processes over again to a succession of visiting amateurs.

If it is true that there are as many U.N.'s as there are member states, since each has its own distinctive view of the Organization, yet there is one member state whose presence at the New York headquarters is so pervasive, so overpowering, as to make it appear at times as if its view of the Organization were the only one that mattered. There are moments when every observer is bound to ask himself, Is the U.N. an American institution? A thousand sights and sounds can prompt the inquiry—the impressive United States delegation building immediately across the road from the U.N.; the reactions of the galleries to a Stars-and-Stripes-waving speech from the floor; the notice-board in the Secretariat post office with its advertisements for United States defence bonds; the cuisine in the delegates' dining-room. The U.N. enclave itself, for all its glitter and its thirty-eight-storey eminence, seems dwarfed on one side by the beetling cliffs of Manhattan and mocked on the other by the Pepsi-Cola sky-sign across the East River; when night falls its denizens are swallowed up in the melting-pot of New York or dispersed over its sprawling suburbs.

Nor are these impressions at variance with the role which we have seen the U.S.A. playing in the birth and growth of the U.N. At each stage, at Dumbarton Oaks, at San Francisco, over Palestine, Korea, Suez, and the Congo, American concepts have prevailed—if not in their entirety, at any rate in their essence. Where American official initiative was lacking, other members responded to the latent magnetism of American power, as in the decision to establish the headquarters in the U.S.A. An American gift provided the U.N. with a home; an American loan made possible the building; an American architect had the biggest hand in its planning and construction. From all this a host of con-sequences inevitably followed; language, procedures, working methods, public relations, and that impalpable wrapping which is style, all took on an American tint as naturally as the delegates and the Secretariat breathed American air. At all points, to a degree often unappreciated, American strength has underpinned the Organization. This is most explicit in finance: the American share of the U.N. budget was originally almost 40 per cent. and will still remain at 25 per cent.; 60 per cent. or more of the cost of the U.N.'s voluntary programmes, including 45 per cent. of technical assistance funds, has come from the United States; the main burdens of UNEF and ONUC have been shouldered by the American taxpayer. Less measurable, but even more potent, is the contribution in diplomacy and, in the crucial instance of Korea, in American flesh and blood. Behind this there has been an American interest and often enthusiasm for the U.N. which it would be hard to parallel elsewhere. American membership in the Organization was floated on a huge tide of popular feeling compounded of shame for the past (America's rejection of the League) and hope and pride in the future. From the first the manifold and powerful organs of American opinion have displayed an omnivorous curiosity about U.N. affairs which has indeed left its mark not only on their American audience but also upon more than one aspect of the Organization's processes. Universities and learned foundations have promoted research into U.N. problems on a scale which no other country has approached and along lines which have often been of the most direct assistance to the Organization. Throughout American society, at all levels of simplicity and sophistication, a diversity of pressure groups actively espouses the U.N. cause.

When flaws, however, are detected in the loved one revulsion is all the fiercer, by reason of the devotion that has gone before. In 1951-2, when the Korean crusade failed to result in speedy victory, worse still when it appeared as if the U.N. were trafficking in appeasement while the U.S.A. paid most of the price in American blood and treasure, American resentment became swift and sharp. As on top of this the trails of McCarthyite witch-hunters led, or were portrayed as leading, to the fastness of internationalism on East River, the U.N. took on for many Americans the novel and hideous visage of something 'un-American'. At the height of the storm, when the U.N.'s immunity was invaded and F.B.I. agents were taking the fingerprints of American Secretariat members on the premises, there was a depressing dearth of voices raised in its defence amongst the leaders of American public life. Many strands were woven into this hostility, of party politics in a presidential contest, of unrepentant isolationism raising its head perhaps for the last time, of Korean War weariness, of a new-found fear of a U.S.S.R. equipped with atomic weapons. As peace returned in 1953 and a new Republicanism accepted the burden of free world leadership, the hostility waned and by degrees respect was restored. Respect and even amity, but perhaps never again the full flush of exuberant devotion. Some of this went with the impairment of American security created by the loss of the atomic monopoly, some with the increasing reliance on NATO. When in 1955 U.N. membership leapt from sixty to seventy-six, the U.S.A. lost that assured majority in the General Assembly which helped to offset the Soviet veto in the Security Council and relieved her of the necessity of wooing the 'uncommitted' countries. Votes had to be worked for harder than before, and those to whom the U.N. was principally a weapon in the cold war often found it too cumbersome and prickly for their taste. In 1956 the Suez crisis placed America in the painful position of having to choose between the Charter and two of her major allies. The decision was made in the U.N.'s favour (had it not been, the Organization's future must have been seriously impaired), but many Americans, in and out of government, were left unhappy at such a clash between the right and the good—especially when in Hungary (as later in Czechoslovakia) it synchronized with a display of U.N. impotence in face of acknowledged evil. Moreover, the increase in the 'neutralist' membership, principally from Africa and Asia, necessarily posed many problems for the leader of the free world. Some aspects of the Congo operation were disillusioning, notably the reluctance of either Africans or Europeans to stand firmly by the U.N. when it seemed to offend against what they felt to be their anti-colonialist or ex-colonialist principles. And it was a shock to the U.S.A., proud to claim the title of the first anti-colonialist country, to find itself in the dock after its intervention in Stanleyville in 1964 and over its record in Puerto Rico and the Pacific Islands at the hands of the Committee of Twenty-four. Over Cuba and Santo Domingo the U.S.A. had to fight hard to justify its intentions and to keep the issues within the control of the O.A.S. Over the issue of Article 19 the American experience was painfully educative; even if some of the hurt was self-inflicted, by clumsy management of the crisis, what remained at the end was a perceptible loss of faith—in the willingness of the 'neutralist' members to stand by the Charter and in the U.S.A.'s ability to control their voting in the General Assembly even on issues she judged crucial.

This did not imply any rejection on America's part of the Organization. But as the sixties led into the seventies it did result in an attitude of greater detachment, with fewer illusions about the automatic identity of U.N. decisions and American policy. When in 1970, rather than leave Britain alone to face a Security Council resolution advocating force against Rhodesia, the U.S.A. cast her first veto, it was plausible to argue that it was the crossing of a Rubicon separating idealistic illusions from benevolent realism. The Vietnam experience was another landmark. Although seldom directly debated, it put the U.S.A., when it was under U.N. discussion, on the defensive and in the dock. The Organization by a kind of contagion shared in the slump of idealism that Vietnam induced; like all other institutions of American concern it suffered from the frustration, cynicism, and decline in vitality that were the dominant features of American politics under Nixon. The conservatism of the Nixon administration found expression in a new indifference to U.N. appeals; aid was cut back, Rhodesian sanctions were blatantly violated to maintain U.S. chrome imports, the American contribution to the U.N. budget was reduced from 31 to 25 per cent, payment of dues to the ILO was withheld in protest at a Russian appointment to the Secretariat, the quality of American representation on U.N. delegations perceptibly declined. Yet, despite the down-grading of the Organization that Henry Kissinger's *real-politik* implied, certain indisputable benefits also resulted from it. Without it Peking would not have secured membership, the two Germanies would not have been admitted, with all that implied, and the ravages of the Arab–Israeli conflict in 1973 would have been beyond the capacity of the Organization to handle.

Initially the most remarkable feature about the attitude of the U.S.S.R. towards the U.N. was, quite simply, her continuing membership of it. Its evolution took it along lines the Soviets never intended, its policies were usually harmful for their purposes, the votes of its members were cast overwhelmingly and repeatedly against the causes they held dear. Yet though Soviet vetoes fell thick as autumn leaves (over a hundred in the first twenty-five years), and Soviet walkouts were numerous and Soviet boycotts extensive, there was never any serious question, so far as can be gathered, of Soviet withdrawal from the Organization. Why did the U.S.S.R. and her satellites remain in a *bourgeois* enterprise which so often operated against them?

For the U.S.S.R. the U.N. in 1943-5 was a by-product of the Grand Alliance against Hitler. It was seen as an embodiment, in binding legal form, of the unity of the great victors; at the same time it would sanctify the division of power between them. To Stalin the Security Council was the only part of the U.N. that really mattered; the General Assembly was merely a talking shop for the underlings. Five policemen (he would have preferred it to be three, or even two) would keep the peace; the veto would guarantee that they would act unitedly against anyone else and also that they would take no action against each other. Disputes between the Great Powers were not fit subjects for U.N. treatment because, *ex hypothesi*, the Great Powers were above the law. The security system of the U.N. was seen by the Soviets, more even than by anyone else, in backward-looking terms; it was to prevent a repetition not only of the invasions from the West which Russia had experienced in 1812, 1914, and 1941, but also of that post-1917 war of intervention which all the senior Soviet leaders had personally experienced. This makes perfectly logical that emphasis on respect for national sovereignty which at first sounds so odd on the lips of the leaders of an international movement who are participating in the processes of an international organization.

Holding these views, the Russians were naturally suspicious of all the San Francisco talk about the rights of the smaller nations, the limiting of the veto, the 'no state being judge in its own cause', and the like. They saw in it merely an attempt to tilt the Charter in favour of the capitalist powers, whose 'satellites' were so much more numerous, and whose frontiers remained un-ravaged. When an attempt was immediately made in 1946 to use the machinery of the Security Council against them, in the Iran dispute, these fears were confirmed and the first of the countless Soviet vetoes was employed to ward off the menace. In thus acting the U.S.S.R. did not feel herself to be abusing the veto; it was the other members of the Security Council who were aban-doning the principle of unanimity. Nor, on this view, if the Security Council was stalled, did it make sense to invoke the Assembly. To do this was to try to overthrow the safeguards which the Charter had provided for the sovereign rights of Great Powers. It was also pointless and silly, in that it attempted to substitute an incoherent mass of unequal votes for the real power distribution in the world of sovereign states. How many divisions has the General Assembly? To try to legalize this perversion of the Charter by a 'Uniting for Peace' resolution is worse; it lends an improper endorsement to an illusory claim. Nor does it make sense to complain that the purposes of the U.N. are thwarted by Security Council vetoes. The U.N., in Soviet eyes, is not an embryonic court or an international welfare organization, still less an incipient world government. It is purely and simply a treaty relationship. For this reason the U.S.S.R. has always been highly critical of any expansion of U.N. activities which would strengthen its institutional roots or branches. It opposed Mr. Lie's Field Service; it opposed Mr. Hammarskjöld's UNEF (despite his careful delimitation of its role); it opposed his ONUC even more. It has little or no time for the humanitarian activities of the U.N., and it dislikes economic and social operations like technical assistance—it only agreed to participate in it, in 1953, when it appeared in consequence to be losing in the race for the favour of the 'uncommitted' countries, and then it insisted on making almost all its financial contributions in inconvertible currencies. It is profoundly suspicious of the specialized agencies, save the purely technical ones, and still holds aloof from FAO and ICAO, and of course from the Fund and the Bank. In the

U.N. itself it always presses for economy, smaller staffing, and a restrictive interpretation of the Secretariat's (and the Secretary-General's) role. For years it never came anywhere near claiming the number of Secretariat posts for itself (still less for its satellites) proportionate to its contribution, and for a long time it was surprisingly acquiescent in the by-passing of Russian staff members when important Secretariat assignments were allotted.

The low point of Soviet–U.N. relations was reached in 1949–50 when the U.S.S.R. had to swallow in rapid succession the election of a truant Yugoslavia to the Security Council, the refusal to cede the Kuomintang's seat in the U.N. to the Communist government that replaced them, and the militant response of the Organization to the North Korean challenge. This was the period of the seven months' Soviet boycott of practically all U.N. bodies (except the Court), followed by the 'non-recognition' of Mr. Lie after the 'illegal' extension of his term. By comparison, being censured over Hungary in 1956 was insignificant—and in any case was in part offset by the opportunities afforded the U.S.S.R. to turn censor over Suez.

The truth was that even in its most anti-U.N. phase Soviet consistency in its U.N. policies was not unflawed. Its disapproval of the 'non-security' aspects of the U.N. has not prevented the U.S.S.R. from seizing the opportunities these provide to a Communist state which wishes to fish in troubled capitalist waters. At first it boycotted the Trusteeship Council as a protest at not being admitted as a 'state directly concerned' to the negotiations of all trusteeship agreements, but subsequently returned when it discovered what generous facilities the trusteeship and related activities of the Organization provided for conducting anti-colonialist propaganda. Similarly, its disapproval of the U.N.'s economic and social operations has been coupled with a vigorous use of ECOSOC and the related Assembly committees for the exposure of capitalist malpractices, especially (with a total indifference to Article 2, § 7) in the field of human rights.

With the sixties the new Soviet confidence born of Sputnik and the opportunities provided by the changed membership gave a new impetus to Soviet policy. The U.S.S.R. made common cause with the Afro-Asians in complaining of the dominance exerted in the Organization by the old American-European guard. It began to demand greater representation in the Secretariats both of the U.N. and of the specialized agencies—while still, of course, refusing to allow the U.N. to recruit directly in the U.S.S.R. (it insists on offering a host of government-approved candidates and only allows these to serve on a seconded, short-term basis). Mr. Khrushchev's personal performance at the 1960 General Assembly was an advertisement of Russia's more affirmative attitude and a sustained bid for the 'non-aligned' vote. The notorious 'troika' proposal was cleverly designed both to rob the U.N. of its most creative and dynamic office, the Secretary-Generalship, and to excite the desires of the newer members to get their hands on the executive controls.

The new approach was a failure, just as the whole Soviet attempt to thwart ONUC was a failure, but the same cannot be said of the Soviet stand in the Article 19 controversy. Here the U.S.S.R. was surprisingly successful in escaping the blame it deserved for its refusal to pay its share, while transferring to the Americans the odium of stalling the General Assembly. There is also no doubt that the U.S.S.R. has had some success in its tireless campaign to curb the General Assembly and restore power to the Security Council. Here, however, the assumption of China's seat by Peking has installed the U.S.S.R.'s bitterest foe within the citadel of power. The consequence has been to make the Soviets often join hands with the Americans, even at the price of seeing the leadership of 'the wretched of the earth' pass, in both Council and Assembly, into Chinese hands.

But whether U.N. was going the Soviet way or whether it was working against them, the Soviets seem to have early arrived at a settled conclusion that it was better to be in than out. Their first maxim seems to have been not to let this potentially valuable instrument become the monopoly of their adversaries. And from their point of view they were surely right. The U.N. may sometimes put the U.S.S.R. in the dock, but the U.S.S.R. can always use the U.N. as a soap-box. Which way on any occasion the balance of profit and loss inclines depends not only upon the facts of the case, or even upon the ability of prosecutors and pleaders, but also upon the susceptibilities of the jury. Neither the Soviet nor its rivals can ever control all these variables, but that is no reason, especially for those committed to the belief that the world is going their way, for abandoning the arena to the other side.

When it comes to voting the U.S.S.R. is, of course, at a disadvantage. But it still has its veto in the Security Council and, if it can muster enough support (or abstentions) amongst the 'uncommitted' members, the ten votes of the Communist bloc may prevent the Assembly amassing the two-thirds majority needed for 'important questions'. Moreover, there are gradations of failure. A resolution that cannot be defeated can perhaps be watered down, or delayed. Distasteful developments in the structure or functioning of the Organization can be retarded and in some cases prevented by a firm show of disapproval. These, admittedly, are negative gains, but they are none the less real for that, and they would all be lost were the U.S.S.R. to resign membership out of pique or disappointment. She has learnt at last from her experience with boycotts that resignations, however temporary, produce more loss than profit.

Twenty-six years before the U.N. was launched Britain had embarked upon a venture in international organization at Geneva which, for all its inadequacy, had yet represented at its peak a considerable investment of the nation's best endeavours and aspirations. When the U.N. took the place of the League Britain once again played a part commensurate with her strength at all stages of its construction and development. Proportionately, however, her strength was less and her role was overshadowed at all stages by her greater partner, the United States. Strength apart, something else was lacking. The League in its collapse had taken with it enthusiasms as well as illusions. Its successor might receive a more realistic service, but it could not command an equal affection. There are some *mystiques* which, once shattered, cannot be restored; the League *mystique*, for better or worse, was one of those. For Britons, however sincere their internationalism, nothing could invest New York with the peculiar potency that the syllables 'Geneva' had enjoyed. Moreover, with its translation to the U.S.A. the U.N. became in an important sense lost to Europe. Not only the Atlantic sundered us. The 'dollar curtain' was a further barrier. The U.N. grew up, remote and legendary, in a country which for all its friendliness hardly any Britons could visit and where even newspapers often found it impossible to maintain regular U.N. correspondents. Moreover, reconstruction and readjustment were proceeding simultaneously in so many spheres of British life, at home and in the Commonwealth, that the focus of public attention seldom rested for long upon the Organization at Lake Success. The best talents of the nation could ill be spared to serve in it even when, after an administratively gruelling war, they wished to serve in a public role at all. Of course there was never a moment's doubt in the public mind that the U.N. should be supported; the U.N. was axiomatic where the League had often been contestable. But it was no use hoping too much from it and it was hard to maintain fervent interest in it.

Thus when the Security Council became a casualty of the cold war Britain neither felt the full sharpness of American disappointment nor shared completely their dynamic conviction that the General Assembly could be sharpened as a substitute instrument. European hopes and cares, embodied in OEEC and NATO, came to count for more than the global prospects so faintly limned in the U.N. Nor did the United Kingdom respond to the full challenge of Korea; there was nothing amiss in the contribution of British troops and resources, but there was a less than generous recognition of the American effort. However, just as Korea failed to exalt, so it also failed to depress our view of the U.N.; in Britain the Organization escaped entirely that slump in esteem which it so painfully endured in the United States. Even the great aberration of 1956, though it evoked sharp and bitter criticism of a U.N. 'with double standards', slow and impotent, quickened an awareness and interest in the Organization and left behind astonishingly little resentment.

Two other main lines of U.N. activity have left their mark on British attitudes. Its social and economic programmes have, broadly speaking, been welcomed and supported when they promised tangible results, viewed with suspicion amounting often to dismay when they did not. Unfortunately, the limitations imposed by Britain's own economic stringencies have hitherto generally forced her to play second fiddle, even where her sympathies were most warmly engaged.

As the greatest remaining imperial power Britain has been continuously concerned with U.N. policies in the colonial field. Here the steady expansion of U.N. interests has proceeded almost *pari passu* with the reduction of British imperial control. Of the U.N.'s 144 members 32 have been released from British rule since the war. But although this has meant that at the most fundamental level there is a harmony of aims between a Britain committed to eventual self-government for the whole Commonwealth and a U.N. concerned about the standards and aims of colonial administration everywhere, it has also meant that at the more superficial levels there is an enormous area of potential friction and discord. Britain, proud of her record and confident in her experience, quickly resented any suggestion of being taught her business by any parvenu international talking-shop. The U.N., partial to national self-determination as only an international organization can be, and responsive to the pressures of all the 'anti-colonial' and 'ex-colonial' world, provided a forum in which inevitably the accent fell on criticism, impatience, and suspicion. In such a context Britain could not resist striking a posture that made her look far more crudely imperialist than she was, and the U.N. seemed to be reaching out for a responsibility that it was clearly not competent to assume. Nor has the friction greatly diminished with the progressive and rapid conversion of Britain's imperial dependencies into U.N. members. Indeed as one reads the debates in Turtle Bay and Westminster over Rhodesia, Gibraltar, and the remaining few areas of British overseas rule one sometimes gets the impression that the fewer the territories the greater the furore. Yet furore is not all; the ex-colonials' bark is worse than their bite and in moments of acute difficulty, as over Rhodesia's UDI, Britain has as often been grateful for the U.N.'s support as irritated by its criticism.

Looking over the whole record of British participation in the U.N. one is conscious of a certain ambivalence. Circumstances have often been against us; the centre of our interest has often, not necessarily improperly, lain elsewhere. But opportunities to maximize the advantages of world-wide connexions and long experience in international relations were too often neglected. Public opinion has been under-informed and public talent has been too seldom engaged. Quite apart from Suez, the level of public empathy for the U.N.'s aims and experiments has been too low. It was not until the establishment of the Labour government in 1964 and the appointment of Lord Caradon as our permanent representative that we developed a positive U.N. policy and presented a consistent image there. Unfortunately this coincided with a period of weakness in our balance of payments which prevented the full realization of good intentions in the field of aid; there was also the inescapable legacy of previous policies, particularly in Rhodesia, which could not be discarded and simply had to be lived down. In the seventies domestic maladies and new overseas orientation, conspicuously towards Europe, undoubtedly diminished British responsiveness to the world of the U.N. Neither the Heath government of 1970–4, nor its Wilson successors have treated the Organization with the seriousness or the imaginativeness that it deserved.

With the recognition in 1972 of the Peking government as the rightful occupant of China's seat in the U.N., a long persistent anomaly was rectified and a formidable new power, ruler of a quarter of the earth's population, was admitted to the councils of the Organization. Awaited with misgivings, even by those who fully recognized the justice of her claim, the arrival of Peking at Turtle Bay proved in fact almost an anti-climax. China's initial delegation was a strong team headed by Chiao Kuang-hua, the Deputy Foreign Minister; their permanent representative was Huang Hua, previously ambassador to Canada and a seasoned diplomat. It was regrettable, but not perhaps surprising, that the new arrivals should carry resentment over the expelled Taiwanese to the petty and ridiculous lengths of disbarring

Taiwanese press correspondents and requiring that the U.N. eliminate all references to Taiwan from its publications and documents. And of course Peking declined to pay any of the $16 million of back dues which Taiwan was owing. But Peking agreed to having its own assessment for the U.N. budget raised from 4 to 7 per cent. over the next five years and only took exception to certain trivial items. It insisted, as Taiwan had never done, upon the use of Chinese wherever possible and had it recognized, in 1974, as a 'working language' of the Organization. In Tang Ming-chao, selected to fill the vacancy as Under-Secretary General, they furnished the Secretariat with a sophisticated diplomatic recruit.

As far as policies went, the Chinese followed a predictable ideological line, competing with the U.S.S.R. as leaders of the Third World and foes of capitalism and imperialism. In general, however, their voice was a good deal less strident than had been expected, save where the clash with Russia itself was involved; there nothing could exceed the sustained animosity of the Sino–Soviet relationship. China's presence thus gave the Security Council a new triangularity, which the Chinese none the less forebore in general to push to extremes. Thus although in 1972 they cast their first veto against the admission to membership of Bangladesh (a faithful reflection of their stance on the India–Pakistan conflict), they withdrew their opposition after the end of hostilities and actually voted for admission in 1974. Similarly although vocally very anti-Israel and pro-Arab they abstained in the Security Council and accepted the cease-fire settlements for the 1973 war and permitted the re-creation of UNEF although declining to make any payment towards it. A similar abstention marked their attitude to UNFICYP.

Though space forbids our examining the relations of the remaining member states to the Organization there is one group of states who have come to count for so much in Assembly voting and talking that they require special mention. They are an amorphous entity, as their diversity of names implies. Sometimes they are known as the 'Afro-Asians' from the two continents which they inhabit, sometimes the 'non-aligned' from the attitude to the cold war which they profess, sometimes the 'anti-colonialists' from the critical sentiment they entertain to the European powers whose dependencies (in most cases, though not in all) they once were. The label one applies determines the exact figure at which one numbers them, but, however totalled, they now amount to considerably more than half of the total membership.

The solidarity of this group can easily be exaggerated. There is a vast range of U.N. issues on which they hold views as diverse as their membership. But that there is a certain community of feeling and of attitudes amongst them cannot be denied. Of what does it consist?

In the first place, they are mostly 'new boys'. In the original U.N. coloured Africa was represented by only three members, Egypt, Ethiopia, and Liberia, and Asia (outside the Middle East) only by China, India, Iran, and the Philippines. Most members of the group were very self-conscious about having arrived late in an organization whose structure was shaped with little or no thought of them. Consequently they are generally united by a desire to obtain a larger and more established voice in the main organs of the U.N. Moreover they feel the U.N. to have been, in many cases, their godparent (especially when they came to independence under U.N. auspices after being U.N. trusteeships) and in their desire to escape a new dependence on their old rulers they feel the U.N. to be their best, perhaps their only, friend. For the diplomats of many new Afro-Asian states the U.N. posting is the most important of all.

What they most want from the U.N. is, of course, assistance in their struggle for economic and social improvement. They are therefore ardent advocates of every form of U.N. aid, technical, administrative, and financial. They press for its expansion in every direction and indeed for every leverage the U.N. system may afford for readjusting the balance between the weak and the strong, the poor and the rich.

Hardly less valuable to them is the opportunity the U.N. stage affords them for the assertion of their new-found personalities.

The pursuit of nationhood, in many cases, continues long after the acquisition of independence, and in the U.N. they have a forum where they can, by announcing themselves to the world, discover for themselves an identity. Here too, since each state, however new, however small, however artificial, has one vote, they find themselves courted and taken seriously. (In them, indeed, the discrepancies between power and voting strength are often revealed at their most blatant.) They have one understandable if doubtfully healthy obsession—colonialism—and a powerful disposition to steer clear of all U.N. issues which do not directly involve it. To the conflicts of the older powers they affect an indifference which they do not always feel, but which derives from an assumption that they have nothing to gain and much to lose by taking sides. But to state even this without qualification is to go too far, since the ideological war of democracy and communism has already made itself felt in their midst and powerfully affected their collective unity. Try as they will they cannot escape making certain choices and it is already apparent that they will not all choose alike.

The basic character of the U.N., it should now be apparent, is that of a voluntary association of independent states. The nature and extent of that association is defined by treaty; the purposes of it, though also in part laid down in the original treaty document (the Charter), change and evolve under pressure of circumstances and in response to the demands of the members. Sweeping though the assertions of some of these purposes may be, they do not give the association the power to invade the domestic jurisdiction of states without their consent. Where the external relationships of states are concerned the association has indeed, under certain circumstances, the right and even the obligation to take coercive action in the interests of peace and security. In fact the association has failed to live up to the letter of its founding Charter and both the guarantees it affords to its members and the claims it makes upon them are less solid than its founders anticipated. Its security functions have thus in part—though only in part—devolved upon regional organizations which operate outside the U.N. system. How much on any given occasion the U.N. will itself undertake depends entirely on how much resolve and strength its members put into it. It has no will of its own. It is a forum in which wills can be expressed and harmonized.

So much is true, but it is not the whole truth. It should also by now be apparent that the association which is the U.N. has become an institution which, though it remains the creature of its members, now has in addition a life of its own. In the first place it gives visible and continuing expression to certain canons of behaviour which members have agreed to observe. It provides, furthermore, a setting in which, and a system of procedures according to which, states may confer and debate and through which, in consequence, something approaching a 'U.N. public opinion' can be formed. In itself non-coercive, this may none the less exercise a moral pressure that states cannot easily ignore. Thus, though the U.N. cannot upset the international distribution of power, or even guarantee the weak against the determined depredations of the strong, it can mobilize and maximize the forces which in any given situation favour just or peaceful action, and can put at their disposal for this purpose the most extensive armoury of diplomatic and parliamentary devices so far known. In its Secretariat, and Secretary-General in particular, it has an institutionalized 'conscience' and a set of skilled servants of its will. They can mediate, they can administer, they can encourage, and they can warn. But they are no substitute for the member states themselves. What the Organization has so far achieved justifies its claims to be something more than the sum of its parts. How much more still remains uncertain. Whether it develops from its present embryonic state sufficiently to realize the purposes of its own Charter, depends on how its members behave towards each other and how sedulously they cherish the association they have formed.

SUGGESTED READING

THE official documents of the U.N. constitute, of course, the principal source material for most of the topics treated in this volume. In varying degrees of completeness these are to be found in the principal British libraries and may also be found in the admirable library of the U.N. Information Office in London. For many purposes, however, the very comprehensiveness of these records diminishes their usefulness and often the *Yearbook of the U.N.*, which contains summaries of debates, of the work of the Secretariat, and of the work of the specialized agencies, is to be preferred. An excellent but belated official compendium is also *Everyman's United Nations* (8th ed. 1968), which provides a survey of U.N. activities since 1945. *International Organization*, the quarterly publication of the World Peace Foundation, Boston, U.S.A., provides scholarly articles on various aspects of the U.N. The Carnegie Endowment for International Peace for many years published *International Conciliation*, a monthly, in which U.N. topics were featured frequently, with one invaluable issue each year devoted to issues facing the forthcoming session of the General Assembly. Unfortunately this has been discontinued.

Of single-volume treatments the best are *The United Nations* by Leland M. Goodrich (Stevens, London, 1960), and *The United Nations: Accomplishments and Prospects* by Norman J. Padelford and Leland M. Goodrich (Praeger, New York, 1965). *The United Nations*, ed. by Maurice Waters (Macmillan, New York, 1967), is a useful collection of readings and speeches. A diversity of topics is treated in *The Quest for Peace*, the Dag Hammarskjöld Lecture Series, ed. by Andrew W. Cordier and Wilder Foote (Columbia Univ. Press, 1965), and in *The Evolution of International Institutions* ed. by Evan Luard (Thames & Hudson, London, 1966).

CHAPTER I

C. K. WEBSTER: 'The Making of the Charter of the U.N.' in *The Art and Practice of Diplomacy* (London, Chatto & Windus, 1961).
CORDELL HULL: *Memoirs*, vol. ii (London, Hodder & Stoughton, 1948).
E. R. STETTINIUS: *Roosevelt and the Russians* (London, Cape, 1950).
A. H. VANDENBERG, Jr.: *The Private Papers of Senator Vandenberg* (London, Gollancz, 1952).
H. V. EVATT: *The U.N.* (London, O.U.P., 1948).
RUTH B. RUSSELL: *A History of the U.N. Charter, The Role of the U.S.* (Washington, Brookings Institute, 1958).

CHAPTER 2

LELAND M. GOODRICH: 'From League of Nations to U.N.' in *International Conciliation*, February 1947.

J. L. BRIERLEY: 'The Covenant and the Charter' in *British Year Book of International Law*, 1946 (London, O.U.P.).

A. ZIMMERN: *The League of Nations and the Rule of Law* (London, Macmillan, 1936).

INIS L. CLAUDE: *Swords into Ploughshares* (New York, Random House, 3rd ed. 1964).

C. WILFRED JENKS: *The World Beyond the Charter* (London, Allen & Unwin, 1969).

Detailed commentaries on the Charter are to be found in:

LELAND M. GOODRICH, E. HAMBRO, and ANNE SIMONS: *Charter of the U.N., Commentary and Documents*, 3rd ed. (New York, Columbia Univ. Press, 1969).

CHAPTER 3

Report of the Preparatory Commission of the U.N., with *Commentary* (London, H.M.S.O., Cmd. 6734, 1946).

TRYGVE LIE: *In the Cause of Peace* (New York, Macmillan, 1954). (The first Secretary-General's account of his period of office, 1946–1952.)

CLARK M. EICHELBERGER: *U.N.: The First Fifteen Years* (New York, Harpers, 1961).

BRIAN URQUHART: *Hammarskjöld* (London, Bodley Head, 1973).

CHAPTER 4

ANDREW BOYD: *Fifteen Men on a Powder Keg: a History of the Security Council* (London, Methuen, 1971).

RICHARD HISCOCKS: *The Security Council: a Study in Adolescence* (London, Longmans, 1973).

CHAPTER 5

SYDNEY D. BAILEY: *The General Assembly of the United Nations*, 2nd ed. (London, Stevens, 1964).

JOHN G. HADWEN and JOHAN KAUFMANN: *How United Nation Decisions are Made* (Leyden, Sythoff, 1960).

PHILIP C. JESSUP: *Parliamentary Diplomacy*, lectures published in The Hague Academy of International Law, vol. 89, *Recueil des Cours*, 1956. An original analysis, with case-histories, of General Assembly and Security Council processes.

THOMAS HOVET: *Bloc Politics in the United Nations* (Harvard Univ. Press, 1960).

CHAPTER 6

GERARD J. MANGONE (ed.): *U.N. Administration of Economic and Social Programs* (New York, Columbia University Press, 1966).

WALTER R. SHARP: *The United Nations Economic and Social Council* (New York, Columbia University Press, 1969).

J. H. RICHARDS: *International Economic Institutions* (New York, Holt, Rinehart & Winston, 1970).

The literature on the specialized agencies is disappointingly meagre. Monographs include:

ROBERT BERKOV: *The World Health Organisation* (Geneva and Paris, 1957).

The First Ten Years of the World Health Organization (W.H.O., Geneva, 1958). *The Second Ten Years* was published in 1968.

GEORGE A. CODDING: *The I.T.U.* (Leyden, 1952).

W. H. C. LAVES and C. A. THOMSON: *UNESCO : Purpose, Progress, Prospects* (London, Denis Dobson, 1958).

JOSEPH M. JONES: *The United Nations at Work* (Oxford, Pergamon, 1965). Mainly devoted to F.A.O.

DAVID W. WAINHOUSE: *Remnants of Empire: the U.N. and the End of Colonialism* (New York, Harper & Row, 1964).

SHABTAI ROSENNE: *The International Court of Justice* (Leyden, A. W. Sijthoff, 1957).

CHAPTER 7

TRYGVE LIE: *In the Cause of Peace* (New York, Macmillan, 1954).

S. M. SCHWEBEL: *The Secretary-General of the U.N.* (Cambridge, Mass., Harvard, 1952).

SYDNEY D. BAILEY: *The Secretariat of the United Nations* (New York, Praeger, 1964).

LEON GORDENKER: *The U.N. Secretary-General and the Maintenance of Peace* (New York, Columbia Univ. Press, 1967).

DAG HAMMARSKJÖLD: *The International Civil Servant in Law and in Fact*, a Lecture (O.U.P., 1961).

BRIAN URQUHART: *Hammarskjöld* (London, Bodley Head, 1973).

A. LOVEDAY: *Reflections on International Administration* (Oxford, Clarendon Press, 1956).

CATHERINE HOSKYNS: *The Congo since Independence* (O.U.P., London, 1965) tells something of the story of the Congo operation.

D. W. BOWETT: *United Nations Forces* (London, Stevens, 1964).

LINCOLN P. BLOOMFIELD et al.: *International Military Forces* (Boston, Little Brown, 1964).

A. L. BURNS and NINA HEATHCOTE: *Peace-Keeping by U.N. Forces from Suez to the Congo* (London and New York, Praeger, 1963).

ROSALYN HIGGINS: *United Nations Peacekeeping, 1946-1967. Documents and Commentary*, 2 vols. (London, O.U.P., for R.I.I.A. 1969-70).

ALAN JAMES: *The Politics of Peacekeeping* (London, Chatto & Windus, 1969).

LARRY L. FABIAN: *Soldiers Without Enemies* (Washington, Brookings, 1971).

CHAPTER 8

The Carnegie Endowment for International Peace is sponsoring a series of studies on individual states and their relations with the U.N., of which over twenty have so far appeared, including *Britain and the U.N.* by GEOFFREY L. GOODWIN (London, O.U.P., 1957). See also *The United Nations and U.S. Foreign Policy* by LINCOLN P. BLOOMFIELD (Univ. of London Press, 1967) and *The United Nations and United States Security Policy* by RUTH B. RUSSELL (Washington, Brookings, 1968). For the U.S.S.R. see *The Soviets in International Organizations* by ALVIN Z. RUBINSTEIN (Princeton Univ. Press, 1964) and *The Soviet Union at the United Nations* by ALEXANDER DALLIN (New York and London, Praeger, 1962). For the U.N.'s newer membership see DAVID A. KAY: *The New Nations in the United Nations, 1960-1967* (New York, Columbia, 1970).

APPENDIX

CHARTER OF THE UNITED NATIONS

WE THE PEOPLES OF THE UNITED NATIONS DETERMINED

to save succeeding generations from the scourge of war, which twice in our lifetime has brought untold sorrow to mankind, and

to reaffirm faith in fundamental human rights, in the dignity and worth of the human person, in the equal rights of men and women and of nations large and small, and

to establish conditions under which justice and respect for the obligations arising from treaties and other sources of international law can be maintained, and

to promote social progress and better standards of life in larger freedom,

AND FOR THESE ENDS

to practise tolerance and live together in peace with one another as good neighbours, and

to unite our strength to maintain international peace and security, and

to ensure, by the acceptance of principles and the institution of methods, that armed force shall not be used, save in the common interest, and

to employ international machinery for the promotion of the economic and social advancement of all peoples,

HAVE RESOLVED TO COMBINE OUR EFFORTS TO ACCOMPLISH THESE AIMS

Accordingly, our respective Governments, through representatives assembled in the city of San Francisco, who have exhibited their full powers found to be in good and due form, have agreed to the present Charter of the United Nations and do hereby establish an international organization to be known as the United Nations.

CHAPTER I

PURPOSES AND PRINCIPLES

Article 1

The Purposes of the United Nations are:

1. To maintain international peace and security, and to that end: to take effective collective measures for the prevention and removal of threats to the peace, and for the suppression of acts of aggression or other breaches of the peace, and to bring about by peaceful means, and in conformity with the principles of justice and international law, adjustment or settlement of international disputes or situations which might lead to a breach of the peace;

2. To develop friendly relations among nations based on respect for the principle of equal rights and self-determination of peoples, and to take other appropriate measures to strengthen universal peace;

3. To achieve international co-operation in solving international problems of an economic, social, cultural, or humanitarian character, and in promoting and encouraging respect for human rights and for fundamental freedoms for all without distinction as to race, sex, language, or religion; and

4. To be a centre for harmonizing the actions of nations in the attainment of these common ends.

Article 2

The Organization and its Members, in pursuit of the Purposes stated in Article 1, shall act in accordance with the following Principles.

1. The Organization is based on the principle of the sovereign equality of all its Members.

2. All Members, in order to ensure to all of them the rights and benefits resulting from membership, shall fulfil in good faith the obligations assumed by them in accordance with the present Charter.

3. All Members shall settle their international disputes by peaceful means in such a manner that international peace and security, and justice, are not endangered.

4. All Members shall refrain in their international relations from the threat or use of force against the territorial integrity or political independence of any state, or in any other manner inconsistent with the Purposes of the United Nations.

5. All Members shall give the United Nations every assistance in any action it takes in accordance with the present Charter, and shall refrain from giving assistance to any state against which the United Nations is taking preventive or enforcement action.

6. The Organization shall ensure that states which are not Members of the United Nations act in accordance with these Principles so far as may be necessary for the maintenance of international peace and security.

7. Nothing contained in the present Charter shall authorize the United Nations to intervene in matters which are essentially within the domestic jurisdiction of any state or shall require the Members to submit such matters to settlement under the present Charter; but this principle shall not prejudice the application of enforcement measures under Chapter VII.

CHAPTER II

MEMBERSHIP

Article 3

The original Members of the United Nations shall be the states which, having participated in the United Nations Conference on International Organization at San Francisco, or having previously signed the Declaration by United Nations of January 1, 1942, sign the present Charter and ratify it in accordance with Article 110.

Article 4

1. Membership in the United Nations is open to all other peace-loving states which accept the obligations contained in the present Charter and, in the judgment of the Organization, are able and willing to carry out these obligations.

2. The admission of any such state to membership in the United Nations will be effected by a decision of the General Assembly upon the recommendation of the Security Council.

Article 5

A Member of the United Nations against which preventive or enforcement action has been taken by the Security Council may be suspended from the exercise of the rights and privileges of membership by the General Assembly upon the recommendation of the Security Council. The exercise of these rights and privileges may be restored by the Security Council.

Article 6

A Member of the United Nations which has persistently violated the Principles contained in the present Charter may be expelled from the Organization by the General Assembly upon the recommendation of the Security Council.

CHAPTER III

ORGANS

Article 7

1. There are established as the principal organs of the United Nations; a General Assembly, a Security Council, an Economic and Social Council, a Trusteeship Council, an International Court of Justice, and a Secretariat.

2. Such subsidiary organs as may be found necessary may be established in accordance with the present Charter.

Article 8

The United Nations shall place no restrictions on the eligibility of men and women to participate in any capacity and under conditions of equality in its principal and subsidiary organs.

CHAPTER IV

THE GENERAL ASSEMBLY

COMPOSITION

Article 9

1. The General Assembly shall consist of all the Members of the United Nations.

2. Each Member shall have not more than five representatives in the General Assembly.

FUNCTIONS AND POWERS

Article 10

The General Assembly may discuss any questions or any matters within the scope of the present Charter or relating to the powers and functions of any organs provided for in the present Charter, and, except as provided in Article 12, may make recommendations to the Members of the United Nations or to the Security Council or to both on any such questions or matters.

Article 11

1. The General Assembly may consider the general principles of co-operation in the maintenance of international peace and security, including the principles governing disarmament and the regulation of armaments, and may make recommendations with regard to such principles to the Members or to the Security Council or to both.

2. The General Assembly may discuss any questions relating to the maintenance of international peace and security brought before it by any Member of the United Nations, or by the Security Council, or by a state which is not a Member of the United Nations in accordance with Article 35, paragraph 2, and, except as provided in Article 12, may make recommendations with regard to any such question to the state or states concerned or to the Security Council or to both. Any such question on which action is necessary shall be referred to the Security Council by the General Assembly either before or after discussion.

3. The General Assembly may call the attention of the Security Council to situations which are likely to endanger international peace and security.

4. The powers of the General Assembly set forth in this Article shall not limit the general scope of Article 10.

Article 12

1. While the Security Council is exercising in respect of any dispute or situation the functions assigned to it in the present Charter, the General Assembly shall not make any recommendations with regard to that dispute or situation unless the Security Council so requests.

2. The Secretary-General, with the consent of the Security Council, shall notify the General Assembly at each session of any matters relative to the maintenance of international peace and security

which are being dealt with by the Security Council and shall similarly notify the General Assembly, or the Members of the United Nations if the General Assembly is not in session, immediately the Security Council ceases to deal with such matters.

Article 13

1. The General Assembly shall initiate studies and make recommendations for the purpose of:

(a) promoting international co-operation in the political field and encouraging the progressive development of international law and its codification;

(b) promoting international co-operation in the economic, social, cultural, educational, and health fields, and assisting in the realization of human rights and fundamental freedoms for all without distinction as to race, sex, language, or religion.

2. The further responsibilities, functions, and powers of the General Assembly with respect to matters mentioned in paragraph 1 (b) above are set forth in Chapters IX and X.

Article 14

Subject to the provisions of Article 12, the General Assembly may recommend measures for the peaceful adjustment of any situation, regardless of origin, which it deems likely to impair the general welfare or friendly relations among nations, including situations resulting from a violation of the provisions of the present Charter setting forth the Purposes and Principles of the United Nations.

Article 15

1. The General Assembly shall receive and consider annual and special reports from the Security Council; these reports shall include an account of the measures that the Security Council has decided upon or taken to maintain international peace and security.

2. The General Assembly shall receive and consider reports from the other organs of the United Nations.

Article 16

The General Assembly shall perform such functions with respect to the international trusteeship system as are assigned to it under

Chapters XII and XIII, including the approval of the trusteeship agreements for areas not designated as strategic.

Article 17

1. The General Assembly shall consider and approve the budget of the Organization.

2. The expenses of the Organization shall be borne by the Members as apportioned by the General Assembly.

3. The General Assembly shall consider and approve any financial and budgetary arrangements with specialized agencies referred to in Article 57 and shall examine the administrative budgets of such specialized agencies with a view to making recommendations to the agencies concerned.

VOTING

Article 18

1. Each member of the General Assembly shall have one vote.

2. Decisions of the General Assembly on important questions shall be made by a two-thirds majority of the members present and voting. These questions shall include: recommendations with respect to the maintenance of international peace and security, the election of the non-permanent members of the Security Council, the election of the members of the Economic and Social Council, the election of members of the Trusteeship Council in accordance with paragraph 1 (c) of Article 86, the admission of new Members to the United Nations, the suspension of the rights and privileges of membership, the expulsion of Members, questions relating to the operation of the trusteeship system, and budgetary questions.

3. Decisions on other questions, including the determination of additional categories of questions to be decided by a two-thirds majority, shall be made by a majority of the members present and voting.

Article 19

A Member of the United Nations which is in arrears in the payment of its financial contributions to the Organization shall have no vote in the General Assembly if the amount of its arrears equals or exceeds the amount of the contributions due from it for the preceding two full years. The General Assembly may, nevertheless, permit such a Member to vote if it is satisfied that the failure to pay is due to conditions beyond the control of the Member.

PROCEDURE

Article 20

The General Assembly shall meet in regular annual sessions and in such special sessions as occasion may require. Special sessions shall be convoked by the Secretary-General at the request of the Security Council or of a majority of the Members of the United Nations.

Article 21

The General Assembly shall adopt its own rules of procedure. It shall elect its President for each session. '

Article 22

The General Assembly may establish such subsidiary organs as it deems necessary for the performance of its functions.

CHAPTER V

THE SECURITY COUNCIL

COMPOSITION

Article 23

1. The Security Council shall consist of fifteen Members of the United Nations. The Republic of China, France, the Union of Soviet Socialist Republics, the United Kingdom of Great Britain and Northern Ireland, and the United States of America shall be permanent members of the Security Council. The General Assembly shall elect ten other Members of the United Nations to be non-permanent members of the Security Council, due regard being specially paid, in the first instance to the contribution of Members of the United Nations to the maintenance of international peace and security and to the other purposes of the Organization, and also to equitable geographical distribution.

2. The non-permanent members of the Security Council shall be elected for a term of two years. In the first election of the non-permanent members after the increase of the membership of the Security Council from eleven to fifteen, two of the four additional members shall be chosen for a term of one year. A retiring member shall not be eligible for immediate re-election.

3. Each member of the Security Council shall have one representative.

FUNCTIONS AND POWERS

Article 24

1. In order to ensure prompt and effective action by the United Nations, its Members confer on the Security Council primary responsibility for the maintenance of international peace and security, and agree that in carrying out its duties under this responsibility the Security Council acts on their behalf.

2. In discharging these duties the Security Council shall act in accordance with the Purposes and Principles of the United Nations. The specific powers granted to the Security Council for the discharge of these duties are laid down in Chapters VI, VII, VIII, and XII.

3. The Security Council shall submit annual and, when necessary, special reports to the General Assembly for its consideration.

Article 25

The Members of the United Nations agree to accept and carry out the decisions of the Security Council in accordance with the present Charter.

Article 26

In order to promote the establishment and maintenance of international peace and security with the least diversion for armaments of the world's human and economic resources, the Security Council shall be responsible for formulating, with the assistance of the Military Staff Committee referred to in Article 47, plans to be submitted to the Members of the United Nations for the establishment of a system for the regulation of armaments.

VOTING

Article 27

1. Each member of the Security Council shall have one vote.

2. Decisions of the Security Council on procedural matters shall be made by an affirmative vote of nine members.

3. Decisions of the Security Council on all other matters shall be made by an affirmative vote of nine members including the concurring votes of the permanent members; provided that, in decisions under Chapter VI, and under paragraph 3 of Article 52, a party to a dispute shall abstain from voting.

PROCEDURE

Article 28

1. The Security Council shall be so organized as to be able to function continuously. Each member of the Security Council shall for this purpose be represented at all times at the seat of the Organization.

2. The Security Council shall hold periodic meetings at which each of its members may, if it so desires, be represented by a member of the government or by some other specially designated representative.

3. The Security Council may hold meetings at such places other than the seat of the Organization as in its judgment will best facilitate its work.

Article 29

The Security Council may establish such subsidiary organs as it deems necessary for the performance of its functions.

Article 30

The Security Council shall adopt its own rules of procedure, including the method of selecting its President.

Article 31

Any Member of the United Nations which is not a member of the Security Council may participate, without vote, in the discussion of any question brought before the Security Council whenever the latter considers that the interests of that Member are specially affected.

Article 32

Any Member of the United Nations which is not a member of the Security Council or any state which is not a Member of the United Nations, if it is a party to a dispute under consideration by the Security Council, shall be invited to participate, without vote, in the discussion relating to the dispute. The Security Council shall lay down such conditions as it deems just for the participation of a state which is not a Member of the United Nations.

CHAPTER VI

PACIFIC SETTLEMENT OF DISPUTES

Article 33

1. The parties to any dispute, the continuance of which is likely to endanger the maintenance of international peace and security, shall, first of all, seek a solution by negotiation, enquiry, mediation, conciliation, arbitration, judicial settlement, resort to regional agencies or arrangements, or other peaceful means of their own choice.

2. The Security Council shall, when it deems necessary, call upon the parties to settle their dispute by such means.

Article 34

The Security Council may investigate any dispute, or any situation which might lead to international friction or give rise to a dispute, in order to determine whether the continuance of the dispute or situation is likely to endanger the maintenance of international peace and security.

Article 35

1. Any Member of the United Nations may bring any dispute, or any situation of the nature referred to in Article 34, to the attention of the Security Council or of the General Assembly.

· 2. A state which is not a Member of the United Nations may bring to the attention of the Security Council or of the General Assembly any dispute to which it is a party if it accepts in advance, for the purposes of the dispute, the obligations of pacific settlement provided in the present Charter.

3. The proceedings of the General Assembly in respect of matters brought to its attention under this Article will be subject to the provisions of Articles 11 and 12.

Article 36

1. The Security Council may, at any stage of a dispute of the nature referred to in Article 33 or of a situation of like nature, recommend appropriate procedures or methods of adjustment.

2. The Security Council should take into consideration any procedures for the settlement of the dispute which have already been adopted by the parties.

3. In making recommendations under this Article the Security Council should also take into consideration that legal disputes should as a general rule be referred by the parties to the International Court of Justice in accordance with the provisions of the Statute of the Court.

Article 37

1. Should the parties to a dispute of the nature referred to in Article 33 fail to settle it by the means indicated in that Article, they shall refer it to the Security Council.

2. If the Security Council deems that the continuance of the dispute is in fact likely to endanger the maintenance of international peace and security, it shall decide whether to take action under Article 36 or to recommend such terms of settlement as it may consider appropriate.

Article 38

Without prejudice to the provisions of Articles 33 to 37, the Security Council may, if all the parties to any dispute so request, make recommendations to the parties with a view to a pacific settlement of the dispute.

CHAPTER VII

ACTION WITH RESPECT TO THREATS TO THE PEACE, BREACHES OF THE PEACE, AND ACTS OF AGGRESSION

Article 39

The Security Council shall determine the existence of any threat to the peace, breach of the peace, or act of aggression and shall make recommendations, or decide what measures shall be taken in accordance with Articles 41 and 42, to maintain or restore international peace and security.

Article 40

In order to prevent an aggravation of the situation, the Security Council may, before making the recommendations or deciding upon the measures provided for in Article 39, call upon the parties concerned to comply with such provisional measures as it deems necessary or desirable. Such provisional measures shall be without prejudice to the rights, claims, or position of the parties concerned. The Security Council shall duly take account of failure to comply with such provisional measures.

Article 41

The Security Council may decide what measures not involving the use of armed force are to be employed to give effect to its decisions, and it may call upon the Members of the United Nations to apply such measures. These may include complete or partial interruption of economic relations and of rail, sea, air, postal, telegraphic, radio, and other means of communication, and the severance of diplomatic relations.

Article 42

Should the Security Council consider that measures provided for in Article 41 would be inadequate or have proved to be inadequate, it may take such action by air, sea, or land forces as may be necessary to maintain or restore international peace and security. Such action may include demonstrations, blockade, and other operations by air, sea, or land forces of Members of the United Nations.

Article 43

1. All Members of the United Nations, in order to contribute to the maintenance of international peace and security, undertake to make available to the Security Council, on its call and in accordance with a special agreement or agreements, armed forces, assistance, and facilities, including rights of passage, necessary for the purpose of maintaining international peace and security.

2. Such agreement or agreements shall govern the numbers and types of forces, their degree of readiness and general location, and the nature of the facilities and assistance to be provided.

3. The agreement or agreements shall be negotiated as soon as possible on the initiative of the Security Council. They shall be concluded between the Security Council and Members or between the Security Council and groups of Members and shall be subject to ratification by the signatory states in accordance with their respective constitutional processes.

Article 44

When the Security Council has decided to use force it shall, before calling upon a Member not represented on it to provide armed forces in fulfilment of the obligations assumed under Article 43, invite that Member, if the Member so desires, to participate in the decisions of the Security Council concerning the employment of contingents of that Member's armed forces.

Article 45

In order to enable the United Nations to take urgent military measures, Members shall hold immediately available national air-force contingents for combined international enforcement action. The strength and degree of readiness of these contingents and plans for their combined action shall be determined, within the limits laid down in the special agreement or agreements referred to in Article 43, by the Security Council with the assistance of the Military Staff Committee.

Article 46

Plans for the application of armed force shall be made by the Security Council with the assistance of the Military Staff Committee.

Article 47

1. There shall be established a Military Staff Committee to advise and assist the Security Council on all questions relating to the Security Council's military requirements for the maintenance of international peace and security, the employment and command of forces placed at its disposal, the regulation of armaments, and possible disarmament.

2. The Military Staff Committee shall consist of the Chiefs of Staff of the permanent members of the Security Council or their representatives. Any Member of the United Nations not permanently represented on the Committee shall be invited by the Committee to be associated with it when the efficient discharge of the Committee's responsibilities requires the participation of that Member in its work.

3. The Military Staff Committee shall be responsible under the Security Council for the strategic direction of any armed forces placed at the disposal of the Security Council. Questions relating to the command of such forces shall be worked out subsequently.

4. The Military Staff Committee, with the authorization of the Security Council and after consultation with appropriate regional agencies, may establish regional subcommittees.

Article 48

1. The action required to carry out the decisions of the Security Council for the maintenance of international peace and security shall be taken by all the Members of the United Nations or by some of them, as the Security Council may determine.

2. Such decisions shall be carried out by the Members of the United Nations directly and through their action in the appropriate international agencies of which they are members.

Article 49

The Members of the United Nations shall join in affording mutual assistance in carrying out the measures decided upon by the Security Council.

Article 50

If preventive or enforcement measures against any state are taken by the Security Council, any other state, whether a Member of the United Nations or not, which finds itself confronted with special economic problems arising from the carrying out of those measures shall have the right to consult the Security Council with regard to a solution of those problems.

Article 51

Nothing in the present Charter shall impair the inherent right of individual or collective self-defence if an armed attack occurs against a Member of the United Nations, until the Security Council has taken measures necessary to maintain international peace and security. Measures taken by Members in the exercise of this right of self-defence shall be immediately reported to the Security Council and shall not in any way affect the authority and responsibility of the Security Council under the present Charter to take at any time such action as it deems necessary in order to maintain or restore international peace and security.

CHAPTER VIII

REGIONAL ARRANGEMENTS

Article 52

1. Nothing in the present Charter precludes the existence of regional arrangements or agencies for dealing with such matters relating to the maintenance of international peace and security as are appropriate for regional action, provided that such arrangements or agencies and their activities are consistent with the Purposes and Principles of the United Nations.

2. The Members of the United Nations entering into such arrangements or constituting such agencies shall make every effort to achieve pacific settlement of local disputes through such regional arrangements or by such regional agencies before referring them to the Security Council.

3. The Security Council shall encourage the development of pacific settlement of local disputes through such regional arrangements or by such regional agencies either on the initiative of the states concerned or by reference from the Security Council.

4. This Article in no way impairs the application of Articles 34 and 35.

Article 53

1. The Security Council shall, where appropriate, utilize such regional arrangements or agencies for enforcement action under its authority. But no enforcement action shall be taken under regional arrangements or by regional agencies without the authorization of the Security Council, with the exception of measures against any enemy state, as defined in paragraph 2 of this Article, provided for pursuant to Article 107 or in regional arrangements directed against renewal of aggressive policy on the part of any such state, until such time as the Organization may, on request of the Governments concerned, be charged with the responsibility for preventing further aggression by such a state.

2. The term enemy state as used in paragraph 1 of this Article applies to any state which during the Second World War has been an enemy of any signatory of the present Charter.

Article 54

The Security Council shall at all times be kept fully informed of activities undertaken or in contemplation under regional arrangements or by regional agencies for the maintenance of international peace and security.

CHAPTER IX

INTERNATIONAL ECONOMIC AND SOCIAL CO-OPERATION

Article 55

With a view to the creation of conditions of stability and well-being which are necessary for peaceful and friendly relations among nations based on respect for the principle of equal rights and self-determination of peoples, the United Nations shall promote:

(a) higher standards of living, full employment, and conditions of economic and social progress and development;

(b) solutions of international economic, social, health, and related problems; and international cultural and educational co-operation; and (*c*) universal respect for, and observance of, human rights and fundamental freedoms for all without distinction as to race, sex, language, or religion.

Article 56

All Members pledge themselves to take joint and separate action in co-operation with the Organization for the achievement of the purposes set forth in Article 55.

Article 57

1. The various specialized agencies, established by intergovernmental agreement and having wide international responsibilities, as defined in their basic instruments, in economic, social, cultural, educational, health, and related fields, shall be brought into relationship with the United Nations in accordance with the provisions of Article 63.
2. Such agencies thus brought into relationship with the United Nations are hereinafter referred to as specialized agencies.

Article 58

The Organization shall make recommendations for the co-ordination of the policies and activities of the specialized agencies.

Article 59

The Organization shall, where appropriate, initiate negotiations among the states concerned for the creation of any new specialized agencies required for the accomplishment of the purposes set forth in Article 55.

Article 60

Responsibility for the discharge of the functions of the Organization set forth in this Chapter shall be vested in the General Assembly and, under the authority of the General Assembly, in the Economic and Social Council, which shall have for this purpose the powers set forth in Chapter X.

CHAPTER X

THE ECONOMIC AND SOCIAL COUNCIL

COMPOSITION

Article 61

1. The Economic and Social Council shall consist of fifty-four Members of the United Nations elected by the General Assembly.

2. Subject to the provisions of paragraph 3, eighteen members of the Economic and Social Council shall be elected each year for a term of three years. A retiring member shall be eligible for immediate re-election.

3. At the first election after the increase in the membership of the Economic and Social Council from twenty-seven to fifty-four members, in addition to the members elected in place of the nine members whose term of office expires at the end of that year, twenty-seven additional members shall be elected. Of these twenty-seven additional members, the term of office of nine members so elected shall expire at the end of one year, and of nine other members at the end of two years, in accordance with arrangements made by the General Assembly.

4. Each member of the Economic and Social Council shall have one representative.

FUNCTIONS AND POWERS

Article 62

1. The Economic and Social Council may make or initiate studies and reports with respect to international economic, social, cultural, educational, health, and related matters and may make recommendations with respect to any such matters to the General Assembly, to the Members of the United Nations, and to the specialized agencies concerned.

2. It may make recommendations for the purpose of promoting respect for, and observance of, human rights and fundamental freedoms for all.

3. It may prepare draft conventions for submission to the General Assembly, with respect to matters falling within its competence.

4. It may call, in accordance with the rules prescribed by the United Nations, international conferences on matters falling within its competence.

Article 63

1. The Economic and Social Council may enter into agreements with any of the agencies referred to in Article 57, defining the terms on which the agency concerned shall be brought into relationship with the United Nations. Such agreements shall be subject to approval by the General Assembly.

2. It may co-ordinate the activities of the specialized agencies through consultation with and recommendations to such agencies and through recommendations to the General Assembly and to the Members of the United Nations.

Article 64

1. The Economic and Social Council may take appropriate steps to obtain regular reports from the specialized agencies. It may make arrangements with the Members of the United Nations and with the specialized agencies to obtain reports on the steps taken to give effect to its own recommendations and to recommendations on matters falling within its competence made by the General Assembly.

2. It may communicate its observations on these reports to the General Assembly.

Article 65

The Economic and Social Council may furnish information to the Security Council and shall assist the Security Council upon its request.

Article 66

1. The Economic and Social Council shall perform such functions as fall within its competence in connexion with the carrying out of the recommendations of the General Assembly.

2. It may, with the approval of the General Assembly, perform services at the request of Members of the United Nations and at the request of specialized agencies.

3. It shall perform such other functions as are specified elsewhere in the present Charter or as may be assigned to it by the General Assembly.

VOTING

Article 67

1. Each member of the Economic and Social Council shall have one vote.

2. Decisions of the Economic and Social Council shall be made by a majority of the members present and voting.

PROCEDURE

Article 68

The Economic and Social Council shall set up commissions in economic and social fields and for the promotion of human rights, and such other commissions as may be required for the performance of its functions.

Article 69

The Economic and Social Council shall invite any Member of the United Nations to participate, without vote, in its deliberations on any matter of particular concern to that Member.

Article 70

The Economic and Social Council may make arrangements for representatives of the specialized agencies to participate, without vote, in its deliberations and in those of the commissions established by it, and for its representatives to participate in the deliberations of the specialized agencies.

Article 71

The Economic and Social Council may make suitable arrangements for consultation with non-governmental organizations which are concerned with matters within its competence. Such arrangements may be made with international organizations and, where appropriate, with national organizations after consultation with the Member of the United Nations concerned.

Article 72

1. The Economic and Social Council shall adopt its own rules of procedure, including the method of selecting its President.

2. The Economic and Social Council shall meet as required in accordance with its rules, which shall include provision for the convening of meetings on the request of a majority of its members.

CHAPTER XI

DECLARATION REGARDING NON-SELF-GOVERNING TERRITORIES

Article 73

Members of the United Nations which have or assume responsibilities for the administration of territories whose peoples have not yet attained a full measure of self-government recognize the principle that the interests of the inhabitants of these territories are paramount, and accept as a sacred trust the obligation to promote to the utmost, within the system of international peace and security established by the present Charter, the well-being of the inhabitants of these territories, and, to this end:

(*a*) to ensure, with due respect for the culture of the peoples concerned, their political, economic, social, and educational advancement, their just treatment, and their protection against abuses;

(*b*) to develop self-government, to take due account of the political aspirations of the peoples, and to assist them in the progressive development of their free political institutions, according to the particular circumstances of each territory and its peoples and their varying stages of advancement;

(*c*) to further international peace and security;

(*d*) to promote constructive measures of development, to encourage research, and to co-operate with one another and, when and where appropriate, with specialized international bodies with a view to the practical achievement of the social, economic, and scientific purposes set forth in this Article; and

(*e*) to transmit regularly to the Secretary-General for information purposes, subject to such limitation as security and constitutional considerations may require, statistical and other information of a technical nature relating to economic, social, and educational conditions in the territories for which they are respectively responsible other than those territories to which Chapters XII and XIII apply.

Article 74

Members of the United Nations also agree that their policy in respect of the territories to which this Chapter applies, no less than in respect of their metropolitan areas, must be based on the general principle of good-neighbourliness, due account being taken of the interests and well-being of the rest of the world, in social, economic, and commercial matters.

CHAPTER XII

INTERNATIONAL TRUSTEESHIP SYSTEM

Article 75

The United Nations shall establish under its authority an international trusteeship system for the administration and supervision of such territories as may be placed thereunder by subsequent individual agreements. These territories are hereinafter referred to as trust territories.

Article 76

The basic objectives of the trusteeship system, in accordance with the Purposes of the United Nations laid down in Article 1 of the present Charter, shall be:

(a) to further international peace and security;

(b) to promote the political, economic, social, and educational advancement of the inhabitants of the trust territories, and their progressive development towards self-government or independence as may be appropriate to the particular circumstances of each territory and its peoples and the freely expressed wishes of the peoples concerned, and as may be provided by the terms of each trusteeship agreement;

(c) to encourage respect for human rights and for fundamental freedoms for all without distinction as to race, sex, language, or religion, and to encourage recognition of the interdependence of the peoples of the world; and

(d) to ensure equal treatment in social, economic, and commercial matters for all Members of the United Nations and their nationals, and also equal treatment for the latter in the administration of justice, without prejudice to the attainment of the foregoing objectives and subject to the provisions of Article 80.

Article 77

1. The trusteeship system shall apply to such territories in the following categories as may be placed thereunder by means of trusteeship agreements:

(*a*) territories now held under mandate;

(*b*) territories which may be detached from enemy states as a result of the Second World War; and

(*c*) territories voluntarily placed under the system by states responsible for their administration.

2. It will be a matter for subsequent agreement as to which territories in the foregoing categories will be brought under the trusteeship system and upon what terms.

Article 78

The trusteeship system shall not apply to territories which have become Members of the United Nations, relationship among which shall be based on respect for the principle of sovereign equality.

Article 79

The terms of trusteeship for each territory to be placed under the trusteeship system, including any alteration or amendment, shall be agreed upon by the states directly concerned, including the mandatory power in the case of territories held under mandate by a Member of the United Nations, and shall be approved as provided for in Articles 83 and 85.

Article 80

1. Except as may be agreed upon in individual trusteeship agreements, made under Articles 77, 79, and 81, placing each territory under the trusteeship system, and until such agreements have been concluded, nothing in this Chapter shall be construed in or of itself to alter in any manner the rights whatsoever of any states or any peoples or the terms of existing international instruments to which Members of the United Nations may respectively be parties.

2. Paragraph 1 of this Article shall not be interpreted as giving grounds for delay or postponement of the negotiation and conclusion of agreements for placing mandated and other territories under the trusteeship system as provided for in Article 77.

Article 81

The trusteeship agreement shall in each case include the terms under which the trust territory will be administered and designate the authority which will exercise the administration of the trust territory. Such authority, hereinafter called the administering authority, may be one or more states or the Organization itself.

Article 82

There may be designated, in any trusteeship agreement, a strategic area or areas which may include part or all of the trust territory to which the agreement applies, without prejudice to any special agreement or agreements made under Article 43.

Article 83

1. All functions of the United Nations relating to strategic areas, including the approval of the terms of the trusteeship agreements and of their alteration or amendment, shall be exercised by the Security Council.

2. The basic objectives set forth in Article 76 shall be applicable to the people of each strategic area.

3. The Security Council shall, subject to the provisions of the trusteeship agreements and without prejudice to security considerations, avail itself of the assistance of the Trusteeship Council to perform those functions of the United Nations under the trusteeship system relating to political, economic, social, and educational matters in the strategic areas.

Article 84

It shall be the duty of the administering authority to ensure that the trust territory shall play its part in the maintenance of international peace and security. To this end the administering authority may make use of volunteer forces, facilities, and assistance from the trust territory in carrying out the obligations towards the Security Council undertaken in this regard by the administering authority, as well as for local defence and the maintenance of law and order within the trust territory.

Article 85

1. The functions of the United Nations with regard to trusteeship agreements for all areas not designated as strategic, including the approval of the terms of the trusteeship agreements and of their alteration or amendment, shall be exercised by the General Assembly.

2. The Trusteeship Council, operating under the authority of the General Assembly, shall assist the General Assembly in carrying out these functions.

CHAPTER XIII

THE TRUSTEESHIP COUNCIL

COMPOSITION

Article 86

1. The Trusteeship Council shall consist of the following Members of the United Nations:

(*a*) those Members administering trust territories;

(*b*) such of those Members mentioned by name in Article 23 as are not administering trust territories; and

(*c*) as many other Members elected for three-year terms by the General Assembly as may be necessary to ensure that the total number of members of the Trusteeship Council is equally divided between those Members of the United Nations which administer trust territories and those which do not.

2. Each member of the Trusteeship Council shall designate one specially qualified person to represent it therein.

FUNCTIONS AND POWERS

Article 87

The General Assembly and, under its authority, the Trusteeship Council, in carrying out their functions, may:

(*a*) consider reports submitted by the administering authority;

(*b*) accept petitions and examine them in consultation with the administering authority;

(*c*) provide for periodic visits to the respective trust territories at times agreed upon with the administering authority; and

(*d*) take these and other actions in conformity with the terms of the trusteeship agreements.

Article 88

The Trusteeship Council shall formulate a questionnaire on the political, economic, social, and educational advancement of the inhabitants of each trust territory, and the administering authority for each trust territory within the competence of the General Assembly shall make an annual report to the General Assembly upon the basis of such questionnaire.

VOTING

Article 89

1. Each member of the Trusteeship Council shall have one vote.

2. Decisions of the Trusteeship Council shall be made by a majority of the members present and voting.

PROCEDURE

Article 90

1. The Trusteeship Council shall adopt its own rules of procedure, including the method of selecting its President.

2. The Trusteeship Council shall meet as required in accordance with its rules, which shall include provision for the convening of meetings on the request of a majority of its members.

Article 91

The Trusteeship Council shall, when appropriate, avail itself of the assistance of the Economic and Social Council and of the specialized agencies in regard to matters with which they are respectively concerned.

CHAPTER XIV

THE INTERNATIONAL COURT OF JUSTICE

Article 92

The International Court of Justice shall be the principal judicial organ of the United Nations. It shall function in accordance with the annexed Statute, which is based upon the Statute of the Permanent Court of International Justice and forms an integral part of the present Charter.

Article 93

1. All Members of the United Nations are *ipso facto* parties to the Statute of the International Court of Justice.
2. A state which is not a Member of the United Nations may become a party to the Statute of the International Court of Justice on condition to be determined in each case by the General Assembly upon the recommendation of the Security Council.

Article 94

1. Each Member of the United Nations undertakes to comply with the decision of the International Court of Justice in any case to which it is a party.
2. If any party to a case fails to perform the obligations incumbent upon it under a judgment rendered by the Court, the other party may have recourse to the Security Council, which may, if it deems necessary, make recommendations or decide upon measures to be taken to give effect to the judgment.

Article 95

Nothing in the present Charter shall prevent Members of the United Nations from entrusting the solution of their differences to other tribunals by virtue of agreements already in existence or which may be concluded in the future.

Article 96

1. The General Assembly or the Security Council may request the

International Court of Justice to give an advisory opinion on any legal question.

2. Other organs of the United Nations and specialized agencies, which may at any time be so authorized by the General Assembly, may also request advisory opinions of the Court on legal questions arising within the scope of their activities.

CHAPTER XV

THE SECRETARIAT

Article 97

The Secretariat shall comprise a Secretary-General and such staff as the Organization may require. The Secretary-General shall be appointed by the General Assembly upon the recommendation of the Security Council. He shall be the chief administrative officer of the Organization.

Article 98

The Secretary-General shall act in that capacity in all meetings of the General Assembly, of the Security Council, of the Economic and Social Council, and of the Trusteeship Council, and shall perform such other functions as are entrusted to him by these organs. The Secretary-General shall make an annual report to the General Assembly on the work of the Organization.

Article 99

The Secretary-General may bring to the attention of the Security Council any matter which in his opinion may threaten the maintenance of international peace and security.

Article 100

1. In the performance of their duties the Secretary-General and the staff shall not seek or receive instructions from any government or from any other authority external to the Organization. They shall refrain from any action which might reflect on their position as international officials responsible only to the Organization.

2. Each Member of the United Nations undertakes to respect the exclusively international character of the responsibilities of the Secretary-General and the staff and not to seek to influence them in the discharge of their responsibilities.

Article 101

1. The staff shall be appointed by the Secretary-General under regulations established by the General Assembly.

2. Appropriate staffs shall be permanently assigned to the Economic and Social Council, the Trusteeship Council, and, as required, to other organs of the United Nations. These staffs shall form a part of the Secretariat.

3. The paramount consideration in the employment of the staff and in the determination of the conditions of service shall be the necessity of securing the highest standards of efficiency, competence, and integrity. Due regard shall be paid to the importance of recruiting the staff on as wide a geographical basis as possible.

CHAPTER XVI

MISCELLANEOUS PROVISIONS

Article 102

1. Every treaty and every international agreement entered into by any Member of the United Nations after the present Charter comes into force shall as soon as possible be registered with the Secretariat and published by it.

2. No party to any such treaty or international agreement which has not been registered in accordance with the provisions of paragraph 1 of this Article may invoke that treaty or agreement before any organ of the United Nations.

Article 103

In the event of a conflict between the obligations of the Members of the United Nations under the present Charter and their obligations under any other international agreement, their obligations under the present Charter shall prevail.

Article 104

The Organization shall enjoy in the territory of each of its Members such legal capacity as may be necessary for the exercise of its functions and the fulfilment of its purposes.

Article 105

1. The Organization shall enjoy in the territory of each of its Members such privileges and immunities as are necessary for the fulfilment of its purposes.

2. Representatives of the Members of the United Nations and officials of the Organization shall similarly enjoy such privileges and immunities as are necessary for the independent exercise of their functions in connexion with the Organization.

3. The General Assembly may make recommendations with a view to determining the details of the application of paragraphs 1 and 2 of this Article or may propose conventions to the Members of the United Nations for this purpose.

CHAPTER XVII

TRANSITIONAL SECURITY ARRANGEMENTS

Article 106

Pending the coming into force of such special agreements referred to in Article 43 as in the opinion of the Security Council enable it to begin the exercise of its responsibilities under Article 42, the parties to the Four-Nation Declaration, signed at Moscow, October 30, 1943, and France, shall, in accordance with the provisions of paragraph 5 of that Declaration, consult with one another and as occasion requires with other Members of the United Nations with a view to such joint action on behalf of the Organization as may be necessary for the purpose of maintaining international peace and security.

Article 107

Nothing in the present Charter shall invalidate or preclude action, in relation to any state which during the Second World War has been an enemy of any signatory to the present Charter, taken or authorized as a result of that war by the Governments having responsibility for such action.

CHAPTER XVIII

AMENDMENTS

Article 108

Amendments to the present Charter shall come into force for all Members of the United Nations when they have been adopted by a vote of two-thirds of the members of the General Assembly and ratified in accordance with their respective constitutional processes by two-thirds of the Members of the United Nations, including all the permanent members of the Security Council.

Article 109

1. A General Conference of the Members of the United Nations for the purpose of reviewing the present Charter may be held at a date and place to be fixed by a two-thirds vote of the members of the General Assembly and by a vote of any nine members of the Security Council. Each Member of the United Nations shall have one vote in the conference.

2. Any alteration of the present Charter recommended by a two-thirds vote of the conference shall take effect when ratified in accordance with their respective constitutional processes by two-thirds of the Members of the United Nations including all the permanent members of the Security Council.

3. If such a conference has not been held before the tenth annual session of the General Assembly following the coming into force of the present Charter, the proposal to call such a conference shall be placed on the agenda of that session of the General Assembly, and the conference shall be held if so decided by a majority vote of the members of the General Assembly and by a vote of any seven members of the Security Council.

CHAPTER XIX

RATIFICATION AND SIGNATURE

Article 110

1. The present Charter shall be ratified by the signatory states in accordance with their respective constitutional processes.

2. The ratifications shall be deposited with the Government of the United States of America, which shall notify all the signatory states of each deposit as well as the Secretary-General of the Organization when he has been appointed.

3. The present Charter shall come into force upon the deposit of ratifications by the Republic of China, France, the Union of Soviet Socialist Republics, the United Kingdom of Great Britain and Northern Ireland, and the United States of America, and by a majority of the other signatory states. A protocol of the ratifications deposited shall thereupon be drawn up by the Government of the United States of America which shall communicate copies thereof to all the signatory states.

4. The states signatory to the present Charter which ratify it after it has come into force will become original Members of the United Nations on the date of the deposit of their respective ratifications.

Article III

The present Charter, of which the Chinese, French, Russian, English, and Spanish texts are equally authentic, shall remain deposited in the archives of the Government of the United States of America. Duly certified copies thereof shall be transmitted by that Government to the Governments of the other signatory states.

IN FAITH WHEREOF the representatives of the Governments of the United Nations have signed the present Charter.

DONE at the city of San Francisco the twenty-sixth day of June, one thousand nine hundred and forty-five.

INDEX